JANE CAMPION

ON

JANE CAMPION

To Pierre Rissient, pathfinder.

OTHER WORKS BY MICHEL CIMENT

Kubrick, Holt, Rinehart, and Winston, USA, 1983; Collins, United Kingdom, 1983; Enlarged edition, Faber & Faber, 2003.

Conversations with Losey, Methuen, 1985.

Kazan on Kazan, Viking, 1974; Secker & Warburg, 1973.

Elia Kazan, An American Odyssey, Bloomsbury, 1988.

John Boorman, Faber & Faber, 1986.

Film World. Interviews with Cinema's Leading Directors, Berg, Oxford and New York, 2009.

JANE CAMPION

ON

JANE CAMPION

MICHEL CIMENT

ABRAMS, NEW YORK

Anna Paquin, Jane Campion,
and Sam Neill on the set of
The Piano *(1993).*

Introduction

The Power of the Image

The emergence in 1989 of Jane Campion with her first feature film *Sweetie* was roughly contemporaneous with that of a group of new American film directors: Joel and Ethan Coen (*Blood Simple*, 1984), Tim Burton (*Pee-wee's Big Adventure*, 1985), Steven Soderbergh (*Sex, Lies, and Videotape*, 1989) and Quentin Tarantino (*Reservoir Dogs*, 1992). Rather than associating her with other female directors or other filmmakers from the antipodes, it seems to me more relevant to see in her films the same belief in the power of the image, the same confidence in the appeal of the story, and the same assertion of a personal approach that is indifferent to the diktats of French theorists (Barthes, Foucault)— very influential in the world of film studies—that in the 1970s were announcing the death of the auteur. Likewise, in opposition to the rejection of narrative that was then being proclaimed by some film-makers (Jean-Luc Godard, Alain Tanner, Jean-Marie Straub), Campion, like these transatlantic "wonder boys," was showing a new vitality and freedom of imagination.

There are many shots in Campion's films whose unique brilliance have marked our cinematic memory: a young woman (Kay, played by Karen Colston) pulling up a shrub in the middle of the night (*Sweetie*, 1989); the adolescent Janet Frame (Alexia Keogh) with her shock of red hair walking along a paved road in the middle of a deserted landscape (*An Angel at My Table*, 1990); Ada (Holly Hunter), her skirts over her head, tied to her piano under water (*The Piano*, 1993); the darkness of the catacomb where Gilbert Osmond (John Malkovich) declares his love for Isabel Archer (*The Portrait of a Lady*, 1996); Ruth (Kate Winslet) appearing to P. J. Waters (Harvey Keitel) like a goddess with multiple arms (*Holy Smoke*, 1999); Frannie (Meg Ryan) holding the severed head of her sister on her lap (*In the Cut*, 2003); Fanny Brawne (Abbie Cornish) standing in a field of bluebells (*Bright Star*, 2009); Tui (Jacqueline Joe) plunging into a lake (*Top of the Lake*, 2013).

Campion belongs to a line of artists—Luis Buñuel (whose work she discovered while still in her teens, with *Belle de jour*, 1967), Roman Polanski, David Lynch (one of her 'modern heroes') and Stanley Kubrick—for whom the strangeness of an image never detracts from the clarity of the story. Their mythopoetic works influenced by psycho-analysis are full of ambiguity and confusion and lend themselves to polysemic interpretations. Like them, Campion is attracted by surprising and moral stories that often have a humorous and playful dimension. The very diversity of the work of these filmmakers is part of their greatness. Like other major film directors, Campion has been criticized for the heterogeneity of her output. But although she has a desire to reinvent and challenge herself, her nine films reveal some recurring features, whether they are original screenplays (*Sweetie, The Piano, Holy Smoke, Top of the Lake*), adaptations (*An Angel at My Table, The Portrait of a Lady, In the Cut, The Power of the Dog*), or an unusual mixture (*Bright Star*, an original screenplay loosely based on a biography and the love letters between John Keats and Fanny Brawne). Like many modern filmmakers, she also likes playing with the notion of gender, subverting it or making it her own, whether in the biopic (*An Angel at My Table*), the costume drama (*The Piano* and *The Portrait of a Lady*), the television series (*Top of the Lake*), or the erotic thriller (*In the Cut*). When she gives free rein to her flirtation with what Edgar Allan Poe would have described as 'the angel of the odd' (*Sweetie, Holy Smoke*), her films are invariably disconcerting in a register that is highly idiosyncratic. Fierce independence is one of her dominant personality traits and sometimes explains the varied reception with which her films are greeted by critics. *Sweetie*, which was shown in competition at the Cannes Film Festival in 1989, was received with equal measures of enthusiasm from some quarters and rejection from others. While Soderbergh's *Sex, Lies, and Videotape*, another debut film, won that year's Palme d'Or, awarded by a jury presided over by Wim Wenders, Campion had managed to so disconcert the critics that she left empty-handed. Later, they were amazed, after the success of *The Piano* (which won the Palme d'Or in

1993), by her decision to create an adaptation of Henry James's classic novel *The Portrait of a Lady*. Although *Holy Smoke* was just as surprising, this time because of the nature of its eccentric inspiration, her next, daringly erotic project, *In the Cut*, once again created a stir. Clearly Campion does exactly as she pleases. Her father, Richard Campion, when he was on the set of *Holy Smoke*, related a conversation he had had with his daughter when she was five years old: "I was doing the parental thing about what she might want to do later on. She looked up at me with those big blue eyes and her golden hair and said, "Dad, I am my own self!" And that's been the basic thing in her work. [...] That's what *Holy Smoke* is about: all in the family lean on this girl, but she finds her own way.[1] We find this same independence in her attitude to her career. While she dedicates herself to her films with passion and determination, she's not worried about whether she should be shooting or not, ready to devote herself to other aspects of her life: for instance, she stopped for several years after making *In the Cut* to commit herself to the education of her daughter, Alice.

A Woman's Take

Without ever claiming to be a standard-bearer for feminism and the like by rejecting 'the woman's film ghetto', Campion has always asserted her femininity. The Palme d'Or that she won for *The Piano* gave her iconic status because no other female director before has ever obtained this prestigious award. Campion is aware of the difficulties a woman faces in this profession and even made it the subject of a three-minute-long satirical tale, *The Lady Bug*, for a film collective celebrating the sixtieth anniversary of the Cannes Film Festival in 2007. A poster marking this celebration shows her jumping into the air alongside Pedro Almodóvar, Wong Kar-wai, Bruce Willis, and Gérard Depardieu, as a tribute to the Festival and to the American photographer Philippe Halsman. Only two other women (one of whom was Juliette Binoche) were part of this celebrity gathering. In another group photograph taken at the same festival, she is the only woman among dozens of male winners of the award, including Manoel de Oliveira, Theo Angelopoulos, Chen Kaige, Ken Loach, Abbas Kiarostami, Wim Wenders, Bille August, Gus Van Sant, and Claude Lelouch.

Femininity is at the center of Campion's life and work. Each of her first eight films focuses on a female protagonist who is struggling for psychological and sensual autonomy and who is in search of her own voice: Kelly in *Two Friends* (1986), Kay in *Sweetie*, Janet Frame in *An Angel at My Table*, Ada in *The Piano*, Isabel Archer in *The Portrait of a Lady*, Ruth in *Holy Smoke*, Frannie in *In the Cut*, Fanny Brawne in *Bright Star*, Robin in *Top of the Lake*. The heroine may also be contrasted with an alter ego, friend, sister, or stepsister: Louise (*Two Friends*), Sweetie (*Sweetie*), and Pauline (*In the Cut*).

So many great directors—from George Cukor to Elia Kazan, Ingmar Bergman and Michelangelo Antonioni—have made a wonderful job of filming women and exploring their inner lives that it would be futile to contrast a female viewpoint with a masculine one and to give the former an advantage over the latter in this art of portraiture. But Campion's approach to female sexuality and her heightened sensibility bring a special resonance to her treatment of women that perhaps only Agnès Varda had previously attempted—in films such as *Cléo de 5 à 7* (*Cléo from 5 to 7*, 1962) or *L'Opéra-mouffe* (*Diary of a Pregnant Woman*, 1958). Campion films her heroines without idealizing them, portraying them, indeed, with all their imperfections and vulnerability, and without passing over the most basic actions—urinating, defecating—which she captures in their most extreme materiality. She also knows how to portray, like no one else, the body of a woman desirous of the opposite sex. The central place of her heroines in no way reduces the importance of her male characters. Although confrontations in male–female relationships are exposed very directly, and often with much violence, her films do not portray a battle between the sexes from a woman's point of view in the parallel way that misogyny is present in many films about couples. The force that enables Campion's heroines to continue to live is expressed in heterosexual relationships. In *Sweetie*, Kay, after the death of her sister, rediscovers her identity with Louis; Ada experiences a semblance of peace with Baines in *The Piano*; in *Holy Smoke*, Ruth can live with P. J. once he has embraced his feminine side; Frannie, having defeated her attacker in *In the Cut*, finds her lover again; in *Bright Star*, Fanny Brawne will remain unswervingly attached to Keats after his death; and Robin renews her relationship with Johnno, her childhood sweetheart, in *Top of the Lake*. There are no happy endings, but over and above the suffering, trauma, and violence experienced by her female characters, there's the affirmation of a belief in life, albeit a fragile one. This vision of the world from a female perspective leads Campion to surround herself with women in her working life: Sally Bongers, cinematographer on her short films and *Sweetie*; Jan Chapman, producer of *Two Friends*, *The Piano*, *Holy Smoke*, and *Bright Star*; Laura Jones, scriptwriter of *An Angel at My Table* and *The Portrait of a Lady*; her sister Anna (co-scriptwriter of *Holy Smoke*); Helen Garner, scriptwriter of *Two Friends*; and Veronika Jenet, who for a long time was her regular editor. Campion is not only a woman, but also an Australasian woman. The geography of her work is set around two polarities. Firstly there is the antipodes, with on one side New Zealand, where she was born and raised, and on the other Australia, where she went to live and work. Within New Zealand another polarity is evident, that of the colonists who arrived from Europe—the 'Pakehas', a Maori word to describe the settlers from the Old Continent—and the Maoris themselves, two communities that are present in *The Piano*. Another polarity contrasts the New World with the Old: Janet Frame in *An Angel at My Table* leaves her native country to tour Europe before returning to New Zealand; Ada in *The Piano* leaves Scotland to travel to New Zealand where she will live following a shipwreck. In *The Portrait of a Lady*, Isabel Archer leaves New England (another version of the New World) behind her to go to Great Britain, then Italy—a further witness of two value systems that will come into conflict. The choice to cast Australian actress Nicole Kidman in the role of an American heroine serves to underline the link between these two new worlds set against old Europe. Ruth in *Holy Smoke* goes to India to regenerate before returning, transformed, to Australia. In the back of a truck, she cradles the body, bloody but still alive, of the *other* that she tried to abandon in the desert but with whom she is reconciled, like two opposing forces finding each other beyond good and evil. To be an Australian woman is to have independence of mind and an ability to affect the world, as is evidenced not only by Ruth but also by Janet Frame and the 'innocent' American Isabel Archer.

At the Heart of a Work

Campion has often contrasted New Zealand (known as Aotearoa by the Maoris) with Australia, the former being governed by a Protestant work ethic and a refusal to accept that one might be better than other people, the cardinal sin. "New Zealanders believe in modesty at all times, and we all thought Australians were vulgar and coarse. But I enjoy the way Australians are."[2] Although verbally Campion has often contrasted warm, relaxed, open Australians with serious, withdrawn, and introverted New Zealanders, her films tell a different story. Those shot in Australia are dominated by insular suburbs, ugly interiors, diminished prospects, and arid terrains parched by the sun, while the verdant landscapes that translate the nostalgia of a wild and invigorating

nature are evident in the works made in New Zealand (*An Angel at My Table*, *The Piano*, *Top of the Lake*). The conflicting ties that characterize the filmmaker's relationships with the two countries that have formed her are reflected in her vision of the family unit, at the heart of her work, an object of both detachment and attraction. Furthermore, the film credits reveal her attachment to her own family: *Sweetie* is dedicated to her sister Anna, *The Piano* to her mother Edith, *The Portrait of a Lady* to her son Jasper (who died eleven days after his birth), while her father is thanked repeatedly. Research carried out by Alistair Fox has shown that Campion's work is intimately tied to her own life history, not in the form of autobiography but by a series of condensations, allusions, and transferences, as well as frequent identifications with her heroines.[3] Her work thus echoes Valéry's *mauvaise pensée* that "Everything you say speaks about yourself, especially when you are speaking about someone else."[4]

1 Howard Feinstein, 'The Jane Mutiny', *Guardian Unlimited*, 2 April 1999 (available online at http://www.theguardian.com/film/1999/apr/02/features).
2 Campion quoted in Katherine Tulich, *The Daily Telegraph* (Sydney), 23 September 1990.
3 Alistair Fox, *Jane Campion: Authorship and Personal Cinema*, Indiana University Press, Bloomington, 2011.
4 'Tout ce que tu dis parle de toi : singulièrement quand tu parles d'un autre.' Paul Valéry, *Mauvaises pensées et autres*, Gallimard, Paris, 1942.

Jane Campion by Patrick Swirc, 2009.

Jane
Before
Campion

*Edith and Richard Campion
in the 1950s.*

*The New Zealand Players
theater company in the 1950s.*

*Richard Campion, Ruth Alley,
and Diane Rhodes in 1953.*

*Jane, Edith, and Anna
Campion in 1954.*

Edith Campion in 1955.

*Jane (age about nine months)
and Anna Campion at the
house at Makererua Street,
Ngaio, Wellington.*

*Edith and Jane Campion
(age about nine months)
at Karehana Bay, Plimmerton.*

1920s

A Family of Actors

Jane Campion was born in Wellington, the capital of New Zealand, on April 30, 1954, the second daughter of producer and director Richard Campion and actress and writer Edith Campion. She is the younger sister of Anna, born a year and a half earlier, and the older sister of Michael, born in 1961 and who, as a businessman, is the only one of the family not connected to the world of entertainment and literature. Edith Hannah, Jane's mother, born in 1923, was the only child of George and Jessie Hannah and the granddaughter of Robert Hannah, a shoe manufacturer and one of the country's major industrialists.[1] Edith had a troubled childhood: both her parents drank, and both died prematurely. Richard came from more humble origins. One of a family of eight children, he was brought up in a puritanical atmosphere: his parents were members of the Exclusive Brethren, an evangelical Christian denomination. He escaped the religious confinement of home by working for a newspaper, the *Evening Post*, and by taking refuge in the public library to read, his family home being devoid of books.

1940s

The couple met at drama classes that enabled them to form their own identities while reacting against the upbringings their backgrounds had imposed on them. They married in 1945 and joined the Unity Theatre, originally an agitprop theatre company created in 1942 and inspired by the radical ideas of the Group Theater, which had been founded ten years earlier in New York by Harold Clurman, Lee Strasberg, and Cheryl Crawford. Among other roles, Richard played that of the knight in T. S. Eliot's *Murder in the Cathedral*, and he also staged *King Lear*, while Edith performed many parts, including Mary Boyle in *Juno and the Peacock* by Sean O'Casey.

1950s

Like lots of Australians—including later their daughter Jane—they took a trip to Europe, studying at the Old Vic in London before joining the touring company of the Young Vic. Their first child died prematurely a few days after his birth, like Jane's son Jasper after her marriage to Colin Englert. On their return to New Zealand in 1951, thanks to a substantial inheritance Edith received from her grandfather (like Isabel Archer in *The Portrait of a Lady*), the couple founded the country's first professional theatre company, the New Zealand Players, with the help of Nola Miller, a local director. The new company was launched in 1953 and organized tours in the island with six plays a year. They staged a total of thirty plays, five of them by New Zealand playwrights. The company's mission would have been approved by the future filmmaker: "To present the best plays of all kinds and, while not pandering to box-office appeal, not to present plays that cause loss of touch with the audience," and "To find a way of acting, fresh, bold, and sincere, which sprang from and appealed to the people of New Zealand." [2] Included in their repertoire were *Saint Joan* by George Bernard Shaw (with Edith in the title role), Shakespeare's *Twelfth Night*, and *The Solid Gold Cadillac* by Howard Teichmann and George S. Kaufman.

1957

Despite some major hits, the company gradually lost money, and, in 1957, Richard resigned and joined Wellington College the following year. His relationship with his wife was becoming strained. Alistair Fox mentions numerous adulterous affairs he had with his actresses, including Margaret Turnbull, and sees an echo in Jane's later work. Jane has a half-sister from one of his liaisons, which for a long time was a family secret. Ruth in *Holy Smoke* speaks to her father of a love child and, in her adaptation of *In the Cut*, the filmmaker introduces a half-sister who doesn't exist in Susanna Moore's original novel. In fact, both Anna and Jane suffered in childhood from their parents' frequent absences, monopolized as they were by their work. Moreover, according to Jane, her parents in their earlier years of marriage were very much in love, and their children took second place. Feeling neglected, the children sought their parents' attention.

1961

Family Life

After the birth of their third child, Michael, Edith abandoned the theatre. Jane remembers: "After a while, we kind of saw that that wasn't a good decision. It didn't help. My father only did what he wanted to do, and of course he enjoyed it."[3] After retiring from the stage Edith devoted herself to writing and published poems, short stories and a novel. She communicated to her daughter her love of the great novels of the nineteenth century that would influence Jane's writing of *The Piano* and would lead to her choice of Henry James's *The Portrait of a Lady* for a film adaptation. However, the mental illness and depression that Edith suffered following her marital problems (she divorced her husband in 1984) had an effect on her daughter. In a television documentary by Lina Safro on the problem of depression, Campion admits that when she was a teenager, her mother's view of the world was so contagious that one day she said to her: "Look Mum, if you really would like to die, if you think you would be happier, I'll be with you. I'll help you." And she said to me "I don't want to die, I don't want to die. I want to feel good about this." And that was a real turning point for me." [4] Edith's influence on Jane cannot be underestimated. The close relationship that Jane had with her mother is revealed in *The Audition* (1989), the documentary made by her sister Anna, where Jane has her mother audition for her role as the teacher in *An Angel at My Table*. Her mother speaks to her about the fear she feels every morning on waking, a fear born out of the absence of a father (who died when she was very young) and the failure of her marriage. The electric shock therapy that Edith underwent in psychiatric hospitals in the 1980s found an emotional echo in the treatments inflicted on Janet Frame in *An Angel at My Table*.

Jane Campion age two or three (c.1956).

Jane Campion age seven (1961).

Anna, Michael, Edith, and Jane Campion in 1962.

Jane Campion age nine (1963).

Jane Campion age twelve (1966).

Edith, Jane, and Anna Campion at Te Kowhai Farm in 1965.

The recurring presentation of family dysfunctions in Campion's films raises questions about the relationships they have with her own life story. The filmmaker has denied any such inspiration: 'If my family was really weird I think I'd have found it very hard to do stories that reveal what can go wrong with the family unit.'[5] Certainly, the link is doubtless not a direct one, but the issue is revived, transformed, disguised, and changed again in the conflictual father–daughter, mother–daughter, and father–mother relationships. The same is true of sister–sister relationships, too, given the rivalry between Anna and Jane that marked their childhood: "We hated each other growing up. I hated everything about her, her competitiveness. [...] I was so sick of the fighting, the competition. I just wanted her to let me be."[6] Her relationship with her older sister later changed radically, to the point that they collaborated on *Holy Smoke* at a time when Anna herself had already begun directing films. To an extent, these buried traumas and emotional problems have continued to fuel Campion's work—in the sense in which Baudelaire explained that "Genius is no more than childhood recaptured at will, childhood equipped now with man's physical means to express itself, and with the analytical mind that enables it to bring order into the sum of experience, involuntarily amassed."[7]

1974

Moving Toward Films

Campion's rebellious sprit and fierce independence that has often been apparent in her life has its origins in her relationships with her family—with her sister but also with her parents. This was evident when, before she turned twenty, she decided to have no more to do with their theatrical world—the idea of doing the same as them was detestable to her—but instead to enroll for a degree in anthropology at Wellington's Victoria University. She developed her interest in mythic thought and the nonrational while studying the work of Marcel Mauss and Claude Lévi-Strauss. The rite-of-passage trip she took to Europe, like lots of young Australians, proved disappointing, and once again she found herself at odds. Disappointed in particular by British reserve ("I had to hide who I was, I was too much for them"), she learned at least one lesson from her trip, at the Chelsea School of Art in London, and on returning to Sydney, enrolled at the Sydney College of the Arts in 1977. Like David Lynch and Tim Burton, she made her first creative experiments in painting and drawing, and, by her own admission, it was at art college that she learned everything. She was influenced by Frida Kahlo (who provided the inspiration for the character of Ada in *The Piano*) and her exploration of female sexuality, and also by Joseph Beuys and his relationship with violence and ritual. She discovered surrealism, with its ability to make the familiar strange, its often black humor and its exploration of dreams, which is also what attracts her to certain filmmakers who have influenced her (Buñuel, Polanski, Fellini, Lynch). She created some narrative paintings annotated with dialogue and text. Quite naturally, she turned to the cinema and the Australian Film, Television and Radio School (AFTRS), which enabled her to practice filmmaking from 1981 onwards.

1981

The AFTRS had been created in 1973 along the lines of major film schools in the USA and Europe. Headed by the Polish critic and historian Jerzy Toeplitz, it had as its mission to promote 'the intelligence and imagination of directors', despite resistance from the Australian film industry, who would have preferred an exclusively technical school. The purpose of this school was to foster the development

Jane Campion at the time of making Sweetie,
in 1989.

*Jane Campion at the Acropolis
in 1970.*

*Campion, age fourteen, play-
ing the role of Andromache in*
The Trojan Women *by
Euripides.*

*Janet Frame (in the background),
cinematographer Stuart Dryburgh (behind the camera),
Jane Campion, and cast and crew members on
the set of* An Angel at My Table *(1990).*

*Jane Campion and her daugh-
ter Alice in front of their house
in Vaucluse, Sydney (1997).*

*Campion posing for John
Lethbridge at her parents' farm in
New Zealand (1979).*

Jane Campion and Mother Yoga,
around 2004.

Jane Campion and Gerard Lee in 1981.

Jane Campion on the set of
The Water Diary *(2005).*

Abbie Cornish, Jane Campion,
and Ben Whishaw on the set
of Bright Star *(2009).*

Jane Campion on the set
of In the Cut *(2002).*

Jane Campion and some of the directors of Chacun son cinéma
at the Cannes Film Festival in 2007.
Top to bottom, left to right: David Cronenberg, Jean-Pierre
and Luc Dardenne, Nanni Moretti, Ethan and Joel Coen,
Manoel de Oliveira, and Amos Gitaï.

Cinematographer Adam Arkapaw
and Jane Campion on the set
of Top of the Lake *in 2012.*

of a national film industry that could compete internationally. Its first intake comprised a dozen students, who included the future filmmakers Gillian Armstrong, Phillip Noyce, and Chris Noonan. Coming from the fine art world, Campion was pursuing creative autonomy and a personal style that were destined to conflict with its more prescriptive style of teaching. Both Campion and fellow student Sally Bongers (later Campion's cinematographer) have noted that their work, which was deemed too excessive, didn't really meet with the approval of the teaching staff, and that they, in turn, found the establishment too conservative. But the filmmaker nevertheless recognized that the AFTRS gave her the opportunity to take advantage of sophisticated equipment, to make contact with other students and, thanks to regular screenings, to acquaint herself with the work of major film directors.

1982

In the 1980s, women became increasingly prominent in the Australian film world. Between 1974 and 1982, only one female director had been able to make a film—Gillian Armstrong, with *My Brilliant Career* (1979)—as opposed to eighty-one men. There were sixteen female scriptwriters to 132 male scriptwriters and thirty-two female producers to eighty-seven male producers. To compensate for this discrepancy, the Women's Film Fund (1976–88) created the Women's Film Unit. It was in this favourable environment that Campion was able to flourish. Her short films were noticed by Pierre Rissient, an advisor to the Cannes Film Festival, while on a visit to Sydney. He selected *Peel* (1982), *Passionless Moments* (1983), and *A Girl's Own Story* (1984), and also her feature-length film *Two Friends* (1986), made for the television channel ABC. In 1986 *Peel* was awarded the Short Film Palme d'Or at the Cannes Film Festival, and her other three films confirmed her place among the most promising directors of her generation. The rest, as they say, is history.

1 I owe much of this biographical information to Alistair Fox's *Jane Campion: Authorship and Personal Cinema* (Indiana University Press, Bloomington, 2011) and to *Jane Campion: Interviews*, edited by Virginia Wright Wexman (University Press of Mississippi, Jackson, 1999).
2 Quoted in Kathleen McHugh, *Jane Campion*, University of Illinois Press, Urbana and Chicago, 2007.
3 Campion quoted in Ellen Cheshire, *Jane Campion*, Pocket Essentials, Harpenden UK, 2000.
4 Lina Safro, Brainstorm, video, SBS Television, 1995. Quoted in Sue Williams, *The Australian* (Sydney), 2 May 1995.
5 Campion quoted in Sandra Hall, *The Bulletin* (Sydney), 26 October 1993.
6 Campion quoted in Suzie Mackenzie, 'Beloved rivals', *Guardian Unlimited*, 5 June 1999.
7 Charles Baudelaire, *The Painter Of Modern Life And Other Essays*, 1863.

Short and Medium-length Films
(1980–1986)

"A Certain Irony
About Life."

Mishaps of Seduction and Conquest
(1981)

Peel—An Exercise in Discipline
(1982)

Passionless Moments
(1983)

A Girl's Own Story
(1984)

After Hours
(1985)

Dancing Daze
(1986)

Rebecca Stewart in Passionless Moments *(1983).*

Graeme (John Godden) and his sister Gloria (Marina Knight) in A Girl's Own Story *(1984).*

The beginnings of a body of work

Very few directors—Roman Polanski and Alain Resnais are the first who spring to mind—have been able to create from the very start, as Campion has done, short films that so brilliantly presage their future work. In 1980, before entering the Australian Film Television and Radio School (AFTRS), she shot a film in Super 8 called *Tissues*, now lost, that analyzed the sexual abuse of children and that was based on the story of a man arrested for this crime. This preoccupation of the filmmaker's reappears in one form or another in certain of her later works. Shot over a period of four years while she was at AFTRS, *Mishaps of Seduction and Conquest*, *Peel*, *Passionless Moments*, and *A Girl's Own Story*, and later *After Hours*, established from the outset an original tone and a highly personal intention.

Mishaps of Seduction and Conquest (1981)

This experimental video has two brothers talking to each other in parallel montage via their correspondence: the first, George Mallory (Stuart Campbell), is unsuccessfully trying to climb Everest in 1924, while the second, Geoffrey (Richard Evans), a fictional character, fervently hopes to seduce Emma (Deborah Kennedy), a writer who shows little interest in him. The men on the expedition speak of the mountain as a temptress, and the closer they get to it the less they want it. The emotional conquest unfolds like an echo of this physical conquest. Even in her style of filming, Campion contrasts two worlds: that of Emma's London interior, which is reminiscent of bourgeois apartments of 1920s cinema, particularly those featured in *Kammerspiel* films, and that of the Himalayan ascent, made up of archival documentaries of the time.

The film opens with a scene of voyeurism. At the end of a corridor, a man bends down to look through a keyhole and to gaze at a woman sitting at her desk writing. In the third shot, the man walks toward the camera and sits down, looking preoccupied, near a door. We learn from a voice-over that he is married ("I trust only that my visits remain unnoticed and Elizabeth unsuspicious"). In this black-and-white film, the filmmaker introduces touches of red that suggest desire and passion: the desire of the man, which decreases the more the conquest becomes possible; the passion of the woman, at first indifferent, who loses the power to write after she has been seduced and then abandoned by her lover. At the end of the film she plays with Geoffrey's scarf, which she has wrapped around her neck, the only token left of this now-absent man.

At twenty-six years old, Campion laid the foundations of her world: an independent woman who makes a living by writing, a man who cheats on his wife, the vagaries of love, the exchange of letters (as would follow in *Two Friends, Holy Smoke, Bright Star*) and no doubt reminiscences—even unwitting—of family tragedies. "At the age of twenty-five," she admitted much later, "I began to work in a rather idiosyncratic way and to develop a relationship with my subconscious. This was when I was writing my first film. After three pages it was finished, I couldn't go any further. So I let my subconscious take over. But for this process to work, you have to believe that there are possible solutions."[1]

Peel—An Exercise in Discipline (1982)

With *Peel* the director presented her style more radically, with the help once again of her cinematographer Sally Bongers, a film-school friend with whom she fought against the much more classical aesthetic advocated by her teachers, who rejected her iconoclastic approach. The opening credits announce "A true story/a true family," and Campion actually asked the Pye family—the father, Tim; his son, Ben; and Tim's sister, Katie—to play the roles in the story. The same credits also presage the triangular relationship that will generate a series of conflicts. The chosen arrangement appears to pastiche the kinship structures of the ethnologist Claude Lévi-Strauss, an author that the director holds in high regard.

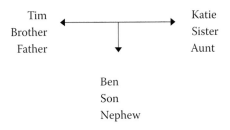

Tim — Brother — Father   Katie — Sister — Aunt

Ben — Son — Nephew

Ben Martin (Son/Nephew) and Tim Pye
(Brother/Father) in Peel *(1982).*

The only film made during her film school years that is in color, *Peel* brings together two red-headed males and a woman with brown hair. Set in the claustrophobic atmosphere of a car journey, it reveals the tensions at the heart of this family unit and the power struggles that make them alternately turn against each other, all joined and yet separated from each other. The subtitle of the work, *An Exercise in Discipline*, highlights the father's will to impose his rule not only on his son, who he orders to pick up the orange peelings he has thrown out of the car window, but also on his sister, who is struggling with this male chauvinist domination, blaming her brother for not paying any attention to what she thinks of a house they have visited and for making them late, which means she'll miss watching her favorite television program. As is often the case in Campion's films, conflicts between adults generate conflicts with children. In nine minutes, Campion affects a series of permutations— Tim against Ben, Ben against Katie, Katie against Tim—all of which are characterized by a rejection of authority and a spirit of rebellion.

From the first shot, the director masterfully makes use of the power of sound when the child repeatedly throws an orange against the car windscreen, a throbbing effect that foretells the tensions, resentment, and anger to come. Dana Polan has demonstrated the central role of the orange (the colour of which mirrors the father's shirt and the red hair of the two males), into which the son sticks his finger.[2] This phallic image evokes a sexual act and is linked with the condom that the boy inflates when he picks it up on the roadside and that brings to mind a giant penis. The presence of sexuality beneath the surface of social relationships would become a recurring feature of Campion's future work. *Peel* asserts with panache Campion's desire to seek the unusual in the ordinariness of people's lives. With this undercurrent of surrealism, Campion consorts with a satirical grotesqueness of the kind that Edgar Allan Poe developed in his short story 'The Angel of the Odd' and cultivates a sense of strangeness. Encouraged by the boldness of Bongers behind the camera, she breaks up the space with unexpected framing, editing effects, and high and low-angle shots. Also in line with experiments taking place in contemporary photography, often more audacious than film, she distanced herself right from the start from the realism that dominated the depiction of the problems of everyday life. In the formal quality of her work, she embodies the same independent and rebellious spirit as her characters, including the son and sister in *Peel*, who reject the rules and pressures being placed on them.

Passionless Moments (1983)

Passionless Moments might seem to contradict the filmmaker's vision as characterized by strong feelings, as seen in *Peel*. Claiming that the film was written by Gerard Lee (Campion's partner at that time), though nevertheless assisted by her, some commentators, such as Alistair Fox, have seen fit to dismiss it in their analysis, considering it to be outside the filmmaker's usual thematic concerns.[3] But aside from the fact that she made it, this film, which is rather longer than the previous one (twelve minutes), appears, on the contrary, to show the same interest in moments of insight amid the banality of everyday life. It comprises short minimalist fragments accompanied by a wry voice-over narration that nevertheless communicates a real affection for the characters. The ten sequences of just a few shots combine a trivial premise with possible repercussions:

1—*Ibrahim Makes Sense Of It*: A man is practicing yoga and from a slogan written on the wall, 'sex is a wonderful and natural thing', retains only the two words 'sex thing'.
2—*An Exciting One*: Lindsay, a small boy, has bought some string beans and imagines that they will explode unless in twenty seconds he plunges them into the nitroglycerine-immune area in his kitchen.
3—*No Woodpeckers in Australia*: Mrs Gilbert is wondering about a noise that is coming from the garden of her neighbour, Mrs Vitacek, and realizes that there are no woodpeckers in her country.
4—*Focal Lengths*: Sean and Arnold, two homosexuals, are having communication problems that augur their separation.
5—*A Neighborly Misunderstanding*: Two neighbors who have never spoken wave to each after a misinterpreted gesture.
6—*Clear Up Sleepy Jeans*: While washing his underpants, Jim is listening to a ten-year-old pop song and wonders about its meaning.
7—*Angela Eats Meats*: A woman who is about to eat some ham remembers her uncle's pig.
8—*Ed Played Front Row At School*: On Sundays, Ed irons his shirts for the week. As he goes to get another beer he thinks about how good he was at sports and decides to stop drinking and get back into shape.
9—*What His Mother Said*: Gavin, a bachelor, is listening to the beating in his eardrum and staring at the ceiling where he sees dust particles. He remembers that his mother used to tell him they were angels.
10—*Scotties, Part of Grand Design of the Universe*: Young Julie, who is sick, is spending the day at home. She discovers that Monopoly notes fit perfectly on a box of tissues.

The original tone of the voice-over, which seems to pastiche that of American postwar crime thrillers such as *The Naked City* (Jules Dassin, 1948), introduces an offbeat humour: "There are one million moments in your neighborhood, but as the filmmakers discovered, each has a fragile presence which fades almost as it forms." Campion reveals the same rigour here as in *Peel*, a self-imposed discipline with regard to form and a concern with depicting the absurdity at the heart of reality.

A Girl's Own Story (1984)

Her last film-school film, and the longest, *A Girl's Own Story* has much more personal resonances and paved the way for the feature films. Although Campion has always downplayed the direct relationship of her films with her own life, she admitted in an interview that she had used a dress belonging to her mother in the film: "My mother hadn't noticed it until my sister said to her, "Don't you see? We're all in this film.""[4] Alistair Fox has analysed strikingly the links between *A Girl's Own Story* and the director's biography.

*Pam (Gabrielle Shornegg) flanked by Stella
(Geraldine Haywood) and Gloria in*
A Girl's Own Story.

One of the first shots in the film shows Pam (Gabrielle Shornegg) and a friend tracing with a finger the outline of a drawing of a man's erect penis, underneath which is the caption: 'This sight may shock young girls.' Campion admits that during her time at art school she had made some very crude pornographic paintings, both funny and particularly ugly, but that no one had told her to stop.[5] Set during 1960s Beatlemania, *A Girl's Own Story* is a portrait of a young girl, her family, her friendships, and her loneliness. This is the first time the director had placed a female character at the centre of her story, and she drew on her own personal memories. Such is the case with the mother of Pam (Colleen Fitzpatrick), who has many similarities to Edith, Campion's own mother, including her marital problems and the infidelities of her husband, her depressive behavior, and her love of cats. In addition, the incessant arguments between Pam and her sister Prue (Joanne Gabbe) echo the quarrels that opposed Jane and Anna.

The film is steeped in sexuality. Her father's liaison with a younger woman, Deidre, disturbs Pam, who is attracted by the possibility of sexual activity yet fears it. The fear of transgression is also expressed in the scene where Pam's father (Paul Chubb) is taking her out to a restaurant for her birthday and he invites Deidre (Jane Edwards) to come along too. Similarly, a parallel plot with Gloria and her brother Graeme is tinged with incest, notably in a sequence where they undress while pretending to be cats. In another (dream) scene, a younger Pam is pushed into a car by a strange man who invites her to stroke his kitten.

The epilogue, where Pam and young girls in white dresses, superimposed with images of skating, are singing 'I feel the cold / I fear it's here to stay / There is no end to this lake of ice / I want to melt away', expresses the heroine's frigidity and her need for human warmth.

With *A Girl's Own Story*, Campion created a work that laid a foundation for her cinema by evoking the passage from teenage years to adulthood, the construction of an identity associated with the fear of masculine sexuality in a climate of vulnerability and anxiety. More psychological than her previous films, this final student work also avoids the norms of the realist chronicle. The directing reflects the same freedom, constantly surprises by its formal stance, and enshrouds certain moments of the story with a dreamlike quality, as though Campion was making Gérard de Nerval's famous phrase in *Aurélia*—"the outpouring of the dream world into real life"– her own.

After Hours (1985)

On leaving film school the director undertook a commission from the Women's Film Unit, a feminist organization. *After Hours* deals with sexual harassment and, although Campion has distanced herself from the film, it in no way conforms to a militant viewpoint. In fact, the film fits perfectly with her other work, and only the conditions of its creation can explain her reservations.

Pam in A Girl's Own Story.

A young office worker, Lorraine (Danielle Pearse), is exposed to the advances of her boss, John Phillips (Don Reid), and seeks the help of an investigator. Far from complying with the didactic intentions of the film's sponsors, Campion makes her subject more complex by refusing to show the least female solidarity: Phillips's secretary is entranced by him, Lorraine's mother comments on the miniskirt she had worn to work, and her boyfriend shows no more understanding, while her work colleagues treat her with indifference. Even the investigator eventually dissuades her from going to court. The behaviour of Lorraine herself is not unambiguous, and in this way reflects that of other protagonists of the filmmaker in relation to sex. Having told her boss she feels unwell, Lorraine encourages him to touch her stomach, telling him that this is where the pain is, and stays the evening with him in his office rather than going home, both frightened and attracted by this father figure. This pessimistic film includes Lorraine's renunciation and her resignedly telling her mother she wants to forget the whole affair. Formally more classical than the film-school works, *After Hours* nevertheless has a highly aesthetic sophistication, from the fluorescent blue of the office scenes to the shots of Lorraine descending to the bottom of the swimming pool and floating passively.

Dancing Daze (1986)

The following year, Campion shot her first film for television, the fifth episode in the series *Dancing Daze*. Anita (Melissa Docker), who has devoted her life to dance, is denied a position in a ballet company. Meanwhile, the members of a contemporary dance company, the Greens, hear that they will lose their rehearsal space unless they can manage to convince an entertainment company to hire them. Everything seems lost until one of the star dancers is injured and Anita takes her place, saving the company's future. It was this film that led the same production company, Australian Broadcasting Corporation (ABC), to finance for the small screen Campion's first feature film, *Two Friends*.

1 Campion in an interview with Marie Colmant, 'Jane et Janet, face à face', *Libération*, 24 April 1991.
2 Dana Polan, *Jane Campion*, British Film Institute, London, 2001.
3 Alistair Fox, *Jane Campion: Authorship and Personal Cinema*, Indiana University Press, Bloomington, 2011.
4 Campion quoted in *Sydney Daily Telegraph*; reprinted in Virginia Wright Wexman (ed.), *Jane Campion: Interviews* (Conversations with Filmmakers), University Press of Mississippi, Jackson, 1999.
5 Campion in an interview with Mark Stiles, 'Jane Campion', *Cinema Papers* (December 1984); reprinted in Virginia Wright Wexman, op. cit.

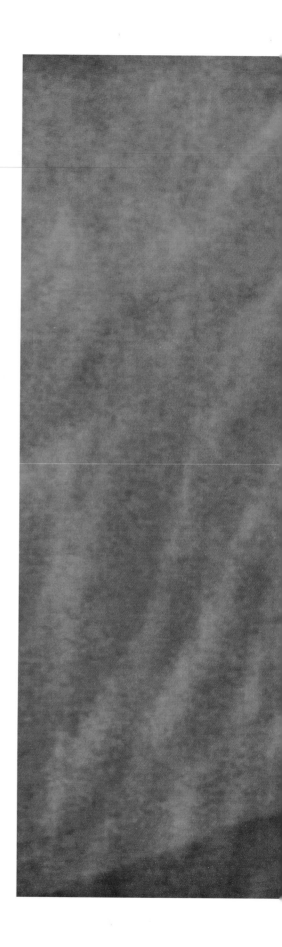

After Hours *(1985): The boss, John Phillips (Don Reid), and his young
employee Lorraine (Danielle Pearse); three of Lorraine's colleagues (Kris
Bidenko, on the left); Lorraine during a swimming training session.*

After Hours *has a highly aesthetic sophistication, from the fluorescent blue of the office scenes to the shots of Lorraine descending to the bottom of the swimming pool and floating passively.*

Interview conducted in Paris, 17 October 1986

You were born in New Zealand. In what sort of environment were you raised?
My parents were in the theater, and their parents had lived in New Zealand for several generations. My mother was an actress, my father a director, and they had both been trained in England. They formed a company in New Zealand, staged Shakespeare and toured the country. After I was born, they stopped and settled in Wellington, the capital. It was there that I was brought up. They then went into farming because they were tired of facing problems in the theatre and they weren't earning much money. From time to time, they returned to the stage. Conversations at home revolved around the classical plays they were staging and the performances of the actors. I myself was passionate about the theatre and tried acting in high school. My brother and sister and I were competing for our parents' attention, but we were good friends at that age. At sixteen, I went to university. But I spent all my youth in both town and country, because in New Zealand, the city is close to the fields.

Why didn't you go into the theater?
I gradually became very critical of the theatre. The actors that I met seemed to me superficial, lacking in naturalness. I decided to tackle something more serious, and I wanted to go to university in Australia. It's the sort of decision you make when you're sixteen. I studied anthropology, having tried psychology and education, which I didn't like much. My diploma didn't really lead to anything, but we had a fantastic teacher, a Dutchman named Power. He had studied with Lévi-Strauss, and talked to us about structural anthropology and linguistic problems. What interested me about anthropology was that I was able to study 'officially' things I was already curious about: how we think, the mythic aspects of our thoughts that have nothing to do with logic, human behaviour. Actually, I think I've got an anthropologist's eye, a sense of observation. I liked both the theory and the poetry of anthropology.

Yet your short films differ from a lot of other Australian films that take into account the presence of Aborigines and the role of myths. You are closer to a behavioural study of the characters.
Actually, I don't think that the great Aboriginal myths are really part of Australian culture. People talk about them, but superficially. I'm very interested in them, as in everything else that relates to human beings, but they're not part of my vision of the world. On the other hand, I think that Man thinks he's a rational being when he's not, when he's actually governed by something else entirely. And that's what interests me. So I finished my studies and graduated. But I realized that if I continued on that path, I would eventually be expressing myself in a way that would be comprehensible only to other anthropologists. And I wanted, rather, to communicate with people and to find common symbols, to see what could be achieved by telling stories. That's when I decided to go to Europe. It was there that my heritage lay, the history that I'd learned about at school. I was curious to discover what it was really like. I also wanted to study painting, which is what I did in London while working as an assistant on a film. But I didn't much like this city where I lived for a year. I went back to Australia because the fees for the art school, as well as the cost of living, were too high in London. Everyone looked a bit lost when I was studying art, including the teachers! On the other hand, my experience at Sydney College of the Arts was marvelous. The teachers were young, had a clear idea what they wanted, and weren't burdened with all the traditions that prevailed in England. What interested me, in fact, was the relationship between art and life, how we react visually to an experience.

What kind of painting did you do?
I wanted to paint what was important to me, and I ended up telling little stories on the canvas. It was figurative. As I also liked to write, I captioned my paintings. At the same time, I was also staging plays that told love stories and stories of disappointing experiences. They were videotaped, and I acted in them. I thought they were really bad, and I didn't like myself as an actress. So I decided to make films myself in Super 8, directing actors in roles I had written for them. It was very ambitious of me as I knew nothing about film, everything came out of a textbook. But I was very motivated because I wanted to tell my stories. The result wasn't very satisfactory, as Super 8 needed a lot of precision and I lacked experience. I made two films like this. One was called *Tissues* and lasted about twenty minutes, the second, *Eden*, I didn't really finish as I never added the sound. *Tissues* was almost a precursor to *A Girl's Own Story*. People liked it because I had put a lot of energy into it, but visually it was horrible, because I didn't really understand what a shot was!

What were your tastes in films?
I wasn't really a film buff. My trips to the cinema were pretty unplanned. But I remember that I was completely crazy about Buñuel and tried to see everything he'd done. I also loved people like Antonioni and Bertolucci. On the whole, I was more attracted to European cinema and the likes of Kurosawa than to the world of Hollywood.

What did you decide to do after art school?
I didn't know what the next step would be. I didn't see how I could make contact with people in the film industry, nor with those in the Australian Film Corporation. One day they seem to have confidence in you and the next they no longer believe in you. So I decided to go to the Australian Film Television and Radio School, and from day one tried to make as many short films as I could during the three years I was there. I shot *Peel* in the first year, *Passionless Moments* in the second and third, and *A Girl's Own Story* in the third year.

What was the idea behind your first film, *Peel*?
I knew a very odd family and thought it would be interesting to film them. They were people who didn't seem able to control themselves. I suggested scenes to them, and as they were very honest, they realized that they were revealing their true nature. It's a very short film, about nine minutes long.

***Passionless Moments* was more developed.**
It was the result of a collaboration with one of my friends, Gerard Lee. The original idea was his, and then we wrote and directed the film together. Once we had the framework of the film—a series of vignettes—we tried to come up with as many stories as possible that would be told with a certain ironic detachment. Finally, we wrote ten of them. Gerard and I wanted to show mild, ordinary people who you rarely see on screen and who have more charm than many famous artists. They also had a comic aspect that appealed to us. The film was filmed in five days, two episodes a day. I was also responsible for shooting, and I realized the benefits of the film school where in two hours I had learned about lighting and gained an understanding of the possibilities of the camera.

What all of these short films have in common is the sense of observation, the choice of

Gabrielle Shornegg and Jane Campion on the set of A Girl's Own Story.

moments, epiphanies in which behaviours are revealed.

That has always interested me. I remember that at film school, my classmates wanted to deal with big subjects or spectacular scenes involving car crashes. That was the last thing I wanted to do.

You like Katherine Mansfield, your fellow countrywoman, who was likewise interested in observing details.

Yes. I love her books. When I was a child in New Zealand, I used to play near her memorial, which was in a park near our house.

To what extent is *A Girl's Own Story* inspired by your childhood and adolescence?

I wanted to pay tribute to that period of life when we feel lost and lonely. It's very characteristic of youth. It's a very curious stage in our development when we feel adult emotions but lack experience. With experience, it's easier to deal with your emotions. The smallest things

seem like huge obstacles when you're very young. I had had lots of experiences that I had never seen represented. For example, in class, everyone used to kiss each other, and as soon as we grew up, we stopped. Everyone behaved as though it had never happened. I also wanted to talk about the Beatles, whose music affected my generation as I was born in 1954. The episode about incest wasn't a personal experience, but I remember that a very young neighbour had been made pregnant by a classmate and the scandal that that had created.

Did the actors bring elements to their parts, or was everything written down from the outset?

Of course, actors always contribute something. But in this case, the teenagers thought I was really very odd and swore to me that they had never done anything like this. In fact, they essentially read from the script. I had trouble finding performers. The first one I chose didn't feel comfortable about the incest. She was too

immature, and I had to find someone older but who looked younger than she was. Officially, filming took ten days, but I managed to 'steal' some extra time. The whole film crew was made up of students, and we didn't have much experience, but the film had a good reception in Australia and even won some awards. When it was screened, the reaction was very good, people laughed a lot, to the point where you could barely hear the dialogue. That touched me, because the teachers had never supported my work. They were very conservative people who thought that this sort of film was too strange to enable me to find a job.

It was after leaving the film school that you made *After Hours*.

Yes. Based on my short films, the Women's Film Unit asked me to write and direct this film. I don't like *After Hours* very much because I felt like my motives for making it were compromised. There was a conflict in me between the project and my artistic conscience. The film,

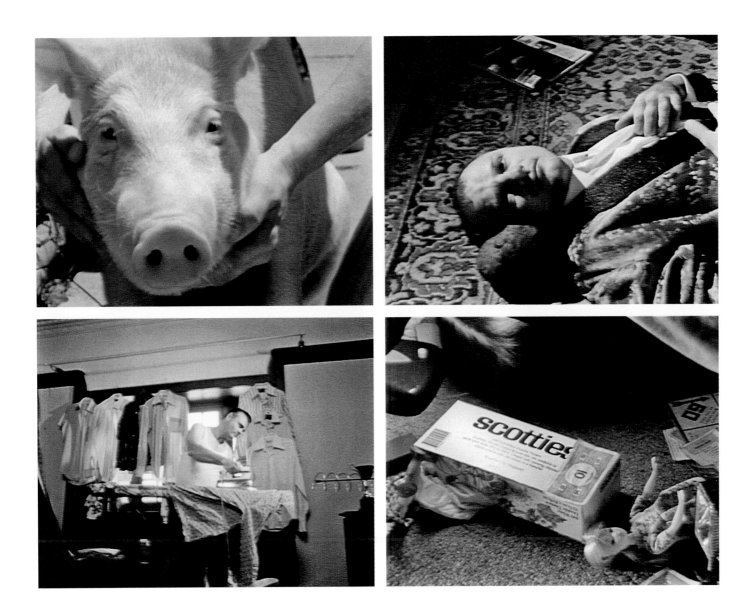

The ten sequences of Passionless Moments *(1983, see page 25).*
<u>*Top to bottom, left to right:*</u>
1—Ibrahim Makes Sense Of It
2—An Exciting One
3—No Woodpeckers in Australia
4—Focal Lengths
5—A Neighborly Misunderstanding
6—Clear Up Sleepy Jeans
7—Angelica Eats Meat
8—Ed Played Front Row At School
9—What His Mother Said
10—Scotties, Part of Grand Design of the Universe

34

Geoffrey (Richard Evans) and
Emma (Deborah Kennedy) in
Mishaps of Seduction and Conquest *(1981).*

commissioned by the Women's Film Unit, had to be overtly feminist as it spoke about sexual abuse of women in the workplace. I wasn't very comfortable with that because I don't like films that tell people how they should or should not behave. I think the world is more complicated than that. I prefer to look at people and study their behaviour without judging them. I would have preferred to put this film away in a cupboard, but it toured the world! I like shooting films that I would like to watch myself, and that's not the case with *After Hours*, but it was important for me to make it.

You then directed an episode of *Dancing Daze* for ABC.
It was a commission, light entertainment for television. I was writing a project for a television series on the New Zealand writer Janet Frame and I wanted to know what it was like to work for television. It was an interesting experience, even though I'm not keen on the film, because it enabled me to meet Jan Chapman, who later produced *Two Friends*. I had to work fast to shoot a fifty-minute film with song and dance numbers in seven days. It was the classic story of a group of young people in 1986 who want to start a dance company. I had to be visually inventive, which was fun, and it gave me confidence in my relationship with commercial cinema.

Shortly afterward, you shot *Two Friends*.
I had to move fast, as ABC had a crew available and a gap in its production schedule. The preparation time was short. The screenplay by Helen Garner was offered to me, as I've told you, by producer Jan Chapman. We agreed on the objectives, and we had a relationship of mutual trust. I also loved the screenplay, even though the idea of telling a story by going back in time wasn't what I would have preferred. What I liked was the freshness of its observation and the realism of the situations. I felt that I could make something of it. Helen Garner had drawn her inspiration from the experiences of her daughter and one of her friends. I went to Melbourne to meet them. The schoolgirl who was playing her daughter had blonde hair, and we thought she didn't look serious enough. We gave her brown hair and cut it like a boy's. On the whole, I think it's not that difficult working with teenagers, even though some days their emotions are very muddled.

To what extent do objects, which are numerous in your films, help the actors in their work?
I like first of all to watch what they do normally in life, and I remind them of that when we're shooting so that their acting is natural and comes from their personal experience.

Do you work a lot with the camera?
I like looking through the viewfinder because I'm very clear on the frame I want. When we were shooting *Two Friends*, the camera crew felt some resentment towards me because they weren't used to the director doing that. My director of photography didn't really understand what I was wanting, and I had to be very obstinate to impose my views. On the other hand, I had a very good rapport with Sally Bongers, a friend who had studied with me and who shot *Peel* and *A Girl's Own Story*. But for *Two Friends*, I had to use the television camera crew. They were very competent but simply had a different way of filming.

Do you do a lot of takes?
No. For *Two Friends*, for example, we'd decided on the visual style, we knew there'd be virtually no close-ups, and as soon as the actors had played the scene with the right tone, we moved onto the next shot. I didn't 'cover' myself, if you like. On the whole, it was a very economical shoot.

Do you plan to continue in this vein of personal stories?
I hope that my films will always have the same sense of observation, because I think that it's a strength, but I'm not sure that my stories will remain so intimate. I have a great desire to work on a larger scale with stronger stories, different material. At the moment, I'm working on a project that's close to the spirit and mood of a Grimms fairy tale. It's a love story set in New Zealand around 1850 with quite a dark mood.

Did you choose to portray youth in *A Girl's Own Story* and *Two Friends* because it was reassuring, when you were starting out, to deal with themes you were familiar with?
In the case of *A Girl's Own Story*, I wanted, indeed, to talk about a world I knew well. Also, I love young people: I find them free and open. But it's not an obsession on my part! Of course, every time someone has written a story with young girls, they think of me to direct it. But every generation interests me. In fact, I'd like to tell all sorts of stories. At the moment,

I'm rereading *Treasure Island* and I'm really enjoying it. I love its strength, it audacity, and also its sense of observation. In any case, I think I'll always retain a certain irony about life.

Two Friends
(1986)

Sweetie
(1989)

"Things Are Rarely
What They Seem."

*Louise (Emma Coles) and Kelly
(Kris Bidenko) in* Two Friends *(1986).*

*Dawn, nicknamed 'Sweetie' (Genevieve
Lemon), and Kay (Karen Colston) in*
Sweetie *(1989).*

Finding Her Way

A New Tone

Although *Sweetie* was Campion's first film for the cinema and one of the most brilliant debut films of the 1980s, it had been preceded three years earlier by *Two Friends*, a feature-length film for television that, along with three of her short films, established her name at the 1986 Cannes Film Festival. For the first time, the filmmaker was inspired by an existing text—a short story by the Australian novelist Helen Garner based on a real-life experience of her daughter and one of her friends—but Campion proved, as she has done frequently since, that she is good at incorporating material by writers other than herself, from Janet Frame to Henry James, into her personal world. The film continues and develops the subject of *A Girl's Own Story*, giving an account of two young girls who are leaving adolescence and facing up to dysfunctional families. The narration is driven by reverse chronology—July, February (five months earlier), January (one month earlier), December (one month earlier), October (two months earlier)—a method that had already been used by Harold Pinter in his play *Betrayal* (1978) and that would be taken up again by filmmakers Lee Chang-dong in *Peppermint Candy* (1999) and François Ozon in *5×2* (2004). The first sequence, which is thus the end of the story, sees Louise (Emma Coles) receiving a letter of reconciliation from her friend Kelly (Kris Bidenko). We are presented with Louise's indecision as to how to reply: since she goes over to a piano, which she begins to play, the music partially covers the voice-over of Kelly reading her letter. Shortly before, the very beginning of the film showed us her mother (Kris McQuade) and her father (Stephen Leeder) attending a meeting where people were mourning the death of a young girl, a gloomy note that cast a pessimistic light, announcing perhaps the same fate for Kelly, whose complicated relationships with her divorced parents have led her into vagrancy, taking drugs, and possible delinquency.

If Campion's earlier short films revealed the influence of Polanski and Lynch, even of Kubrick—for example, the bedroom in *A Girl's Own Story* littered with semi-naked Barbie dolls in provocative poses, like the mannequins of *Killer's Kiss* (1955)—*Two Friends* shows signs of the shooting style of Antonioni—particularly that of *Le Amiche* (1955)— with its long sequence shots, depths of field, ellipses, and a liking for the unsaid and empty shots. Campion once again focuses on the family story. Her two female leads have ambiguous relationships with their fathers, both of whom are separated from their mothers. Louise, alone

at a restaurant with her father (a scene resembling that in *A Girl's Own Story*) says to him, "Dad, do you think anyone would mistake us for girlfriend and boyfriend?" Meanwhile, Kelly, exposed to the animosity of her stepfather (Peter Hehir), has gone to visit her father in his apartment, when he leaves her alone with a friend to go and meet his mistress. The fantasized romances that the teenage girls imagine with their fathers express a need for affection that is not being satisfied. But Campion also knows how to portray the complexity of intergenerational relationships. Louise silences her mother, who wants to talk to her and isolates her on the seat on a bus, turning her back on her to chat with Kelly. Kelly, meanwhile, wants attention from her mother that the latter reserves for her new partner, and ends up smashing the ceramic vase she had bought her for her birthday. Feelings of exclusion and loneliness are shared by adults and teenagers. After her father goes out, Kelly remains at his apartment with his friend and slips into bed with him before fleeing his advances. Once again, the attraction and repulsion that sex holds for adolescents asserts itself as a recurrent motif in Campion's cinema. *Two Friends* presents a new tone, previously unknown in her work, a melancholy that alludes to a friendship that is falling apart, paths that are diverging, even though Kelly, the more fragile of the two, makes a last appeal for their reunion.

Tragic and Grotesque

Sweetie takes up the stylistic devices and thematic issues of the short films to give them a new dimension, establishing Campion internationally with her debut feature film for the cinema. Kay (Karen Colston), the narrator who provides the thread running through the story, is a cousin of Pam, who 'feels the cold' in *A Girl's Own Story*, and of Lorraine, abandoned to loneliness after being sexually harassed in *After Hours*. Kay, in the first shots, confesses in a voice-over that she is afraid of the trees because she imagines their roots crawling right under her bed. In fact, Kay is afraid of her family tree, of secrets buried like roots that can't be seen. *Sweetie* is a new exploration of a dysfunctional family whose past we speculate about and keys to which we are given gradually. Kay has suffered from a lack of affection and an inability to connect to the world. She goes to see a psychic (Jean Hadgraft), takes refuge in magic and superstition, and believes in the prophecy she's been given when it tells her that the man she will love will have a question mark on his face. On meeting Louis (Tom Lycos), she notices a strand of hair that joins

40

Two Friends *(1986).*
Top and centre: Louise (Emma Coles);
Bottom: Kelly (Kris Bidenko).

Two Friends.
Top: Kelly and her boyfriend Panky (Peter Bowden);
Centre: Malcolm (Peter Hehir) and his stepdaughter Kelly;
Bottom: Kelly, Louise, and Janet, Louise's mother (Kris McQuade).

Kelly and Louise in Two Friends.

42

Kay believes in the prophecy given to her by a psychic, which tells her that the man she will love will have a question mark on his face.

Sweetie's voracious appetite is also manifest when, for revenge, she tries to eat the horse figurines that are Kay's most precious possessions.

*Campion's use of documentary images of tumid plants
to interpret Kay's nightmare (above right) is reminiscent
of the way in which Luis Buñuel introduced an extract from a
nature film about scorpions in* L'Âge d'or *(1930, above left).*

up with a birthmark, suggesting this punctuation mark. Evidence thus provided, she steals him from the arms of the girl to whom he's recently become engaged and makes love with him under a car in an underground car park. When Louis, who comes to live with her, plants a shrub in her garden, she digs it up and hides it in the house, substantiating further her phobia of nature and its proliferation.

The first third of *Sweetie* gives priority to the perspective of Kay, the narrator, and her view of the world and her family. Then we are introduced to Dawn (Genevieve Lemon), nicknamed "Sweetie" (after whom the film is named), the sister who breaks into the story much as she enters Kay's house at night with her boyfriend by smashing a window. One of the components of the family's neurosis is the relationship between the two sisters, one of the recurring features of Campion's films. While Kay is lacking love, Sweetie has suffered from a surfeit of it, their father (Jon Darling) having encouraged her dreams of stardom and professional success in the world of dance. He has made her a palace fit for a princess in the tree that her sister so detests. Kay's fear of sex—she refuses Louis and goes to sleep in the guest room—becomes more extreme after the arrival of Sweetie, who overflows with sexuality, making love noisily with her drug-addict boyfriend, physically seducing Louis on the beach in Kay's absence, and behaving like an animal in asking her lover to imitate a horse, barking like a dog, urinating and breaking wind in public and painting herself black like a baboon when she takes refuge in her 'palace'. This regression also finds expression in her friendship with little Clayton (Andre Pataczek), the neighbours' child. Sweetie's voracious appetite is also manifest when, for revenge, she ingests the porcelain horse figurines that are Kay's most precious possessions and that have symbolic value as representing the sexuality that she otherwise rejects. When Kay sees Sweetie bathing her father and touching him between his legs, she goes to bed and, in a fit of modesty, pulls the sheets up to her chin. The incestuous fantasy was noted from the moment of *Sweetie*'s release by Françoise Audé, who argues that Kay is jealous not only of a favored sister, but also of her father, who has excluded her from a phallic relationship.[1] The screenplay for *Sweetie*

was written with Gerard Lee, who was the director's boyfriend at the time. The character of Flo (Dorothy Barry), the mother of Sweetie and Kay, was inspired by his mother, who had left her husband, as also happens in the film. Campion's own parents, Edith and Richard, had divorced a few years previously. Another indirectly autobiographical element can be seen in the selection of actor Tom Lycos for the part of Kay's boyfriend, a choice influenced by his physical resemblance to Gerard Lee. The third part of the film opens with a pastoral scene, Flo having found a job working in a canteen for farm labourers in the Australian outback. It's here that Kay, Louis, and Gordon, Flo's husband, meet up with her after having given the slip to Sweetie, who they've left alone at home. It is as though Gordon needs to break the exclusive and unhealthy relationship he has with Sweetie to find his wife again. Indeed, we see him, come nightfall, dancing tranquilly among the labourers, while in an earlier scene, Flo, Kay, and Louis swim together in the refreshing waters of a lake. Water plays a particularly important role here, as elsewhere in Campion's films. Flo is portrayed as the only balanced person in the family. It is she who confesses: 'I can't imagine living without my trees. They give me hope.' These airy, simply shot outdoor scenes have a Western tone that contrasts with the rest of the film, with its constantly bold formal quality, fragmented and sometimes frenetic editing, unbalanced framing, ellipses, wide-angle shots, and disturbing lighting. For example, in the first shots, Kay is cut in half; we see only her legs. Everything competes stylistically to create a feeling of strangeness heightened by a claustrophobic atmosphere that expresses the protagonist's instability and anxiety. To convey Kay's nightmare after Louis has planted the shrub, Campion inserts documentary images of tumid plants, seeds germinating, protrusions, reminiscent of the way in which Buñuel introduced an extract from a nature film about scorpions at the beginning of *L'Âge d'or* (1930).

After the rural sequence, Campion returns to her bizarre aesthetic where the grotesque blends with the tragic to depict Sweetie's increasing delinquency after being abandoned by her family. She takes refuge in her palace at the top of the tree with her young friend, the neighbours'

*Sweetie takes refuge in her palace
at the top of the tree.*

son, before a fatal fall. Kay, who Louis has left after becoming aware of her phobias and denouncing her as abnormal when he discovers the shrub hidden under the bed, throws herself on her sister's bruised and bloodied body as though she is the only one who wants to save her. It is as though her guilt is intensified by her restored equilibrium and her reconciliation with Louis. At Sweetie's funeral, the coffin cannot be placed in the ground because of a protruding root that has to be sawn off. The white gospel choir, the Café of the Gate of Salvation, which has been heard elsewhere in the film, accompanies the burial, singing, not without irony: 'Love will never, never let you fall.' The film ends with two short sequences: in the first, a high-angle shot frames the legs of Louis and Kay, who are stroking each other with their feet; in the second, Gordon, walking in the backyard, passes the tree where Sweetie as a child, standing next to a fence, dressed in pink and wearing white gloves, sings 'Every Beat of My Heart', showing her undying love for the one for whom the song is destined, that is to say, her father.

The Doors of Poetry

Sweetie, a family story, is one of the director's most personal films; through a series of projections and displacements, she speaks of very intimate things. She has given a very prosaic explanation (see the interview on page 48) for her final dedication: "For my sister." We can see here a sign of love for Anna, after a difficult relationship during their childhood and adolescence when they vied for their parents' attention. Alistair Fox suggests that these two sisters are two halves of the same personality, and links this to the theory of "the shadow aspect" promulgated by Jung, whom Campion admires: We suppress the more unacceptable traits of our personality by relegating them to our unconscious, and that unacknowledged part of us, the shadow (also evoked by Kubrick in *Full Metal Jacket*, 1987), surfaces in dreams and visions.[2] We deny its existence in ourselves by projecting it onto others. Sweetie has access to this animal part of her that Kay is too

afraid to face. The whole first part of the film is shot with a bluish light that gives the portrait of Kay a dreamlike quality. Like the directors she admires—Buñuel (*Belle de jour*, 1967), Polanski (*Repulsion*, 1965), Lynch (*Blue Velvet*, 1986)—Campion films the mind, which opens the doors of poetry. The ugliness of the Sydney suburban interiors, with their floral motifs on the walls and floors, garish colours and repellently run-of-the-mill furniture, only serve to highlight the powers of the imagination. The cracks in the asphalt pavements and in the ceiling that mark Kay are like a reminder of the scars of her childhood, just as her destruction of the shrub in the yard of their suburban home betrays her desire to prevent her unconscious from emerging. Like Louis, Sweetie, and her father, she can't face reality. Sweetie still dreams of the career on the stage that her father has instilled into her, and introduces her lover as her manager; Gordon hides the attraction he feels for his daughter and creates false hopes for her future; Louis takes refuge in meditation and the study of tantric sex.

Campion's rebellious personality is particularly evident in *Sweetie*, which is like the synthesis of her short films, with its revolt against all forms of repression that prohibit emotion and desire. This rejection of conventions can be found in her aesthetic approach, which eschews bland, consensual cinema. In this sense, the film can be seen as a catharsis, echoing the first a cappella gospel song of the opening credits: 'Somebody told me about an endless journey, and I can say I feel it clearly now.' This journey is the one that the director took on her first film for the cinema, a therapy for her inner demons and an attempt to understand the world. And it is a search that she continued with *An Angel at My Table*, the story of a woman's quest to find her way.

1 Françoise Audé, 'Les malheurs de S', *Positif*, 347 (January 1990), p. 11.
2 Alistair Fox, *Jane Campion: Authorship and Personal Cinema*, Indiana University Press, Bloomington, 2011.

The two final sequences of Sweetie*.*
<u>*Top:*</u> *Gordon (Jon Darling) passes the tree where Sweetie*
as a child expresses her undying love for her father.
<u>*Bottom:*</u> *A high-angle shot frames the legs of Louis and*
Kay, who are stroking each other with their feet.

*Kay, in a fit of modesty, pulls
the sheets up to her chin.*

Interview conducted in Cannes, 17 May 1989

What were you doing during the three years between your short films and *Sweetie*?
After the presentation of my films at the Cannes Film Festival, I thought about what I was going to embark on in as much as opportunities were opening up to me. The first project that I wanted to do was *Sweetie* because it seemed to me to have the most modern and provocative point of view. In addition, it was feasible financially. I was also thinking that after a more 'serious' film, it would be difficult to make *Sweetie*! I sense there's a provocative side to me, and I really enjoyed tackling this subject. I began to develop the story with my co-screenwriter Gerard Lee, the friend who had already written *Passionless Moments* with me and who is someone very intelligent. It was material he knew well, that belonged to both of us, and we were on the same wavelength. It took me three years to make *Sweetie*, because during this period I developed other projects, including *The Piano Lesson*, a very romantic subject in the register of the Brontë sisters that I would like to shoot later, and also Janet Frame, which will be my next film, the portrait of a New Zealand writer who wrote several volumes of autobiography that revolve around what it's like to grow up and also deal with the issues of creation. I love the style of her autobiographical trilogy: *To the Is-Land*, which is about her childhood, full of originality and the most appealing of the three, *An Angel at My Table*, and *The Envoy from Mirror City*, in which many of the events take place in Europe. That's why I recently spent time scouting locations on your continent. I'll be shooting three parts of an hour each for television, with the possibility of a cinema version.

Did you have any trouble financing *Sweetie*?
Finding the money to write these three projects wasn't difficult. As for the production of *Sweetie*, it happened without too many problems as the film was very cheap, less than a million dollars. The script was written from this perspective. It was inspired by people and events that I knew. I always work like that. It gives me more authority to write, and even if I later diverge from these experiences, I always have a base to which I can return. The character of Sweetie was inspired by a man, but for family reasons we changed the sex. I was disappointed about that to begin with but I respected the feelings of my co-writer. What I liked about Sweetie was the potential that she had and the way in

which she fell apart. That happens to all of us. One day we're exploring what we could be, then the day passes and it's too late. She's a poignant character who lacks hope.

In a sense, Kay is the central character. The others connect with her story gradually—first Louis, then Sweetie, then her parents.
We called the film *Sweetie* because it's a nice title, not because she's the heroine of the story. Kay evolves, she feels braver. I also believe that you can't love without there being a real basis to that love, otherwise you're just loving an illusion, and that doesn't work. But most of us create a certain degree of illusion around what we do. We have an idea in our heads about who our partner is, and it's difficult for us to accept that they're different from this idea.

Did you always have the idea that you would begin with a voice-over and by what's going on in Kay's head?
No. At the beginning I'd thought of opening with shots of trees. They were very beautiful shots, but I thought that would disorientate the audience, that there were too many elements to bring together. At the same time, when I'm filming, I feel that I can do anything, that I'm completely free as long as it contributes to the story, that there's a sense to it. I love it when things are fresh and surprising. With Kay's voice-over we were wanting to show, right from the beginning, that we were interested not only in what the characters do but also in what they think and feel.

Whereabouts in Australia does the action take place?
For the most part in Willoughby, a suburb north of Sydney. The scenes where they're going to visit the mother were shot in Warren in the north of New South Wales, a fantastic town, a centre for cotton picking and sheep farming. I loved filming there. We trampled the ground to give it the dry, desert aspect of certain regions of Australia where we didn't have the budget to shoot.

In Kafka's *The Metamorphosis*, everything's seen from the perspective of the 'abnormal' son. Here, it's rather that of the family faced with Sweetie's otherness.
I thought, however, that from time to time it would be good to feel what Sweetie is thinking or feeling, such as when the family leaves to go west and we understand from her reaction what a baby she is. Her father is a treacherous

bastard who creates a vain hope. He knows that if he takes Sweetie, he'll never be able to bring back his wife. I remember that the actor who was playing Gordon [Jon Darling] had the same reactions as his character; he felt really in trouble at that point!

Did you study psychiatric cases and read books on the subject?
No, not really. We had living examples around us. And we used to talk a lot about people we used to know who'd gone mad. We also sent Genevieve Lemon [who played Sweetie] to a rehabilitation centre to observe the patients. We wanted her to feel the menace. She had trouble coping with the experience; there was one patient in particular who constantly threatened her with a razor blade. You couldn't say that we did in-depth research, but we borrowed a lot from personal experiences. It was a subject that I thought about for about a year. I didn't want to stick to the usual narrative formula but rather to deal with mental states and emotions. I wanted to talk about the difficulty of loving while subtly introducing darker undercurrents. That's when I had the idea of superstition. I also wanted to use metaphors because I think people think a lot more often that we realize in metaphors and we don't often see that on screen. That seemed to me to give an extra dimension to the film.

Then I asked myself what sort of story we were wanting to tell. It was at that point that Gerard and I got a bit of money together and went and spent a fortnight in a house facing the beach, where we discussed and acted out, both of us, the different roles. What was important to us was to find the tone of each scene, the way in which people were going to speak. The screenplay developed organically. I didn't know that Sweetie was going to eat ceramic horses until we arrived at that moment in the story where I asked myself what she could do. We never knew what the following step would be until we got there. It was certainly true that we had a lot of trouble reordering the story; it was like a chain where we couldn't move the links around.

Did you work with the actors on their lines?
Everything was scripted, but we had a lot of rehearsals, which was especially useful for getting to know them and for them to have confidence in me, and also for us to know how to support each other. It was also an opportunity to explore all the possibilities of their roles. Each actor is different, and I worked

<u>*Left, top and bottom:*</u> *Sweetie in the garden with her neighbours.*
<u>*Top right:*</u> *A rural scene with farm labourers in the outback.*
<u>*Bottom right:*</u> *Sweetie at the beach with her boyfriend.*

One of the components of the family's neurosis is the relationship between the two sisters, a recurring feature in Campion's films: while Kay lacks love, Sweetie suffers from a surfeit of it.

with their differences. Genevieve liked me to tell her exactly what she needed to do. I had to trick her, to put her in situations where she would discover for herself what we needed. Karen Colston [Kay], on the other hand, knew exactly, at each moment, who she was and what she needed. My method with her was to ask her opinion on what Kay would do and think at a particular moment. In general, she got it right every time. What is curious is that in real life, Genevieve is a very strong and very intelligent woman.

The subject could have given rise to a pessimistic film. Yet you film ugliness and vulgarity while stylizing them.
The art director deliberately created dull, ugly sets. We thought about the interiors, bearing in mind the fact that people bring their own furniture into apartments or they move in while keeping items that belonged to the previous tenants, so there's a mix of styles. What is ugly can also be seen with style depending on the lighting or the framing. It's a mark of sympathy. It's more poignant for me than a 'pretty' décor, which offers fewer possible contrasts.

Your framing is astonishing. Were the frames preset or were they inspired while shooting?
I had nothing to lose; it was a small budget and we could be daring, take risks. We were shooting for our own pleasure. Lots of things were worked out in advance. Sally Bongers, my director of photography, thinks like me. We talk together, drink tea, laugh, imagine shots, look around us to see what we can steal. We're both very visually oriented, and our aesthetic sense is very similar. Sally also has a lot of common sense about the scenes: she frames according to the dramatic situation to create a touching emotion, but she's careful to ensure that that doesn't distract the viewer's attention too much. We've made those sorts of mistakes. In some scenes, we felt the characters weren't talking to each other because they were at the extreme edge of the frame! We had to reshoot them. I am very good friends with Sally Bongers, although that doesn't mean we don't argue; we both like to have our own way. She is very stubborn, very strong, and sometimes wants certain things. And as I'm like her and I sometimes have contrary ideas, conflict is inevitable! They're not really disagreements but rather the result of the pressures that result from shooting.

As far as the lighting is concerned, Sally was mainly responsible, and she's very intuitive. But we had discussed it beforehand and we wanted a soft light on faces because that's how we felt towards the characters. At the beginning I was afraid that my framing would seem pretentious, but I no longer have that horrible feeling. What I wanted was to cross the line that allows the framing to create the poignancy of a situation, as in photography, which is a much more adventurous art in this respect. There's a sensibility, a sophistication in photography that you don't often find in film, and I want to be able to continue to juggle this visual exploration with the development of the narrative.

Were the nature scenes, like the swimming one or the nighttime dance in the country, envisaged as you've filmed them?
I made a storyboard that helped me see what I needed to do but we often modified it depending on what happened. For example, the shot where the two cowboys teach each other to dance comes from what I'd observed between two actors, one of whom was teaching the other a dance step. I thought that had charm and decided to introduce it into the film. You need to be constantly on the lookout so you can capture details that give the feel of things, but, of course, the big obstacle is time. We had lots of other ideas that we were unable to shoot during those forty days of filming. Eight weeks isn't very short according to the usual criteria, but with our way of filming it was pretty restrictive.

The scene with the clairvoyant whose son is mentally disabled announces the appearance of Sweetie.
Except that he's really mentally disabled. I liked the idea that this old woman accepts her son's status so easily. You often find that with clairvoyants: contrary to what you might think, they're often very down-to-earth. Sweetie's parents behave very differently.

The cemetery scene at the end, with the tree in the wind, the tracking shot of the very regular trees, then the shot of the open grave, which has a tree root growing into its side, was that entirely conceived in advance?
It was different in the script. But when I saw the cemetery, I loved the formal character of the place and I wanted to highlight it. I also noticed this tree that seemed to be breathing. But it was especially during editing that its living character became so apparent. I spend a lot of time editing; twelve hours a day, six days a week. I love editing—it's a stage where you can still add a lot, where original ideas appear. The first rough cut was two and a half hours, but I always intended that the film be not much longer than an hour and a half.

Where does the music come from?
It's an Australian group of thirty singers, Café of the Gate of Salvation, which isn't religious. They're original compositions that come from the white gospel tradition. They're very human singers who have a great sense of orchestration, meet for the pleasure of being together and don't work for money. They're growing stronger and stronger, and being in a room with them and hearing them sing is a very powerful experience. The last song isn't their lyrics but is adapted from the Jewish prayer book. We were concerned that these songs would appear religious, but once we'd used one when they were making love in the car park, our worries vanished! I'm not systematically in favor of music in film, but there are moments when it really makes the difference. Like, precisely, this sequence in the parking lot with Kay and Louis, when it enables us to establish our ironic point of view regarding these characters at this precise moment.

The danger in this sort of film is being condescending.
I thought that the characters, being very vulnerable, very exposed, would eventually win the viewer's sympathy. I wanted the public to end up by identifying with them. I think, in life, people are both funny and tragic, and I don't have a problem with laughing when they're in a difficult situation. Sometimes they're grateful to you because it enables them to see that there are two sides of the coin. We take our lives too seriously, when there needs to be a limit to that. It's even only due to a certain way of thinking that we think of certain events as being tragic. I'm not at all respectful of the misfortune of others, but at the same time, I'm very sensitive to it. I myself tend to complain a lot about things that happen to me, and others find it hilarious and laugh!

Are you aware of a difference between your short and medium-length films and *Sweetie*?
Not really. Except that *Sweetie* is the best and most powerful thing that I've done. It's a film that I was less in control of, that led me to places I didn't really know I was going, and in that sense it was a great adventure. In that respect, I'm satisfied.

Clayton (Andre Pataczek),
the neighbour's child who
Sweetie seeks out as a friend.

Are there films where you've sensed there's a pursuit similar to your own, a desire to describe mental states?

It's common in literature, and I don't see why one wouldn't do it in film. One just needs to want to do it, to desire to accomplish it, like David Lynch. You don't discover truth simply by developing a plot but by exploring several levels. I don't want simply to look at behaviour but to discover thoughts and emotions, as in some of the novels by Duras and Flannery O'Connor. I find the latter exquisite, ruthless, and honest. "A Good Man is Hard to Find" is an extraordinary story that is both hilarious and horrific. I feel completely innocent in relation to stories like that! I really liked John Huston's adaptation of *Wise Blood* [1979]. In fact, I like John Huston's films generally.

I think people are very symbolic in their understanding of the world. Things are rarely what they seem; they're the metaphor of what is or what could be. And that is equally true of our internal torments. One day a friend came to live with me because she was very troubled. She didn't know how to choose between two men. I remember that the whole world became a metaphor of her personal problem. When we went shopping together and she noticed some extravagant shoes, that meant to her that she should live with the more adventurous guy, or, on the other hand, that her own adventurous spirit needed the one who was the more stable of the two. When we were driving and she saw a licence plate beginning with J, that meant that she should live with John. We all do that to a greater or lesser extent.

Do you know Emily Dickinson's poetic work, with its mixture of metaphysical and tangible?

No, but I like the mix!

With your films, too, we get a cosmic feeling from small material details—a tree root, for example, and you suggest a link between the mind and the outside world.

That's how I feel things. I believe my generation is attracted by the spiritual and is less willing to participate in world movement. I myself have been meditating for five years. It helps me to exercise self-restraint. I am also more aware of my true emotions. Very often we're simply driven to do things that in fact don't resonate with our inner self.

Your characters are all very lonely.

Not Sweetie. She communicates a lot in her way, and sometimes dishonestly! She immediately makes friends with the neighbours and takes Louis to the beach. Nobody understands the threat posed by Sweetie except Kay, who is the most vulnerable. It is difficult to know how mentally disabled Sweetie actually is. In my opinion, she's normal, or at least was. Since childhood, she has been gradually pushed by her environment and has ended up losing her balance and her sense of responsibility. In other circumstances, she might have been different.

Was Sweetie barking inspired by a case that you'd observed?

No, I completely made it up. There were a lot of rehearsals for that scene. It took courage for Genevieve to manage to scare everyone. It was a decisive moment in her performance. She really became the character when she felt her power over others and that she was capable of scaring them.

Why did you dedicate the film to your sister?

Because I was very touched by her behaviour. While we were shooting, my mother was very ill, dying, in fact, and I had to decide whether to stop, to let another director finish the film, or to continue. My sister, who was in England, came back to New Zealand to look after her and enable me to continue.

<u>Top:</u> *Jane Campion on the set of* Sweetie *with
the son of the psychic (Paul Livingston).*
<u>Bottom:</u> *Tom Lycos (lying on the sand) and
members of the film crew.*

An Angel at My Table
(1990)

"The Red Wigs
of Autobiography."

From top to bottom: Janet Frame as a child (Alexia Keogh);
as a teenager (Karen Fergusson), with her sisters Myrtle
(Melina Bernecker), Isabel (Samantha Townsley), and June
(Sarah Llewellyn); and as an adult (Kerry Fox).

Fragile and vulnerable

From Word to Image

An Angel at My Table is the first adaptation deliberately chosen by Campion, the previous adaptation—the short film *After Hours*—having been a commission. The autobiography of the New Zealand novelist Janet Frame had attracted Campion at a young age, and she returned to her native country to shoot there for the first time. While a writer has to condense the story of his or her life by making some drastic choices, the screen adaptation written by Laura Jones, with the active participation of the film's director, had in turn to reduce the 450 pages of the book to around eighty pages. Overall, the film remains very faithful to the original, even though it places more emphasis on certain events and leaves out others. Clearly, Campion found many elements in the material that echoed her own personal concerns. It was inevitable, indeed, that she would relate to the odyssey of a woman who had decided to succeed as a writer by learning to depend on no one but herself and by fighting to decide her own future. Originally conceived for New Zealand television, the film respects the three parts of the original work, even though some minor cuts were made for its theatrical release and its presentation at film festivals, notably the Venice International Film Festival, where it won the Grand Special Jury Prize (Silver Lion) in 1990.

The first part, *To the Is-Land*, is devoted to Janet's childhood (the young Janet is played by Alexia Keogh), her family, her experiences at school, and her encounters with friends; and her adolescence (where Janet is played by Karen Fergusson), marked by the death of her older sister Myrtle (Melina Bernecker), who drowned in a swimming accident. The second part, *An Angel at My Table*, marks her passage into adulthood (here Karen Fergusson makes way for Kerry Fox), the absence of home, her experience at university, her short time teaching in a primary school, her crush on a teacher, and then her eight-year incarceration in a psychiatric hospital following another death by drowning, that of her younger sister Isabel (Glynis Angell), which plunges her into depression. In the final part, *The Envoy from Mirror City*, she undertakes a trip to Europe that is marked by her encounters in London, then a brief stay in Paris, and, finally, her experience in Ibiza, where she has a love affair with Bernhard (William Brandt), an American who leaves her to return to the United States. She pursues the literary adventure that she

had begun in New Zealand with the publication of her first poems and stories. The film ends with her return to her native country after she learns of the death of her father (Kevin J. Wilson), some time after the demise of her mother (Iris Churn).

The film has an episodic structure made up of ellipses and short scenes that link a series of thematic echoes to evoke these formative years. In this sense, it differs from the novel format Campion adopted in her two subsequent films, *The Piano* and *The Portrait of a Lady*. The problem posed by *An Angel at My Table* is similar to the one Campion would have to face—which she did no less brilliantly—with *Bright Star*, her portrait of the last months of the life of the poet John Keats: How can one adapt a work devoted to words, to writing, and thus to language, for a visual medium?

The presence of numerous sequences where poems are evoked underlines the powerful influence of literature in the life of the young Janet, which would determine her vocation and lead to her decision to give up teaching to devote herself to a life as a writer. Her sister Myrtle recites Walter de la Mare's "I Met At Eve" in a cemetery. Janet borrows books from the Athenaeum, Dunedin's famous library, to take them back to her family. She listens, fascinated, to her teacher Miss Lindsay (Edith Campion) reading a passage from Alfred Tennyson's *Idylls of the King*, in which a gloved arm rises from the lake brandishing the sword Excalibur, which the child visualizes (John Boorman has made one of the most striking shots of it in his adaptation of the Holy Grail). Later, with her classmates, she is captivated by the sad face of Shirley as she sings Schubert's *lied* "An die Musik" ("hast thou borne my soul above to realms of rest"), which strikes a chord in her. Other moments are equally significant: the mention of Matthew Arnold's "The Scholar Gipsy" Karl and Kay reciting Keats, Janet silently reading George Borrow's *Lavengro* ("Life is sweet, Jasper"; Campion would give this name to her first child, who died a few days after he was born), writing lines of Shakespeare's *Cymbeline* on the walls of her hospital cell and reciting Shelley's "Ode to the West Wind" looking out over the Mediterranean in Ibiza. Most of these many references are from nineteenth-century English literature, cherished as much by the Campion family as by the Frames, in particular by Edith, Jane's mother,

60

The opening of the film: 'This is the story of my childhood. In
August 1924, I was born: Janet Paterson Frame.'

who was of the same generation as Janet Frame. The film is equally steeped in the same poetic world.

Proximity and Detachment

The other problem inherent in a biopic that recounts several stages of a single life is finding different actors to play the same character from childhood to adulthood. The choices of Alexia Keogh, Karen Fergusson, and Kerry Fox, each sporting similar red hair, turned out to be the right ones in terms not only of the quality of their portrayals of the character but also in establishing a fluid continuity that renders the transition from one to another virtually imperceptible. This is accomplished each time by a unique moment of voice-over narration: Janet as a child is introduced by an adult narrator (the Janet Frame author of her memoirs) in the opening sequence; Janet as a teenager, with her back to the camera, speaks of the tears she shed reading 'The Scholar Gipsy'; finally, the adult Janet, again with her back to the camera, walks along a rail track, holding an open book from which she reads the conversation with Jasper.

The beginning of the film is marked by fragmented images as muddled memories: a mother with her arms open, a baby taking her first steps in the grass, then a little girl with red hair walking towards the camera in the middle of a verdant landscape, accompanied by a voice-over ('This is the story of my childhood. In August 1924, I was born: Janet Paterson Frame'). The camera frames her face in close-up, in the same way that Kay was framed at the beginning of *Sweetie*. This film, too, is the exploration of a personality, except that this time the heroine turns back and runs away at full pelt, as though fleeing our gaze, as if to say 'No Trespassing'. Here Campion establishes the aesthetic principle that will govern *An Angel at My Table*: proximity and detachment. As Kathleen McHugh has noted, she alternates between subjectivity and objectivity.[1] Frame is observed in the first part, she observes herself in the second, and, having become an artist, observes the world and explores her imagination in the third. As in her earlier films, Campion focuses on a fragile and vulnerable character.

Janet is looking for affection. In one of the first scenes in the film she steals some money from her father's coat pocket to buy chewing gum for her classmates and so gain their friendship. The gesture earns her the humiliation of being exposed by the schoolteacher. Her family's poverty, her unkempt appearance, and her decaying teeth isolate her. She is consumed with shame and by her obsession with the perception she believes others have of her. 'Too shy to mix, too scared to enter the union building. I was more and more alone. My only romance was in poetry and literature', recalls Janet in voice-over. Later, after she has become a teacher, she is petrified at the sight of an inspector sitting at the back of the class while she stares, unable to move, at a piece of chalk that she is holding in her hand. Campion has probably never gone as far in her depiction of human suffering as she did in portraying the mental asylum where Janet was committed. The book's author was reticent about her addressing this period of her life, which is mentioned only

briefly in her autobiography, but clearly the filmmaker wanted to retain this passage, which is at the heart of her film and achieves a particularly powerful intensity in her depiction of its dereliction. She had to borrow the elements she needed from one of Frame's novels, *Faces in the Water*, about a woman in an institution for the mentally ill.

Two Father Figures

As with all the filmmaker's female protagonists, Janet's experience of sexuality is an important aspect of the development of her personality. Her best friend Poppy (Carla Hedgeman, then Caroline Somerville) tells her how babies are made; the two girls discover Myrtle and Ted, Poppy's brother, making love in a wood; Janet gets her first period and feels a new sense of shame. Shortly before she is initiated in physical love in Ibiza, she confesses that she feels 'as asexual as a lump of wood'. As Eithne O'Neill has pointed out, the trials she encounters are linked to the colour red: menstruation stains, a nose bleed after she attempts suicide by overdosing on aspirin, the colour of her drowned sister's dress that she holds to her.[2] Bernhard, the man who introduces her to sex and who breaks her heart for the first time, turns out to be a mediocre poet and a disappointing lover, quick to interrupt their lovemaking to read her his latest literary creation. Earlier, a teacher she had admired and whom she had likened to Ashley in *Gone with the Wind* became the agent of her incarceration.

However, two men—two father figures that with their almost idealized image have been absent in Campion's work until now—impose their presence in the film. First there is Janet's biological father, Curly, who offers her a notebook in which to write her poems, who tells her he never wants her to leave again when she returns home after her internment, and who later comes to see her to give her advice about her trip to Europe. When she comes home from the Old Country, having learnt of her father's death, Janet takes pleasure in slipping on his old shoes. It is a scene that does not appear in the autobiography and represents her reconciliation with life and her discovery of home. Her literary father is her mentor, Frank Sargeson (Martyn Sanderson), a renowned New Zealand writer to whom Edith Campion was close, who offers his advice when she goes to live in a cottage next to his own to write her first novel. This change in the way that the image of the father is represented—until now, father figures have been shown as ambiguous, unreliable, and sometimes even sexually disturbed—is positive evidence of an evolution, albeit temporary, of the director's vision of the world.

A Bright Tone

Although viewed from many angles, *An Angel at My Table* is a dark film; it shines in sequences where life is exalted, most notably in its depiction of landscapes. Campion was back in her homeland and would celebrate its natural beauty with the help of her new cinematographer, Stuart

Janet and her friend Poppy (Carla Hedgeman)
amuse themselves by lining up rows of bottles and pretending
that they are naughty schoolchildren who must be punished.
<u>Facing page:</u> Janet expresses an irrepressible desire to know herself.

Dryburgh, who had replaced the equally talented Sally Bongers, who had worked on her earlier, more twisted films. Her heroine mirrors the colours of nature with her green eyes and red hair. The outback sequence in *Sweetie* had previously allowed the peaceful nature of a rustic landscape to emerge. The contrast with the town—whose representation is linked with Janet's fall into depression—is even stronger here. Similarly, when Janet finds herself on two other islands during her to trip to Europe, it is the Spain of the Balearic Islands rather than the England of London that is conducive to moments of happiness—such as when, in the splendor of her radiant nakedness, she swims in the ocean.

The film also produces a brighter tone in its depiction of Janet's relationships with her sisters and friends—these relationships between girls where Campion excels like no one else. These scenes are often linked to some sort of entertainment or performance which, like the references to poetry and literature, form the backdrop to Janet's imaginary world. She and Poppy amuse themselves by lining up rows of bottles and pretending that they are naughty schoolchildren who must be punished, so taking symbolic revenge on the power relationships imposed by their teachers. Later, the Frame children act out by moonlight the images they have seen in a book of fairy tales by the Brothers Grimm. Myrtle, meanwhile, plays at being a blond Hollywood vamp of the 1930s, while Janet mimics the Spanish dance of a childhood neighbour. The four sisters turn in unison in their bed. These moments, from the audition for a school play to Janet's sister Myrtle reading a poem on the radio, are moments of solace where the child attracts attention, gains some sort of recognition, and finds fulfilment in imitating life.

If, in the end, *An Angel at My Table*, is brighter in mood than Campion's previous works, it is because, despite the terrible events that her protagonist endures during the course of her life, she learns to grow and prosper by means of words without experiencing the redemption that, in a Hollywood scenario, a male partner could have offered her. Indeed, there are many scenes in which Janet looks at herself in a mirror, not in a narcissistic way, but with an irrepressible desire to know herself. And, in effect, she does eventually come to know and accept herself for who she is. Punctuated by trips—there are train journeys at the beginning and end of the first part and a boat trip at the beginning of the third

part—the film ends with Janet in a trailer home, where, smiling and at peace, she is tapping out her next novel on a typewriter. *An Angel at My Table*, as recounted by both Janet Frame and Jane Campion, is, to paraphrase James Joyce, the portrait of an artist as a young woman.

Very Secret Feelings

An Angel at My Table is also one of the most personal films about an emancipation, in which the director inevitably recognized herself, even though she was distanced from the character's story. Furthermore, it is personal in the relationship that she had with her mother, Edith, to whom she entrusted the role of the teacher Miss Lindsay, who recites Tennyson. Curiously, the adaptation minimizes the role of Janet Frame's mother, herself a poetess, whose domestic chores prevented her from realizing her creativity. Edith, belonging to the same generation as the famous author Janet Frame, cannot have failed to have inspired troubling parallels in her daughter: Frank Sargeson had also been her literary mentor; she too had attempted suicide and undergone treatment in a psychiatric hospital; she lost her first child in London in 1949, like Janet Frame, who had a miscarriage there a few years later. Finally, it was she who sent Jane the book *To the Is-land*, which so moved the director that she immediately decided that she wanted to adapt it. Anna Campion made a short student film called *The Audition* (1989) about the relationship between her sister and their mother at the time that Jane made Edith audition for her role in *An Angel at My Table*. The film reveals not only the affection that they had for each other but also the tensions that existed between them and their different points of view on life, with Edith accusing her daughter of bullying her and Jane coming across as more optimistic than her mother. This codicil to *An Angel at My Table* confirms the very intimate nature of a film that, as is often the case with adaptations, allows the director to better hide herself in order to reveal her innermost thoughts and feelings.

1 Kathleen McHugh, *Jane Campion* (Contemporary Film Directors), University of Illinois Press, Urbana and Chicago, 2007.
2 Eithne O'Neill, 'Jane Campion filme Janet Frame', *Positif*, 616 (June 2012).

Top: Janet confesses to her sister the attraction she has for her teacher.
Bottom: Back to New Zealand.

During her trip to Ibiza, Janet liberates herself and loses her inhibitions
in her affair with Bernhard (William Brandt).
<u>*Following pages:*</u> *Kerry Fox, Jane Campion, and cinematographer*
Stuart Dryburgh on the set of An Angel at My Table.

68

Interview conducted in Venice, 14 September 1990

What did Janet Frame represent for you before you thought of adapting her book?

I remember when I was thirteen and I used to read her books lying on my bed, and the impact they had on me. There were lots of poetic passages in her novel _Owls Do Cry_, like "sings Daphne from the dead room," which had a peculiar quality of sadness and evoked the world of madness. Her family had experienced many tragedies. In _Owls Do Cry_, the sister falls into a burning rubbish heap and dies. In her autobiography, she drowns herself, but this triggers the same feeling of terror. When you're very young, at thirteen, you're very impressionable and particularly affected by what poetically renders the inner life. I must have been really moved because when I wrote stories at school, I named a character Daphne. I also remember what I read about Janet Frame, the explanations that were given about her writing that linked it to schizophrenia. There were lots of rumors, a whole mythology surrounding her, and when I passed by a psychiatric clinic I wondered about Janet Frame, just as she had about the identity of the people she had described. It's why, when I heard that she had written her own account of her life, I had a strong desire to read it. It was thus that I discovered the first volume of her autobiography, _To the Is-Land_, around the age of twenty-eight, when I was at film school. And I then moved from curiosity about what had really happened in her life to the pleasure of discovering the freshness of the narrative and the richness of its detail. It awoke my own memories of my childhood, and, indeed, her book seemed to me to be a sort of essay on New Zealand childhood. I loved it; it was very emotional, and I wanted to share this experience with people.

You had to considerably condense her complete autobiography (three volumes, each one 250 pages).

Indeed, it was a huge undertaking. I believe it was I who originally had the idea for this project. I spoke about it to Bridget Ikin, who at the time was John Maynard's production director. I was visiting a set where they were filming and I talked to her about this autobiography, and she confessed to me that she had loved it, too. I suggested to her that we do it together. It was rather presumptuous of me, as at the time I hadn't done much except _Peel_, my first short film.

Did you originally envisage it for the cinema or for television?

I always thought of it as a film for the small screen. I never imagined that anyone would want to see this story at the cinema. My conception of what a cinema movie should be was doubtless a cliché, but I thought more in terms of action dramas or films with beautiful panoramas, whereas this was a very personal story. I thought it would be very difficult to convince producers that this story could interest lots of people, and we did encounter problems, because a lot of those we spoke to didn't find the Janet Frame that came across in the book very sympathetic! That's difficult to believe now, because in the film she seems intensely likeable! That, in any case, was how Laura Jones, the scriptwriter, Jan Chapman and myself, who collaborated on the script, saw her. Everything about her was marked by discretion and gentleness. Filming went well—unlike for _Sweetie_, which had sometimes been dramatic—and the whole production seemed to be infused with the relaxed atmosphere that Janet Frame creates. I didn't censor myself because I was working for television. The subject didn't lend itself to an experimental style like _Sweetie_. Just the opposite. For me, the story as told by Janet Frame needs the square format of the TV screen. Sometimes you lose the substance of a film when it's shown on television, but not in this case. There are a lot of close-ups, for example, but they are relevant to the story, which is an intimate one. The problem with films made for the small screen is that they're often not carefully enough produced because filming is too quick. For _An Angel at My Table_, we worked in conditions that were similar to those of the cinema: twelve weeks of shooting, including two in Europe. It was hard, conditions weren't quite as good as for a movie, but they were acceptable. The real problem was the number of new actors we had to meet every day because there were such a lot of characters! It was like a series of interviews! Everyone arrived quite anxious, wanting to do the best they could but knowing that, in most cases, they had only a day of filming. The only character who really holds the screen is Janet Frame, but there are very few people with whom she has a long relationship. The main task for me, therefore, was to get the actors up to speed very quickly.

Your mother plays a role in the film.

Yes, she's the teacher who reads Tennyson's 'The Passing of Arthur' about Excalibur. My mother was a very good actress, and you can see the remarkable intensity that she expresses in this scene. She's like that in real life. She doesn't act much anymore, but she is perfectionist to a degree that is almost neurotic. When I told her she had acted really well, she shrugged her shoulders; she thought she was dreadful. I'm like her; when people pay me compliments, I have a tendency to reject them. I told my mother that she should feel pleased with what she'd done and she replied that that was impossible because she knew she could have done much better. In her opinion, if she could be content with herself she'd become lazy!

It was the second of your films, after _Two Friends_, for which you didn't write the screenplay. Did that make a big difference to you when you were filming?

Not really, as I was still closely involved in the writing of _An Angel at My Table_. That made the task easier when it came to shooting, because I already knew the material intimately. I would talk a lot with Laura Jones so that we had a common vision, then she would write, and later, I would make a few changes. In any case, the book was always a mediator between us, which aided the connection in our thinking. I've never done an adaptation on my own, and I don't think I'm tempted to try it. Frankly, I've enjoyed sharing it. It was a simple story, and we thought that anyone could understand it. In that sense, it was a good subject for television, and there was no point in unnecessarily complicating the issue. All we did was read the book many times, lay it aside after each reading, and put down in writing the things we liked the most. Then we would compare our lists, which were actually pretty similar. Next, we studied the way in which the things we'd held on to could fit together. And Laura flowed it together. When I'm working on a script, I don't think about images—that comes later. In the same way, when I'm filming, I need to be completely steeped in the text so that I can concentrate only on the visual, and that's why I collaborate so closely on the screenplay when I'm not the author. Also, I was directing _Sweetie_ while Laura was writing _An Angel at My Table_, which prevented me from taking on the task. The film wasn't an experimental or intellectual challenge for me. I needed to be as simple and as honest as I could with the narrative. From this point of view, there were real differences in approach between _Sweetie_ and _An Angel at My Table_. I love _Sweetie_, I love that tragedy. I think that it's a film with depth, which in parts is obscure and difficult, that its emotions are more complex,

Top: Kerry Fox, Janet Frame, and scriptwriter Laura Jones
on the set of the film.
Bottom: Jane Campion directs her mother, Edith, who plays
Miss Lindsay, Janet's English teacher, in the film.

Janet Frame with the three actresses who portray
her in An Angel at My Table: *Kerry Fox, Alexia Keogh,*
and Karen Fergusson.

less accessible, and that it's a film that remains with you for longer. On the other hand, *An Angel at My Table* establishes a great rapport with the audience by speaking the language of the heart. From a human point of view, it's all I wish for; from a cinematic point of view, it's less exciting for me than *Sweetie*. But with my next film, people should prepare themselves for a shock, as I will be much less mannerly than with *An Angel at My Table*!

What it has in common with *Sweetie* is your sense of ellipsis. On the one hand, you have a fluid narrative development, and on the other, you make some stark breaks.
That has a lot to do with the way the screenplay is written. And also because I come up with lots of things during rehearsals. I had a huge amount of material at the end of the shoot. I would imagine different beginnings and endings of scenes, and during editing, I loved making cuts in the middle of sequences. Hence the abrupt, elliptical feel of certain passages.

One of the more remarkable aspects of the film is the continuity you've established between the three actresses that play Janet at different stages of her life: Alexia Keogh, Karen Fergusson, and Kerry Fox.
Their red hair helped us a lot with the resemblance! When little Alexia Keogh put her wig on for the third time, she started crying. It was so horrifying for her to have hair that colour! It was funny seeing all three of them with their wigs at lunchtime. It was undoubtedly one of the most difficult problems to resolve. I remember that we discussed it a lot, having seen Bertolucci's *The Last Emperor* and the way they had passed from one age to another. The one that I liked best was the actor who played the emperor at the intermediate stage. He expressed his feeling of having privileges very well. I became very attached to him and had trouble moving on to the next one because I'd connected with the character. I was afraid the same thing would happen with the young Janet in *An Angel at My Table* and that the viewer would be sorry to leave her. We thought about these transitions a lot, both at the scriptwriting stage and when we were casting, and then when we were filming. Finally, at the editing stage, Veronika Haussler showed me that we needed to shoot more to ensure a better flow. I decided she was right and I filmed the shot of the second Janet on the hillside reading her poems

from a journal so that the audience would have a moment alone with her. In fact, each of the three Janets has an instant like this: the youngest when she comes towards us on the road and the third when she's reading a poem near the railway. The transition from the second Janet, Karen Fergusson, to the third, Kerry Fox, was difficult because children and teenagers are so honest and innocent that it's difficult for an actress to measure up to the absolute charm possessed by the very young. We had to work hard with Kerry in order to choose the moment when she would appear so that didn't come across as dull. It was important for the audience to like her immediately, for there to be no problem. Karen Fergusson, who is on screen before Kerry Fox, is an incredibly shy and very intelligent girl. We chose her from a class where she was reading Keats's "Ode to a Nightingale" with her classmates. She was the only one to know it by heart after two readings, and she had an incredible ability to cry. She is more capable of empathy than any other teenager I've ever met. I loved her. She was fourteen when we were shooting, the same age as Melina Bernecker, who played Myrtle, her sister. Melina, like her character, was very sexy, very into boys, whereas Karen, like Janet Frame, was very reserved, dressed in a little cardigan and a plain skirt. There was something fascinating about watching these three Janets, who were playing the same character, sitting together, the youngest enjoying being mothered by the two older ones.

Was Janet Frame in touch with you during the making of the film?
She read the screenplay, which she liked very much, and she came to visit us during filming. We were very anxious to see how she would react to our adaptation. But she is a very mature woman who knows that the narrative of her life is also a fiction. She was even generous enough to tell Laura Jones that her screenplay was better than her book. For her, being on set was a big event, as she hardly ever travels. She came on the train with my godmother, who is one of her best friends. They made an odd couple, and Janet, who is interested in everything, didn't give my godmother a moment's peace during the journey, continually drawing her attention to everything that was going on. At the beginning, on set, she was very shy, but by the end of the week she was much closer to us. Sometimes she made remarks about what

her father was saying in the film and suggested changes to us.

The film is faithful to her autobiography, but it also ties in with the themes and concerns of your other films, as well as with events in your own life, such as your discovery of Europe in your youth.
Everyone in New Zealand goes to the Old Continent at some stage! But it's true that I'm generally interested in ignored, neglected characters to whom little interest is shown. And I liked Janet for that reason. I'm not aware of my choices. I suppose it's like falling in love: you don't question it, you just do it. And you're grateful for being able to love something or someone. With this film, I wanted at first to serve Janet Frame and her vision. There's certainly more of me in the final result than I was aware of when I started out. My aim was to capture on screen the emotions I'd felt when reading the book. I don't know how much of me can be found in *An Angel at My Table*. I'm a bit like an actress who chooses projects and enjoys doing different things. You're certainly better placed than I am to comment on what I do!

Did you have a colour palette? Did Janet's red hair determine the colour range of the film?
I always thought of green and red for *An Angel at My Table*. Green is the colour of New Zealand, and red is that of Janet's hair. They were the primary colours. Beginning with the red hair, I could play with a palette of soft, muted tones, or, on the other hand, brighten the film by clashing the red with vivid colours such as green, which was the solution I adopted. If you go to New Zealand, you're aware of the difference in light. The first European painters— English and Dutch—who returned with paintings from their travels to New Zealand faced scepticism from their fellow countrymen. Everyone thought the colours were exaggerated; they didn't believe them because the light in northern Europe is much softer and more diffuse. There is also a lot of wind in New Zealand, and it sweeps everything away. The air is clear here, and from Wellington you can see mountains 250 miles away. Because of that, shadows are so dark that you can't distinguish anything in them. This intensity captivates me, and the contrasts are so strong that it's difficult to film. For some childhood sequences, we used filters to obtain yellow or golden brown colours.

In what part of New Zealand did you shoot?

It was a lie as far as the autobiography is concerned as we shot around Auckland, whereas Janet Frame grew up in a completely different region near Oamaru. Nevertheless, I found the landscapes similar. It's not the same type of nature, but the feeling evoked is the same.

How did you approach the scenes in Europe? Were you not afraid of exoticism in shooting in Ibiza, London, and Paris?

I was aware of the danger of tourist clichés as I don't know Europe intimately in the way that I do my own country or Australia. However, I did live in London for a while. Paris posed a problem as we were there for only half a day, and for that reason I filmed as a tourist. To me, Paris is totally exotic. We didn't go to Ibiza because the place doesn't look anything like it did in the 1950s. We found an equivalent at Cadaqués on Spain's Costa Brava. My cinematographer and I tried to find odd, different places, with a mixture of old and new, to avoid clichés. My favourite from the European sequences is the scene where Janet is walking while reading a poem by Shelley.

For the hospital scenes, rather than adopting a naturalistic style, you've attempted a sort of stylization while highlighting the cruelty of the psychiatric treatment.

I think it's traumatic enough like that! Adding more wouldn't have made the scenes any more convincing. I wanted to show her gradual decline, from a normal state in the beginning to a form of madness at the end. She doesn't describe her stay in the mental institution at all in her autobiography. But she does talk about it in one of her novels, *Faces in the Water*, which inspired us. There was some fascinating material in this book that, in the beginning, Janet Frame wasn't very willing to let us use. But she eventually agreed.

You never explain in words her progressive decent into depression linked with the death of her sister, her brother's epileptic fits, etc. It's suggested, evoked, but there's no speech from a doctor, for example, as in a lot of films, that help the audience to understand its evolution.

I don't like explaining things. What I was wanting was to create a feeling of intimacy with Janet's state rather than giving the reasons for that state. For me, explanations always destroy the dramatic essence of a story, but clearly the danger is that the viewer doesn't really understand what's going on! I don't like being lectured as a viewer. I want the filmmaker to find a more subtle way of leading me to discover the keys of a behaviour.

One of the problems faced by films about artists is how to show them creating. It's almost impossible to film.

Towards the end of filming, I was very troubled that I'd made a film about a writer that we never saw writing. I therefore filmed a few typewriter shots. It's true that this absence bothered me. On the other hand, how do you film the act of writing? There are, of course, the physical details: Janet Frame has an almost neurotic fear of noise while she's writing. Apparently Kipling liked to write with ink that was as black as possible and liked the smell of orange peel. Others drink very strong coffee. Everyone needs a sort of conditioning and comfort to allow their subconscious free rein. I've recently read a lot of literary autobiographies, but how to show visually the process of writing still seems just as difficult to me.

You also convey the artist's profound loneliness very strongly. At school, at home with her family or with her friends, Janet Frame is still utterly alone.

When she read the screenplay, Janet was afraid that people would pity her. She told me that she didn't feel alone, that the sky, nature, were living presences for her, and that she felt intimately connected to them. I had to show that, despite everything, she wasn't unhappy. On the other hand, I don't think that Janet could have had an ongoing relationship with anyone. It was too complicated for her. But I don't believe it was as serious as all that, and in any case, it's too complicated for most of us as well!

Punctuated by journeys, An Angel at My
Table *also celebrates the beauty of Campion's
homeland.*

The Piano

(1993)

"More Barbarian
than Aesthete!"

Harvey Keitel and Holly Hunter in The Piano.

Clockwise from left: Ada (Holly Hunter) and her daughter, Flora (Anna Paquin); Baines (Harvey Keitel); Stewart (Sam Neill).

The redemptive power of love

Dark Colors

The journey towards the light, the fulfilment of a woman in control of her own destiny, took on a new expression in *The Piano*, which achieved irrevocable recognition for Campion, who in 1993 with this film became the first woman to win the Palme d'Or at the Cannes Film Festival. The inspiration for *The Piano*, however, is different from her previous films: it is profoundly romantic in that it mines a whole tradition of nineteenth-century gothic literature, including Emily Brontë's *Wuthering Heights*, which associates passion with dark colours. Having in her previous films explored family relationships—daughter–father, daughter–mother, sister–sister—the filmmaker pursues and develops her focus on the relationships between men and women, a subject already present in the Ibiza episode of *An Angel at My Table*. Before she even started shooting *An Angel at My Table*, its producers offered her a project in a similar vein. This was the adaptation of a book by a New Zealand writer, Jane Marder, called *The Story of a New Zealand River*, published in the 1920s, about a single mother who leaves Europe with her young daughter to travel to the antipodes to marry a man she doesn't love and to whom she prefers a bushwhacker. Despite its superficial resemblances to this original story, *The Piano* is a radically independent work, with a romantic scope that was new for the director.

Ada McGrath (Holly Hunter), a young Scottish woman who is mute (an invention crucial to the screenplay) arrives in New Zealand with her ten-year-old daughter Flora, (Anna Paquin), and her piano to join Alisdair Stewart (Sam Neill), a husband chosen by her father. But it is a neighbour, George Baines (Harvey Keitel), who is close to the Maori community, who proves sensitive to her music and attracts her attention. Baines buys the piano from Stewart in exchange for a piece of land and allows Ada to reclaim her precious instrument if she will consent to barter: for each erotic liberty she allows him, she will buy back in exchange one or more black keys of her piano.

The choice Ada makes of black keys is not insignificant. It corresponds to her clothes, which give her a severe, straight-laced appearance, the pallor of her complexion and her muteness, which reflects a frigidity in common with previous female protagonists and for which we will be given no explanation. Ada is in touch with her subconscious through her instrument: it is her piano that arouses masculine desire, that enters into an auditory, visual, and tactile relationship with Baines, that enables the piano tuner to detect the smell of Ada and of sea salt. Her piano is both the projection of her own body and the catalyst of her emotions. In this sense, one of the most powerful sequences is where Baines, naked, walks around the instrument, caressing it with a garment. In *An Angel at My Table*, Janet Frame blossomed as a writer; *The Piano* shows Ada's emotional and erotic fulfilment. Her muteness can be seen as a desire for independence, a resistance to a world that doesn't understand her, a woman forced to contend with a patriarchal society in the form of her father in Scotland and her husband, a settler in New Zealand, who treats her as an object. In the colonial community in which she finds herself, she is viewed with incomprehension; her face is inscrutable, and her mysteriousness makes men impatient. Her fear of phallic power will turn into sexual liberation when Baines relinquishes the bargain he has subjected her to and which, by his own admission, is making her a whore and him wretched.

Romantic Richness

The romantic richness of the story comes from the interweaving of several thematic threads. It reveals, in fact, the working of a capitalist colonialist society. It is the desire to possess that drives Stewart, who is eager to acquire new land—a plot belonging to Baines, for which he gives the piano in exchange, but also a piece of land on which lies a burial ground sacred to the Maoris, who refuse to yield it to him. (This is reminiscent of the American Indian burial ground, the site of a genocide, beneath the Overlook Hotel in Stanley Kubrick's *The Shining*.) The natives, like Ada, present the same resistance to Stewart's irrepressible desire. Outsiders, they are viewed with the same incomprehension as she is by the white community, represented in particular by Stewart's aunt Morag (Kerry Walker) and her daughter, Nessie (Genevieve Lemon), who form a sort of grotesque counterpoint to Ada and Flora. Baines, meanwhile, whose face bears the moko, a Maori tattoo, represents the bushwhacker (rather like the gamekeeper in *Lady Chatterley's Lover*); sensual and virile, he too arousing the

The opening shot of The Piano.

suspicion of the other settlers because of his closeness to the Maoris. Between two worlds, that of his origins and that which he has adopted, he is differentiated by his casual style of dress (in contrast to the austere clothing worn by Stewart) and his lack of inhibition. He lives in a wood cabin in the middle of the lush vegetation of a virgin forest, while Stewart, as Thomas Bourguignon has noted, has burnt all the trees surrounding his house, "a scorched clearing as dead as his sexuality is sterile and perverse."[1]

A Vibrant Work

The film opens, like *Sweetie* and *An Angel at My Table*, with a close-up of the heroine's face, which we glimpse this time through her fingers, as if to signify her introversion. A voice-over, that of Ada, who we will hear again at the end of the film ('The voice you hear is not my speaking voice but my mind's voice. I have not spoken since I was six years old. No one knows why, not even me'), speaks to us in the same way that Janet Frame did. There follow several subjective shots of her previous life in Scotland: Flora on horseback with her grandfather; then skating in the corridor of her house; then, suddenly, the face of a woman that fixes her. We discover nothing more, either about the father or her child or the reasons for her arranged marriage. But what the early scenes present with undeniable lyricism is the dialogue with nature and the beauty of the New Zealand landscapes, to which Campion draws attention even more than she did in *An Angel at My Table*. The incongruous placing of a grand piano, more readily associated with Victorian or Biedermeier style interiors than with a windswept coastline under attack from a stormy sea, is enough to highlight the inherent exoticism of this part of the world. The director contrasts the wild black-sand beach of New Zealand's west coast near Auckland and New Plymouth with the world of the bush. Flora associates the coast with her mother and the bush with Stewart,

her adopted father). To evoke the bush, Campion asked her cinematographer, Stuart Dryburgh, to use a monochrome blue that brings to mind an oppressive undersea world, harking forward to the film's finale, and that had already characterized some of her previous works.

The filmmaker, who had shown restraint in *An Angel at My Table*, both out of respect for Janet Frame's work and to meet the requirements of television, here frees herself, with sweeping and soaring camera moves, to scan the woods with their gnarled trees, combined with high-angle shots like the one that overlooks the piano abandoned at the water's edge. The highly mobile camera movements combined with the ellipses favoured by Campion make *The Piano* a vibrant work that is in tune with the passion of human relationships and avoids the pitfalls of academicism. What is striking is the complexity of the subject and the simplicity of the form, or, to use Yann Tobin's finely turned phrase, "a film that is desperately enigmatic while providing blinding clarity."[2] Although this work, more so than any other film that Campion had previously made, draws the viewer into becoming emotionally involved (which no doubt explains why it met with such unprecedented popular acclaim), it nevertheless shows a certain detachment, notably in the differing points of view of the four main characters.

Subversions

The legend of Bluebeard, which the Reverend Campbell stages at Christmas, plays ironically on the phenomenon of audience identification with a performance. At the moment when Bluebeard is ready with his axe to kill his young wife, the appalled Maori spectators rush onto the stage to prevent the murder. The scene also heralds the one in which Stewart, driven mad by his wife's infidelity, cuts off one of her fingers with an axe. The play is reminiscent, too, of the performances based

*Ada, flanked by Morag, Stewart's aunt
(Kerry Walker, on the right), and her daughter, Nessie (Genevieve Lemon, on the left).*

The amateur theatrical production of Bluebeard.
*<u>Following pages:</u> Ada asks Baines, through Flora,
to take them to the beach where her piano has been left.*

82

*Baines gets Ada to agree to a barter: for each erotic
liberty she allows him, she will buy back one or more
black keys of her piano.*

The small silhouette of Flora running along the ridge of a hill
(above right) would not be out of place in Charles Laughton's The
Night of the Hunter *(1955, above left).*

on Grimms' fairy tales that the Frame family plays out in *An Angel at My Table*. Although it is rooted in a specific historical context—during the mid-nineteenth century, when thousands of British settlers bought land from the native people for a pittance and widened the gulf with the islands' inhabitants—the film nevertheless has the features of a fable, of a mythopoeic story, which has led some academics to allude to the film *The Night of the Hunter* (1955). The extreme long shot where we see the small silhouette of Flora running along the ridge of a hill would not be out of place in Charles Laughton's masterpiece. The episode of Bluebeard, the seducer who brings a succession of young wives to his castle before doing away with them, also links the film to a gothic tradition characteristic of Romanticism and that Campion subverts. Dana Pola suggests in this regard a relationship with the films noirs of the 1940s, such as Hitchcock's *Rebecca* (1940) and *Suspicion* (1941), George Cukor's *Gaslight* (1944), Joseph L. Mankiewicz's *Dragonwyck* (1946), and particularly Fritz Lang's *Secret Beyond the Door* (1947), where a woman allows a stranger into her life, marries him and is taken to a remote place where she finds herself a prisoner and suspects him of wanting her dead.[3] This scenario is altered in *The Piano*. Stewart is not particularly physically attractive (the Maoris call him "dry balls") and the place lacks charm. As Polan points out, it is his rival, Baines, who offers Ada the thrills of love.

Equally subversive is the filmmaker's treatment of sexuality. Unlike many of her fellow directors, she doesn't glamorize the body of her heroine, admirably portrayed by Holly Hunter. Indeed, she even gives her a surly look and takes pains not to make her an object of desire. She also reverses the perspective by eroticizing the male body and feminizing Baines. The woman ceases to be an object; rather, her gaze is trained on the virile body that has now become an object. Her lover's sensuality engages her own. When she goes back to her husband, she caresses his body, uncovering his buttocks to explore their contours, causing him to shy away prudishly from his wife's advances. Here too, Campion does not allow herself to indulge in clichés. Rather than simplistically opposing husband and lover, she gradually shows Stewart to be a fragile, vulnerable being, the victim of an image of virility in keeping with his upbringing. Although, transformed into a Peeping Tom, he discovers Ada and Baines making love, he really reacts only when he reads the love token that his wife has sent to her lover. It is words (words that the illiterate Baines would be unable to understand) that make him truly aware of the situation and that provoke his vengeful fury before he eventually allows Ada to leave with his rival.

Imitation

It is with no less subtlety that Campion portrays Flora, children always having been one of her favourite subjects. Flora is at one with her mother on the beach on which they land, dresses in the same style of black clothing, snuggles up in her arms, sleeps with her under the crinoline made into a makeshift tent, and deplores the father who has been imposed on her. 'I'm not going to call him Papa. I'm not going to call him anything. I'm not even going to look at him.' She discovers sexuality with the young Maoris, rubbing up against tree trunks with them, as though mimicking lovemaking, provoking the wrath of Stewart, who makes her whitewash the trees. But her mother's growing passion for Baines, which leads her to neglect her daughter, drives Flora to betray her and, like a malicious Cupid, to hand over to Stewart the love token that was destined for Baines. Still wearing the angel wings that she wore to perform in Bluebeard, she is both an angel of light with her mother and an angel of doom in becoming responsible, out of her jealousy, for her mother's amputation. Exuberant and spontaneous, she also makes up stories, inventing for herself a mother who was a singer before she became mute and a father who was an orchestral conductor until he was struck by lightning—she imagines him going up in flames in an animated shot that the director, with characteristic freedom, inserted into the film.

Flora imitates her mother in classic fashion, but mimicry extends to other characters, too. Nessie, who echoes her mother, Aunt Morag,

Top: Flora gives Stewart the love token from her
mother that was destined for Baines.
Bottom: Stewart discovers the affair.

finishes or repeats her sentences; the Maoris mockingly parody Stewart; Baines behaves like the natives to get closer to them. Repetition is also imitation: Stewart watches Ada and Baines embracing after Flora has done the same. And mirrors, even more so than in Campion's other films, play a crucial role: Ada, in her narcissism, is constantly trying to find herself by gazing in one, while Stewart looks at her image in a small portrait of her that he carries and combs his hair while reflected in the glass protecting it. The web of visual echoes and narrative rhymes that Campion weaves gives the film a rare density.

Uncertainty

The Piano presents an extraordinary view of the complexity of human relationships and the ambivalence of individuals. If the film can rightly be described as romantic, which had not been a characteristic of her work up to this point, it is probably due to the fact that it was made during a particularly happy period of her life: the previous year, she had married Colin Englert, who also worked as the second unit director on the film. The work has a happy ending. Ada's voice is heard for the first time. She is now teaching the piano in Nelson. George has fashioned her a metal fingertip. 'I'm quite the town freak, which satisfies', she says. However, although Ada was ready to abandon her piano to the sea once it had ceased to be a substitute for her desire for love, she places her foot in the coil of rope that is holding the instrument, and is thus tempted to allow herself to be engulfed by the waves. In a final gasp, she chooses life and rises to the surface, aided by the Maoris, but the temptation to suicide lurks at the heart of the finally attained happiness, for the film ends with a dreamlike shot of Ada floating above her piano at the bottom of the sea, while a voice-over recites an extract from the sonnet 'Silence' by Thomas Hood:

> There is a silence where hath been no sound
> There is a silence where no sound may be,
> In the cold grave—under the deep, deep sea [. . .]

Does the feeling of emptiness linked to the loss of the piano that haunts her dream speak of an uncertainty about the future? This poem had been given to Campion by her mother (to whom the film is dedicated), who, following an attempted suicide, had, like Ada, chosen life. Campion has often said that her mother was a true romantic who believed in the power of romantic love, something of which *The Piano* gives no definite assurance.

1 Thomas Bourguignon, '*La Leçon de Piano*: Un ange au piano', *Positif*, 387 (May 1993).
2 Yann Tobin, '*La Leçon de Piano*: Maîtresse', *Positif*, 387 (May 1993).
3 Dana Polan, *Jane Campion*, British Film Institute, London, 2001.

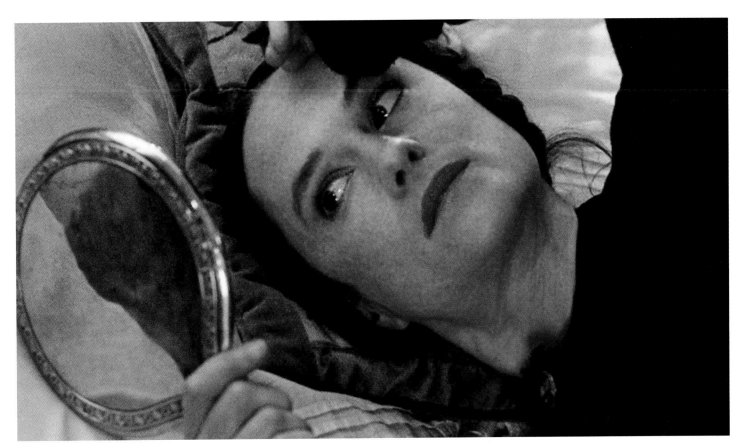

Ada is constantly trying to find herself by gazing into mirrors.

Interview conducted in Paris, 23 April 1993

The Piano is your oldest project; you were thinking about it even before beginning Sweetie. What was the starting point?

After my studies at film school I thought about the next step, which, naturally, was to be a fiction film. I had two ideas: *The Piano* and another, *Ebb*, which was more fantastic, more my sort of thing at the time. *The Piano* seemed more commercial as it was a love story, but also a narrative that needed more maturity. I wrote nearly half of it, but it seemed to me that although I could handle it on a small scale, money would be needed to do justice to the landscape. Moreover, I didn't have enough experience as a director, and I wasn't able to really understand all the themes I wanted to deal with—this archetypal story, the relationship between primitivism and civilization, a whole construction based on oppositions. I therefore decided to leave the project to rest. Meanwhile, I met Pierre Rissient, who had shown my short films at Cannes. It was an important experience for me as I realized—which I hadn't seen in Australia—that there was an audience with whom I could make my voice heard without having to alter it. So I returned to Australia to make *Sweetie*, which was a continuation of my work at film school and seemed to fit my mood at the time, something more provocative, more in rebellion against cinema.

What was Ebb about?

It was an imaginary story set in a country where one day the sea leaves, never to return, and the way in which people have to find a spiritual solution to the problem. The natural world had become artificial and unpredictable, and the film spoke about belief and doubt. The people of this country tended to develop a certain form of spirituality, to hear voices and have visions. At the end, the father of a family at the heart of the story, the man least likely to have a spiritual adventure, had the most extraordinary experiences. Because it was thanks to him that the sea returned and his tongue began to taste of salt! He became a sacrificial victim.

What has changed in The Piano since your first ideas about the film?

To begin with, there were simply piano lessons. But the conclusion was very traditional, with the story climaxing in a violent act. After *Sweetie* and *An Angel at My Table,* I returned to this project, and I thought that the central idea was too good for such a predictable ending. Talking with my producer, Jan Chapman, and with Billy MacKinnon, who helped me with the writing of the screenplay, I asked myself why we had so many reservations—especially me! Stewart had been killed by Baines, more fingers had been cut off, it was much more violent. So we decided to go more deeply into the psychology of the story. In the second version of the screenplay, Ada came back to Baines; Stewart saw them together, he fell in love with her and became more vulnerable. Changes were made, particularly in the last fifty pages. We introduced the characters of the aunts and made the protagonists less rigid as they were too like characters in a fairy tale.

The fairy tale mirrors the story of Bluebeard shown in the shadow play.

This sequence corresponded to a certain type of experience for the viewer, but I wanted the central story to be as strong and as emotional as possible. The sequence in the school hall has always been in the script. I had been struck by the photograph of a woman of the colonial period whose head appears between the sheets. These amateur plays have always seemed to me remarkably skilful. The scene sums up for me the power of the made-up story: we know it's an imaginary world, and yet we believe in it. It's the essence of the show. People love to play along. When the little girl tells the aunt her father's story, the aunt believes it even though she knows it's a lie. The desire to believe is stronger than everything.

In this story of Flora's, there's a shot where you use animation to show the father burned by the flames.

We had found a wonderful picture book that had belonged to a child of this period and we decided that in the story it would belong to Flora; it was the place where it was possible to introduce this amazing illustration. A member of the technical team also believed firmly in the story told by Flora. There was also a practical reason for this animation shot: it allowed us to make a link between two shots in which Anna Paquin [who played Flora] had given the best of herself.

How did you approach the problem of an historical film?

I did a lot of research. I have a good ear for dialogue; I can imitate people really well, and my husband is even better at it. But with these characters, I had no models; they weren't based on anyone I know. Making them human and using my skills of observation in the film was a real problem. I read diaries written by women in the nineteenth century, as well as accounts of the arrival of Europeans in New Zealand. I tried to discover their voices and their ways of thinking. I also read novels from this period, until I decided to solve these problems in my head. I suppose that I needed to feel protected, because this classic story presented a number of obstacles that I couldn't solve with my narrative technique of the diversion that isn't really leading anywhere. I wanted to work in a classic tragedy style, but I wasn't really equipped for it and needed to develop new skills. Every scene presented me with problems, and, unlike in *Sweetie*, I couldn't go off in all directions. I had to follow a set path.

Did you do any research on the relationships between Maoris and Anglo-Saxon colonists?

I couldn't study these contacts because no one really knows what went on. But we can see the consequences today. I don't feel I'm much of an expert in this field, and there were things that I wanted to say in the film that my Maori advisors convinced me were nonsense! Of course, I talked to specialists, especially as there is a renaissance of Maori culture. There's a tendency for some Maoris to have a heroic view of their past, and that's not what I wanted to portray. Moreover, points of view are often very different from each other. I preferred to look around me and observe people's behaviour. For example, having a homosexual Maori character in the film was a crisis for this community. They claimed that if there had been a homosexual at that time, they would have killed him! But they clearly flaunt their sexuality, people are always talking about their genitals; it's part of how they view others, and there's none of the prudishness of Protestant culture.

The Maori background is like an objective correlate of what the heroine is feeling: Maori culture embraces the spiritual and sexual as well as the purely material.

Yes. They highlight the puritanical side of the colonists. Their relationship with nature is much more balanced and much stronger. The Anglo-Saxons haven't resolved the relationship between the animal, sexual part of their nature and their rationality. Baines is between the two, belonging neither to the whites nor to the Maoris. He was probably a whaler who settled there, and his unfinished tattoo shows a desire for integration that wasn't completely successful. He has also made an effort to learn their language and acts as an interpreter between the Maoris and the Europeans. In fact,

*Exuberant and spontaneous, Flora invents for herself a mother who was a
singer before she became mute and a father who was
an orchestral conductor until he was struck by lightning—she imagines him
going up in flames in an animated shot inserted into the film.*

*Tempted to allow herself to be engulfed by the
waves with her piano, Ada, in a final gasp, chooses
life and rises to the surface.*

*'We wanted to give the bush scenes underwater colours
to link them to the final sequence.'*

Harvey Keitel learned to speak Maori and knew more than most of the extras! He was a very good student, whereas many of the indigenous people no longer spoke their language very well.

How did you come to quote the poet Thomas Hood?

In fact, I asked my mother, who reads much more poetry than me, to find me a quotation about the sea. Initially, I was going to use it for *Ebb*, because originally *The Piano* didn't end with the present sequence. Then I placed it at the end of *The Piano*. The film closed with a concert. Baines arrived, took Ada from the school hall, and escaped with her and her daughter. Stewart realized they were missing and went looking for them. A postscript said that he had disappeared in the bush and that he hadn't been found. There were no scenes where we saw them making love. He was more of a one-dimensional character, jealous and angry. In the final version, he is much more human and vulnerable.

You use slow motion several times.

There's one moment where I use it when it goes unnoticed: it's a way of observing characters more closely. Certain passages were even shot slow motion 'in' camera. I could afford myself this licence because this is a romantic story that is treated in a more stylized, dramatic, and poetic way. Slow motion can appear facile or tasteless in some circumstances. Not in others. When she surveys the water, the shots were uninspiring without slow motion, whereas I wanted to communicate the shock this was for her. I think it works.

There are lots of angels in your films: *An Angel at My Table*, Flora dressed up as an angel, and Stewart's remark to Ada, where he acknowledges having clipped her wing.

I don't believe in angels, but I believe in the hope of being an angel, the desire of human beings to be saved and be able to fly. That brings us back to talking about artists. The artist expresses dissatisfaction, the desire to escape from oppression, a form of hope: I don't offer a solution, but I am expressing a state of mind. The people who matter to me are those who give meaning to life, artists, poets who have wanted to understand and ask questions that allow us to know each other better. I can't imagine life without this kind of approach. And yet I'm neither an aesthete nor a cinephile. I quickly lose patience with films that demand too much of my attention. I have a wild side!

Ada is an artist, but I don't believe it's important to her to have an audience. She plays for herself. We created her rather in the image of the Brontë sisters and the imaginary worlds they made up for themselves. I am drawn to Romantic literature and wanted to make my contribution to this genre. In terms of novels, I am thinking particularly of *Wuthering Heights* as well as the poetry of Blake, Tennyson, and Byron. I visited the village where Emily Brontë grew up, walked on the moor and tried to absorb its atmosphere. But obviously I didn't want to make a transposition of *Wuthering Heights*, because I don't think this story can be told today: it's a saga that spans two generations, and also, I'm not English, I belong to a colonial culture and I needed to invent my own fiction. I wanted to talk about the relationship between men and women, the complex nature of love and eroticism, but also of sexual repression. I owe a debt not only to Emily Brontë, but also to many women artists. There are qualities in this film that are peculiarly feminine. Ada is an extremely feminine character with her sense of secrecy and her relationship with her daughter. I also read a lot of Emily Dickinson's poetry while writing the screenplay.

You haven't used the music of Romantic composers such as Schubert or Schumann.

That was never our intention! I wanted a musical identity for the film and not a pastiche of nineteenth-century composers. I needed a personal voice, musical compositions that Ada could have written. Michael Nyman decided to make use of Scottish airs, pieces that Ada might have heard at home and that were in tune with her personality. I don't know much about music, and I asked for advice in choosing a composer. A few friends recommended Michael Nyman, whose work I knew, of course, for Peter Greenaway's films, and in particular for *The Draughtsman's Contract*, where he had captured the tone of the period and at the same time expressed a very personal style.

Michael is not just a composer of film music, he is also a true musician. He has real integrity. It was what I was wanting for this film, not somebody who would use tricks. I am happy with what he did, and especially with the violence of his music.

In the sequence on the sea, you also use Maori songs.

I don't know very much about Maori culture, but I can tell you that that is all authentic. We could have added other elements of Maori

culture into the film, but they wouldn't have fitted into the story. There are disturbing stories and fascinating aspects that we therefore had to abandon. We retained only that which would be at one with our story.

The Romantic aspect of the film is clearly enhanced by the use of nature. How did you choose your landscapes?

I knew the atmosphere and the power of these landscapes, having grown up with them. I used to walk barefoot in the bush, and spend nights there, as is the custom in New Zealand. I walked on long trails with my father, and I loved that. There is such intensity in some parts of the bush that you feel as though you're underwater. It's a landscape that's disturbing, claustrophobic, and mythic, which was enhanced for me during my childhood by the complicated routes we used to take. We wanted to give the bush scenes underwater colours to link them to the final sequence. It's a landscape that unnerved lots of Europeans when they arrived, and because they didn't like it, they cleared much of it to make it look like Europe. I thought that this wild landscape suited my story because Romanticism has been misunderstood in our time, and especially in film. It's become something 'sweet', nice. We've forgotten its severity, its dark side. I wanted to create in the viewer a sense of awe at the power of the natural elements. This is, I believe, the essence of Romanticism: this respect for nature, which is seen as greater than you, your spirit, or even humanity.

How did two American actors come to be chosen for the roles of Ada and Baines?

Mysteriously, in fact. It wasn't my idea to have Americans in this film. Nor New Zealanders either, for that matter, as this is a period that virtually preceded the creation of New Zealand. Initially, we were thinking more of English. I had even imagined having French actors, but it's strange how your fellow countrymen—or at least those I talked to—are reticent about their own actors. I was much more enthusiastic than they were. But I suppose it's the same everywhere: we appreciate less that which belongs to our own culture. I met lots of fabulous French actors, but I did wonder about the problem of the language. In England, too, I met quite a lot of people. Rather than undertake a systematic and methodical search, we picked up actors all over the globe! We were lucky that we finally made the right choices given that our method was rather muddled. In London, for example, I found no one with Harvey Keitel's presence.

Some people thought it odd that I talked to him. Harvey was linked to very powerful memories of films from when I was very young: *Mean Streets, Bad Timing,* and *The Duellists.* I thought he was interested in things that were different, experimental. I was told his age could be a problem. So I watched one of his latest films, *The Two Jakes,* and thought he was very good and that he seemed young. I sent him the screenplay, which he loved. With what was going on in his life at that time, he wanted to act in a film that spoke about the relationships between men and women rather than a new cops-and-thugs story. He's not often been given the chance to express certain tender qualities he has in him. I think that I was intimidated at first, but the more we got to know each other, the more we talked, the more natural and easy the friendship became. He is a shy, thoughtful man, a long way from the macho and brutal image of his films! He found me funny, and I respected him; everything was fine!

I loved Holly Hunter as an actress, but I didn't immediately think of her, probably because, like everyone else, I had a stereotyped idea of a romantic heroine as tall, with exquisite manners. But then I thought it would be more powerful to go against this stereotype. I was lucky to get Holly Hunter, for even though she's beautiful in her own way, she doesn't promote it; she has very strong feelings and relationships with others, and it's not just superficial. She also has a high level of concentration and is very vulnerable. She's a small woman who's immensely powerful.

Does she play the piano herself?
She already played very well before beginning the film. She has a grand piano at home; obviously, that was an asset. I think a lot of people were sceptical of my choice, without daring to say so. I found her wonderful in the film, playing her role in a very restrained way. Moreover, we communicated very easily; we were really on the same wavelength. She has a very practical mind, like me, and neither of us has many theories. I was lucky to have such an enthusiastic collaborator because she really had her work cut out: mastering sign language, playing the music; it wasn't easy.

For the third character you chose Sam Neill.
I chose him very early on; he's a very handsome man, and the idea of making the "bad guy" "Mummy's blue-eyed boy," rather than someone ruddy-faced and physically unattractive, as is often the case with such characters, appealed

to me. It allows the viewer to discover the real qualities he possesses and to see him as a human being. Stewart is a man who transforms himself, and that was difficult to portray. Sam Neill managed to do so despite not having the same acting background as Harvey Keitel—who trained in Method acting at the Actors Studio—or as Holly Hunter. Sam works at home and comes back with choices he's made. I like to protect my actors; I respect their personal conception of acting. I believe, too, that they were enchanted by the natural environment. After we finished filming, Holly spent two weeks traveling in the bush with her sister. I believe that Holly and Harvey have personalities that enable them to work anywhere in the world without missing Hollywood. They don't behave like stars. In any case, that would be impossible in New Zealand, where people would immediately put you in your place. They're not used to associating with stars.

Did editing take a long time?
The normal length of time for a film of this kind; I didn't do a lot of takes even though I used more film than I had for my two previous films. We didn't have a lot of money: a budget of 6.5 million dollars. The film seems richer than it actually cost; the big advantage is that the American dollar is worth three times more than the New Zealand dollar.

The Piano was not the title you originally chose for the film, was it?
I wanted *The Piano Lesson*, but that was already the title of an American play, and we were unable to obtain the rights. We agreed on the title *The Piano* with Ciby 2000, but in France, for example—where the problem of rights was not an issue— it was called *La Leçon de piano.* I'd also thought of *The Sleep of Reason*, but it wasn't very commercial!

What you were saying about Stewart's character could apply to the whole film: it unfolds in an unpredictable way, and our perspective of the action and characters varies constantly, such as when Ada caresses Stewart.
In doing so, she is thinking of Baines, but particularly of her own eroticism. The whole process of the piano lessons has eroticized her. It reveals her sexuality even though she believes she's resisted it. It's the surest way to seduce someone when they're unconscious of a deeper motivation. Ada, of course, has a sexuality, but at some stage it's been repressed.

She doesn't realize that she has feelings for him; he's a sexual object to her. She doesn't really know what she's doing; her behaviour is almost like that of a sleepwalker. This scene is very ambiguous, and I talked to Holly and Sam about it. I'd written it, of course, but I still needed to really understand it with them! When she caresses Sam, she's really trying to find herself. Normally, it's the opposite that occurs: women often feel that they're being treated as objects by men. It may be a cliché, but men often want to have a sexual experience without getting involved. The film wants to show, however, that men are vulnerable, including sexually. They need to be loved and to feel protected.

Ada's past is quite mysterious.
My attitude in this regard is simple. My characters meet each other at a certain moment in their lives, in the same way that we don't know about other people's past, and that's part of the mystery of being with people. We talk with people and their past is within them, in front of us, even if we don't know about it. I, too, have a past, but I'm not sure I understand it, or that I can say how it's made me who I am. However, we do know some things about Ada: she stopped speaking when she was six years old and doesn't know why. I remember having read that Emily Brontë wasn't happy being around people, that she had a certain disdain for society and didn't like speaking in public. Charlotte would take her into society with friends and she wouldn't say a word. Ada's problem is that she's too obstinate; she's romantic to the point that she's so involved in her ideals that she could die for them. In order to live, she needs to compromise her ideals. Young people often have very strong convictions. Curiously, growing up means adapting, and I think that's no bad thing. Pure ideas don't take into account the complexities of being alive. Ada, at the end, can live out her ideals in her imagination, fantasize about herself and be happy in real life. She can separate art from life. Up until then she'd had a poetic vision of herself; she'd been in love with her romantic ideals, which ended up controlling her to the point she could no longer live.

Do you find a lot of yourself in your heroines? Kay, Sweetie's sister, Janet Frame, and Ada, who also correspond to different stages of life?
I don't believe I project my fantasies into my characters, and in any case, I don't know who I am. We are what we do. On the other hand, I

*It is with subtlety that Campion
portrays Flora, children
always having been one of her
favourite subjects.*

The piano is at the heart of the exchange and desire between Ada and Baines.

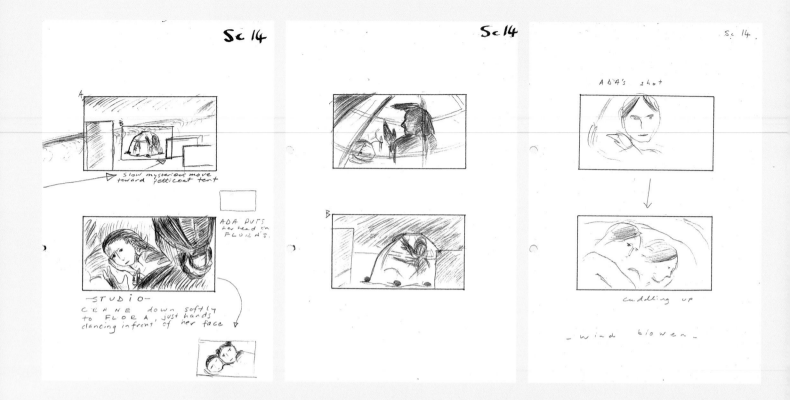

Storyboards, drawn by Jane Campion, of the scene of Ada and Flora's night spent on the beach after their arrival in New Zealand; and the shot of the same scene in the film itself.

have a lot of affection for them, even if none of them represents me, although Kay comes closest to the person I was. What *is* part of me is a certain sense of the absolute and wanting to control things. I've always had trouble understanding the boundaries between myself and the world; the mystery of sexuality, hatred, and passions has always been a problem.

Sweetie was dedicated to your sister, *The Piano* to Edith.
She's my mother. That figures, doesn't it!

At the end you have the words 'kia ora' in the credits.
It means 'thank you' in Maori. It's addressed to the cast and the crew. It's also a way of taking leave.

You had the same cinematographer, Stuart Dryburgh, as on *An Angel at My Table.*
In the earlier film, we were obliged to use a certain restraint with the photography as it wasn't a 'big' story. We didn't want to stifle Janet Frame's autobiography. For *The Piano*, it was nice to have a more flamboyant, more cinematic style.

Some shots have a fairy-tale atmosphere, an eerie quality, like where Flora is running on the hills.
I loved those hills, and I thought of putting the figure of the little girl there. I guess it was a way of controlling the landscape, as sometimes it dominated me so much that I would question how I could interpret it in a personal way. But those hills were so lovely that I wanted to have them in the film. Anna Paquin looked so miniscule on the ridge of the hills that she practically disappeared. We had to replace her with someone bigger so that we could see her. Anna was furious and humiliated!

In your films, death is linked to nature. Sweetie dies jumping from the tree. In *An Angel at My Table,* two sisters die by drowning. Here, Ada nearly perishes at sea.
I've never thought about it, but I'm going to try to come up with a reply! It might be that the story's always the same: We believe we can control nature, but it's stronger than we are. To survive, we have to make a truce with it, be humble and accept the part of nature that is part of us. The human will can become

disproportionate in relation to the world. As children, we think we're the masters of the world, and we need to learn that we're not or we'll be laying up trouble for ourselves.

Ada and Flora have a relationship that is more like that of two friends than of a mother and her daughter.
Their situation is very peculiar: they have neither husband nor father; it's hinted that Flora is illegitimate; Ada doesn't speak and Flora speaks for her, which gives her an importance for her age. She maintains a relationship with the world for both of them. They're virtually inseparable. They conspire together; they have a peculiarly feminine intimacy. When Stewart sees them together, he feels they have a power that he doesn't really understand. Similarly, Ada's relationship with her piano is a mystery to him.

The Piano* is, in some sense, a synthesis of your first two films. It has the poetic force of *Sweetie* and the narrative signification of *An Angel at My Table.
There's actually a lot more narrative in *The Piano*—not only a story but also a plot. There is, I hope, the sense of surprise and the poetry of *Sweetie*. In *An Angel at My Table*, I was faithful to a book I respected. *The Piano*, like *Sweetie*, is more faithful to myself, or to certain aspects of my personality. But *An Angel at My Table* was important not because it fitted my idea of cinema, as I knew I was making it for television, but because it gave me confidence on set. I was relaxed, and I felt able to improvise. I learned to be more understanding with the actors, to give them more space. I believe there are things that I wouldn't have been able to do in *The Piano* had I not had the experience of *An Angel at My Table*.

Do you have projects in mind?
Two actually. The first is the child that I'm going to have in two months' time; that's a big project, and I want to enjoy it. Then I have two adaptations on the horizon: the first is *My Guru and His Disciple* by Christopher Isherwood, for Ciby 2000, the second, *The Portrait of a Lady*, adapted from the novel by Henry James, for the American company Propaganda.

The Portrait of a Lady
(1996)

"A Voyage
of Self-Discovery."

98

Top: Caspar Goodwood (Viggo Mortensen).
Bottom: Isabel Archer (Nicole Kidman)
and Madame Merle (Barbara Hershey).

An indomitable energy

An Antidote

The Portrait of a Lady, Campion's fourth opus, could have been the title of any of her films. After the film based on Janet Frame's autobiography, here was a new adaptation (also with a screenplay by Laura Jones), which continued what has become an alternating pattern of works inspired by books and those with original screenplays (*Sweetie*, *The Piano*, *Holy Smoke*, and *Bright Star*). As it happens, this masterpiece by Henry James is set just twenty years later than *The Piano*, and its adaptation to the screen posed the same problems of condensation: from a novel of more than six hundred pages, Campion and Jones shot a film lasting two hours and twenty-four minutes. One of the most radical choices they made was to cut the first eleven chapters of the novel, which narrate Isabel Archer's early life, beginning the film in media res with her arrival in England. Like *An Angel at My Table* and *The Piano*, the story revolves around a journey the protagonist takes from one continent to another, witnessing her transformation by the end of her travels.

It is the nature of this particular transformation that distinguishes this film from Campion's earlier works. Whereas Ada seemed to have found happiness in love (albeit not without signs of anxiety dreams), Isabel finds herself disillusioned, trapped in a marriage that she had desired and facing the consequences of a bad choice. In this sense, the film may seem like an antidote to the previous one, as the denunciation of a romantic vision of life and of the blindness of an individual to her fate. Ironically, what may be considered as one of Campion's greatest films received a universally guarded reception from critics and was a commercial flop (the film had a budget of 25 million dollars and suffered a loss of 12 million, the most substantial that Campion had ever sustained), as though the filmmaker, like her heroine, had deliberately caused this rebuff. After her Palme d'Or at the Cannes Film Festival, her Oscars at Hollywood and her extraordinary success, Campion had undertaken at great expense a heritage film that, at a superficial glance, fitted in with the contemporary trend for films inspired by the dozens of novels of Jane Austen, Edith Wharton, Joseph Conrad, E. M. Forster, and Henry James, epitomized by directors such as James Ivory. Instead, Campion's work was striking in its rejection of academicism, its focus on the movements of body and soul, its rigor and its avoidance of decorative emphasis. It also confirmed the intrinsically personal nature of the filmmaker's projects.

A Being in a Cage

Isabel Archer (Nicole Kidman) is the sort of woman Campion likes: fierce, independent, fearless, determined to live her life and not to jeopardize it by making a hasty decision. She refuses the advances of Lord Warburton (Richard E. Grant), a rich and brilliant English nobleman; of an American industrialist, Caspar Goodwood (Viggo Mortensen), whose cause is defended by her friend Henrietta (Mary-Louise Parker); and of Ralph Touchett (Martin Donovan), her cousin, who, unbeknownst to her, convinces his father on his deathbed to bequeath her part of his fortune. On a trip to Italy, encouraged by a new friend, Madame Merle (Barbara Hershey), she allows herself be seduced by an American dilettante living in Rome, Gilbert Osmond (John Malkovich), a widower and art collector who lives with his daughter Pansy (Valentina Cervi). When she falls into the trap set for her by her husband, who becomes her nemesis, it is not without a certain masochistic submission, blind as she is to her true personality. Not wanting to be 'a mere sheep in the flock' she finds herself a being in a cage (although, as she says to her cousin Ralph, 'If I like my cage, that needn't trouble you') or, as one of her suitors suggests, like a rare object belonging to an antique collector. In this sense, her trajectory is the opposite of Janet Frame's.

The work's pessimism is reflected in the use of shade. Isabel informs us in an early scene in the film, "I love this time of day just as it gets dark." With her cinematographer, Stuart Dryburgh, the filmmaker turned her back on the choices they had made for *The Piano*: here twilight dominates the story. Thus, Osmond's first attempt to seduce Isabel takes place not in a hotel salon in Rome, as it does in James's novel, but in a catacomb in Caprarola, near Viterbo. The dominant palette is of browns and blues; places, bedrooms, and reception rooms bathe in half-light, and Rome is a city that seems gripped by the cold, while the character of Madame Merle is associated with the rain. Similarly, the scene where Ralph argues with his cousin about her decision to marry takes place in a garden in James's novel, but here the filmmaker moves it to some stables, where, in the twilight, she films the stable's bars as an evocation of her heroine's future imprisonment. The cinematographer has said that he used long focal lengths, 100mm or 200mm, which isolate the characters against an undefined background. He was also inspired by Dutch painters such as Rembrandt, using natural light to create chiaroscuro in

Gilbert Osmond (John Malkovich),
the American seducer living in Rome.

his settings. Campion plays much less than in her other films with the relationship between foreground and background in order to strengthen the focus on the actors in the story. This feeling of suffocation is reflected in the choice of sets—imposing buildings, staircases, balustrades, columns, catacombs, door jambs, and bars—which establish a monumental style, an architectural expression of confinement. The importance of stone in Italy is anticipated in Isabel and Henrietta's visit to the Victoria and Albert Museum in London, where they touch a reclining statue. Similarly, clothing contributes to this feeling of constraint, expressed notably in the ballroom scene at Osmond's house, where corseted young women faint after dancing the quadrille.

The Omnipotence of Desire

The Portrait of a Lady, in contrast with this repressive atmosphere, affirms the omnipotence of desire. James, troubled by sexual issues, deals with them only obliquely in his novels, suggesting in an indirect manner rather than showing, consistent with his puritanical scruples. Campion, on the other hand, announces even as early as the prologue the erotic charge her film will convey. In a provocative manner that is very much in keeping with the spirit of her short films but a long way from what one expects of a costume drama, she presents, against a black screen, voice-overs of seven young women reminiscing about their experience of kissing, what it feels like to be kissed, erotic attraction, and relationships. The first images of the film following this oral introduction are black-and-white shots of young women—black, white, aboriginal, Asian— in a wood (like that of *An Angel at My Table*), who form a circle, are lying on the ground, dance and look directly at the camera, smiling and enigmatic. It's a way for Campion to tell us that the story she's going to relate could happen at any time and in any place, that this is an evocation of the female condition and of erotic experience. Among the voices we

hear, one of them tells us that falling in love is like finding the clearest and most loyal mirror and that that person will shine that love back. This statement, which is both narcissistic, innocent, and idealistic, introduces us quite naturally to a close-up of the face of Isabel (an opening shot in the style of Campion's previous films), who we then see sitting on the branch of a tree on a spring day in the late nineteenth century, wiping the tears from her eyes just before Warburton declares his love for her.

The motifs of finger, hand, kiss, and touch will recur throughout the film, from the middle finger on which the title is written in the opening credits and the hands of Caspar, Warburton, and Ralph that are placed on Isabel, to Osmond's kiss in the catacomb, those kisses with which she covers the dying Ralph's hands and face and Caspar Goodwood's impetuous kiss at the end of the film. These sensual strokes find their erotic expression in Isabel's dream, just after Goodwood, in London, has caressed her face before leaving. In this fantasy, which is, of course, absent, as is every desiring body, in James's novel, she finds herself lying on a bed being kissed by Warburton and Goodwood, watched by Ralph. This ecstasy is also seen in the trip she takes to Greece and the Middle East with Madame Merle shortly before she marries Osmond and that Campion, once again, inserts into her story in a disturbing way. In black and white, like the prologue, this short film pastiches Hollywood's orientalist films (such as George Melford's *The Sheik*, 1921, starring Rudolph Valentino), the holiday home movie with a view of the pyramid, and the surrealist films of her favourite Buñuel, when a plateful of beans (reminiscent of *Passionless Moments*) start to groan, repeating Osmond's declaration: "I'm absolutely in love with you." It's an anachronistic sequence—cinema would not be invented until a quarter of a century later—but one that reflects the heroine's mental state. She envisions Osmond's hand around her waist, appears nude like a Renaissance Venus, and faints in the desert like the young girls will do later in the ballroom scene. It is clear that Campion, while she remains resolutely

Osmond's first attempt to seduce Isabel
takes place in a catacomb in Caprarola,
near Viterbo.

Top: Madame Merle (a less cynical version of Choderlos de Laclos's
Marquise de Merteuil) and Osmond (similarly, a version
of Laclos's Vicomte de Valmont).
Bottom: Pansy (Valentina Cervi) and her father Gilbert Osmond.
Following pages: Madame Merle and Isabel.

faithful to James (she is not the sort of director to choose a classic and then deform it), takes an independent approach with regard to the novel in modulating some of its points of view or, as here, inventing whimsical digressions. For her, the adaptation is a form of critical commentary.

Stylistic Devices

As she did in *The Piano*, but using different stylistic devices here, Campion averts the danger of petrification inherent in the period drama. Her characters are often on the move, even in the most intimate scenes, thus reflecting, in the case of Isabel, her independent, impetuous, and capricious temperament. The camera itself encircles them, revolves around them in order to express, notably with Osmond, his desire to conquer. The constant use of the dolly reflects this perpetual restlessness, which is reminiscent of Max Ophuls's arabesques in his representation of the past. The structure of the screenplay, which operates by a series of references and duplication, shows rigour and invention. The story opens at Garden-court (the Touchett family's country estate), in the springtime, with its bright sunshine, lush lawns, cheerful characters, and Isabel receiving her first marriage proposal. The epilogue takes place in the same place, now covered with snow and ice, devoid of greenery and flowers, the objective correlation of the chill that has seized Isabel following the failure of her marriage. In her final meeting with Goodwood, parallel to her first, she is dressed in black, like Ada in *The Piano*. Campion chose an ending that is more ambiguous, more unresolved than that of James's novel, in which Isabel returns to Rome to rejoin her husband. In this sense, if one accepts the definition of Joseph Conrad, for whom James's books 'end as an episode in life ends. You remain with the sense of the life still going on', Campion is more Jamesian than James himself. In fact, in the film's final scene, we see Isabel leave Goodwood, run in slow motion, and place her hand on a doorknob. If happiness isn't an absolute certainty at the end of *The Piano*, neither is unhappiness here. Isabel kisses Goodwood, but then walks away. She has shed her illusions, come to know herself, and, having disobeyed her husband, who had forbidden her from going to London, it is unlikely she would submit to the standards of middle-class respectability.

In building relationships between the characters, the filmmaker also highlights the device of symmetry and duplication. Thus, Isabel and Madame Merle mirror each other, dressed almost identically. While Madame Merle—a less cynical version of Choderlos de Laclos's Marquise de Merteuile in *Les Liaisons dangereuses*—schemes to throw Isabel into the arms of Osmond—Malkovich also plays the Vicomte de Valmont in Stephen Frears's film *Dangerous Liaisons*), Osmond later tries to manipulate Isabel into persuading his daughter Pansy to marry a man that she doesn't love. It is because of a woman that Isabel chooses Osmond, influenced by the advice of Madame Merle, who she loves and admires, and also because of the intimate relationship Osmond has with Pansy (the first sight she has of them is of the father with his arm around the girl's waist), a relationship and an affection that Isabel, an orphan, lacks.

Once again, Alistair Fox, in his remarkable psychological and critical exploration of the filmmaker and her work, has shown the resonances that James's novel inspired in his adaptor.[1] While *The Piano* corresponded to a period of marital bliss (she had recently married Colin Englert), *The Portrait of a Lady* followed the disintegration of her marriage and the death of Jasper, her infant son (to whom the film is dedicated). This premature death is echoed in Madame Merle's confession that she had a young boy who died two years previously. The attention of a father, which Campion so lacked in her childhood, finds its expression in the relationship between Osmond and Pansy. Isabel is looking for a substitute father in Osmond, which explains the tension she feels deeply between the desire to control her own fate, to be her own mistress, and that of accepting his domination and submitting herself to this father figure, like the wasp we see imprisoned in a glass. Fox, no doubt correctly, believes this film marks a turning point in Campion's work. Having exhausted her curiosity about her mother, she turns towards the father she loved but has also criticised, as *Holy Smoke* and *In the Cut* would confirm. It can also be argued that the filmmaker, who has often confessed to wanting to be loved, identifies with her heroine as much as with the young girls of the prologue, with their impatience, their impulsivity, and their susceptibility to romantic love.

Two secrets

The Portrait of a Lady, like *The Piano*, belongs to the tradition of melodrama that was popular in the nineteenth century, the period in which both these stories are set. While, having portrayed a mute heroine within the setting of a natural world, Campion probably enjoyed the change of register, here presenting abundant dialogue and asserting the theatricality of the indoor scenes, the two films are nevertheless closely linked. There are two secrets at the heart of the story of *The Portrait of a Lady*: Madame Merle is Pansy's real mother and Osmond's former mistress; Ralph persuades his father to bequeath a part of his inheritance to his niece, Isabel. Similarly, the young woman held captive in a large house by her husband—Pygmalion, Dracula, Bluebeard—is a recurring theme of the gothic novel, which is reflected in the fate of Isabel held prisoner in a Roman palazzo and that of Ada in her home in the bush. This morbid theme is highlighted by the melancholic music of Schubert—notably the second movement of his String Quartet No. 14 in D Minor, based on his lied "Death and the Maiden"—played on the piano by Madame Merle, but it is not a death wish that drives *The Portrait of a Lady*. Although the battles that take place in its salons are no less violent than those in the bush in *The Piano*, it is the same indomitable spirit in both female protagonists, even in the midst of their misfortunes, that dominates both films.

---

1 Alistair Fox, *Jane Campion: Authorship and Personal Cinema*, Indiana University Press, Bloomington, 2011.

Interview conducted in Venice, 11 September 1996

Two of your films have had original screen-plays; the other two, written with Laura Jones, are based on literary works. Were the problems of adapting Henry James's novel *The Portrait of a Lady* different from those you encountered bringing Janet Frame's autobiographical work *An Angel at My Table* to the screen?

James's book is a great work of fiction and a narrative with a very complex structure. It also introduces many strong characters, whereas the stories of Janet Frame have, in truth, only one. *An Angel at My Table* follows the course of a life; *The Portrait of a Lady* has philosophical implications—it's really the journey of a young woman towards darkness and the underbelly of life. There is also a mythical dimension, with an awakening at the end. Adapting James's novel for the screen was a difficult task and one that sometimes even scared me, given the magnitude of the work.

When did you discover it?

I don't remember exactly when it was, but it was certainly when I was in my twenties, when I used to devour this kind of fiction. I've been thinking of making it into a film for a long time. I remember talking to a friend when we were amusing ourselves with the idea of founding a production company together to adapt for the screen classic novels like this, and those of Jane Austen, whose complex stories made a change from the boring films we were watching then. It would appear that, over the last few years, lots of people have had the same idea!

Faced with a book of more than six hundred pages, how did you decide on drastic cuts—the early chapters set in New England, for instance?

They were obviously difficult choices to make, and we even wondered at the beginning whether it was possible to do such an adaptation, until I realized, while rereading the novel, that we weren't going to film *The Portrait of a Lady* but rather the story of *The Portrait of a Lady* interpreted by me, with some of the dialogue. I love James's subtle psychological analyses, the way he has of spinning his web around his characters, but obviously you can't do this in film. My strengths were in being able to materialize situations, develop sexual

elements that were only hinted at, and give Isabel fantasies. On the other hand, Laura and I didn't have too much of a problem about sacrificing the first third of the novel, which is a kind of long prologue of conversations about a possible marriage. We started by making a shooting script of it, but it wasn't leading anywhere. However, we had the idea very early on of the symmetry between the tree at the beginning, under which Warburton proposes to Isabel, and the leafless one in winter at the end, where everything seems stripped and vulnerable, like Isabel herself. So many things have happened between and within the characters that lots of people don't notice that it's the same tree.

Your last sequence differs from the end of the book in that it's much more 'open'. In James's novel, Henrietta tells Goodwood that Isabel has gone back to Osmond, although James doesn't rule out a different future for her.

I think that James, too, doesn't want his readers to be sure which path his heroine is going to take. I think there are contradictory tensions in his book, which explains why he leaves us in suspense at the end. On the one hand, there is the fairy tale/melodrama that he is telling, and on the other, the weight of realism that he brings to his story, because James is a realist, and his characters are described in a way that is powerful, intimate, and true. He tries to blend these two tendencies in the epilogue to his novel. Personally, I didn't want to conclude with that, and preferred the symmetry of the two trees and Isabel's slow-motion running.

Isn't there also a conflict in you between a taste for romantic stories and the desire for a "realist" approach?

I like entering into a story like a member of the audience. I like feeling, without restraint, the reality of a drama that I'm telling, because its one of the great pleasures that all fiction gives us. And I strive to share with my actors, and with future viewers, this sense of reality. At the same time, I like the "romance," it's in my nature; I'm very romantic in the way I live my life. I don't mean that from a sentimental point of view, but in a wider sense: fundamentally, I'm an optimist.

Isabel is very like your other heroines. She's exploring life.

She's courageous and searching for truth; it's what drives her. Personally, I feel that

within me, among other things, there are two main forces that guide me: the excitement of discovering the truth about things and people, wherever that might be found, and the desire to be loved. They are two companions that are difficult to reconcile. If, for example, one of my films becomes very popular, I start asking myself how much truth it contains and wondering whether this truth is perhaps just too easy to embrace!

In *The Portrait of a Lady,* you made decisions that were not easy, in particular to do away with the decorative aspects of the reconstruction of the period that are usually found in this kind of adaptation. You concentrate on passions.

It was a very conscious decision. We knew we needed a period background because it was in this setting that the story was taking place, but the real theme was the intimacy of the relationships between the characters. It's a very demanding story, and that's what interested me, rather than the splendour of Italy. We also needed to show the darkness, and that was possible only in winter: the dark face of beautiful Italy, which is like that of Madame Merle and Osmond, of which Isabel sees only the bright side at the beginning. I myself got to know this Italy when I was twenty-one and went to study art in Venice. I spent the winter there, deeply depressed by the cold, the humidity, the confinement, and also my terrible loneliness, as I didn't know anyone there. That was my first existential experience of isolation. That really helped me to understand Isabel's feelings, particularly as the summer before this stay in Venice I had spent a wonderful summer in Perugia, where everyone loved me, the weather was great and I thought I was in heaven. A few months later, I really felt the fragility of my happiness!

You deviate from a "realist" narrative approach three times in the film, starting with the opening credits and the voice-over of young girls in conversation.

I thought I needed to evoke for viewers the romantic hopes of young girls. The decision was taken very early on to have this introduction, which serves as a link with our period, like a poem before a young girl's journey. She begins it with an idealized view of life, and the process of disenchantment will be a very difficult experience. It was then that I had the idea of getting together all the young

<u>Top:</u> *Jane Campion with her daughter, Alice.*
<u>Bottom:</u> *Campion on the set of the film.*

The tree at the beginning of the film,
under which Warburton proposes
to Isabel ...

*... and the leafless tree in winter, at the end,
where everything seems stripped and vulnerable, like Isabel herself.*

*The motifs of finger, hand, kiss and touch recur
throughout the film: here the hands of Caspar,
Warburton (Richard E. Grant) and Ralph (Martin
Donovan) that are placed on Isabel.*

intelligent women that I'd known in Australia during the preparation of the film and asking them to talk ad lib of their aspirations and emotional experiences. Friends, such as Genevieve Lemon, who played Sweetie, joined them. They were absolutely fascinating conversations, of which you hear only fragments and which would make an amazing radio broadcast, if only all the stories of kisses they relate!

There is also the sequence where, in a dream, she makes love to three men. Did you think about introducing other dream sequences like this?

No, not really. The development of the story is so dramatic that I didn't see how I could interrupt it. I did shoot another sequence of this sort, but I didn't keep it during editing. At this point in the story I wanted to show that Isabel was a woman with strong sexual aspirations, who wants to be loved and feels frustrated. Although she talks about something else entirely, about making a career for herself, what she's really searching for is passion. A critic of James's novel wrote—very accurately, I think—that Isabel is divided. On the one hand, as she never knew her father, she's looking for a substitute. On the other, she's fascinated by images of domination and submission. I think her attraction to Osmond took her by surprise, and that she trusted him because this experience seemed so powerful to her. Deep down she likes the idea that her future will no longer rest in her hands and that she can entrust it to this domineering 'genius'.

In one sense, Osmond is a negative mirror image of Isabel's spiritual aspirations. She refuses Warburton, who offers her material security, and Goodwood, with his physical attractions, in favour of Osmond, whom she idealizes.

She believes she's searching for light, whereas she's actually attracted by shadows, by a dark adventure that will engulf her. When Osmond declares his love for her, it's in a place plunged in darkness, with beams of light. The setting seems haunted.

The third imaginary sequence is this voyage in the East, shot in black and white like an old film.

We thought of a mental diary in the form of a home movie. It's very ludic, somewhat in the spirit of *Sweetie.* The shots where isolated

mouths move on their own are risky, but I think it's the sort of thing that either works or it doesn't, and you need to take the risk without asking too many questions afterward about their meaning. The sequence also helps you understand why she falls in love with Osmond, while the viewer tends to see him as a bad choice. The problem is that Isabel is an easy victim as she's so desperate to fall in love. During this journey, she convinces herself to make the fatal decision.

When you chose John Malkovich, you knew, with the rakish image he has on screen, that the audience would discover the true nature of his character before Isabel.

But James, when he introduces the character of Osmond, tells us that there will be no revelation and describes him as he is. I like that idea, because it allows the reader to be in on the secret of the ploy concocted by Madame Merle and Osmond to conquer Isabel. In the same way, I wanted it to be known from the start that Osmond is bad. Readers or viewers have the feeling that the author is revealing everything in advance. Hence their total surprise when they discover that Pansy is the daughter of Osmond and Madame Merle.

You originally thought of asking William Hurt to play Osmond.

Yes, but Hurt would have projected a more subtle image of the 'villain'. He turned down my offer because he was troubled by the idea of playing an evil character with no saving graces. You can't convince an actor to play a role he doesn't want to take, and his refusal was my good luck, because Malkovich was prepared to freely explore a human being's darkest facets. Moreover, we can all identify with Osmond and Madame Merle when, for example, they speak critically of people they know. Another curious thing about Osmond is that he always speaks the truth, even if it's in a sly way.

Madame Merle shows more compassion than in the novel.

To me, she's a great character. And I agree with James when he says that the great characters in literature are great because they understand their own tragedy. Madame Merle has, somewhere inside her, a love for Isabel, and to some degree she's disgusted by what she has undertaken to do in order to protect her daughter.

Nicole Kidman, with her red hair, is reminiscent of Kerry Fox, who plays the Janet Frame as an adult in *An Angel at My Table.*

It was Nicole's idea to have this frizzy hairstyle because she'd had hair like that as a child and didn't like it. She definitely didn't want her character to be a 'beauty'. In real life, Nicole is. She's a very intelligent woman, but she doesn't like to make a show of it and even comes across as very reserved. When Laura Jones, my writer, Janet Patterson, my costume designer, and myself were talking about the character of Isabel, we asked ourselves how she would dress if she were our contemporary. We decided she was the sort of young woman who would wear black tights and men's shoes, who wouldn't dress in a feminine way and would want to be taken seriously for her ideas. There are some very beautiful women who don't want to be elegant. Isabel doesn't know who she is, and while she thinks she's on a journey in search of truth, she's actually exploring who she is. At the end, when she acknowledges to herself that she's in love with Ralph, she's laid bare, honest, and she's sure of her emotions and determined to make him feel the feelings she has for him. She has a revelation of her true self.

You already knew Nicole Kidman before directing her.

We had met several times in Australia but had never really been friends. I had thought of her in 1983 for one of my short films, *A Girl's Own Story*, which I made while studying at the Australian Film Television and Radio School, but she was taking an exam and wasn't free. Later I dreamed of getting her to return from Hollywood to play Isabel in a theatrical production of *The Portrait of a Lady* that I wanted to put on in Sydney. At the time, I didn't think it was possible to make a mainstream film of this novel, and I didn't have enough confidence in myself to brave its complexities in order to translate it visually. The stage seemed to me to be a more appropriate setting. When, finally, I decided to shoot the film, I thought of her because she's a woman who feels she can aspire to anything, that she can claim a right to things, that she's intellectually superior. At the same time, she has serious bouts of modesty and can spend all her time apologizing. In a word, she's very bright. She can be overly frank, then be sorry that she's hurt you. I needed a personality of this kind—strong, courageous, and intelligent—to portray Isabel. She also has a great ability to convey different emotions

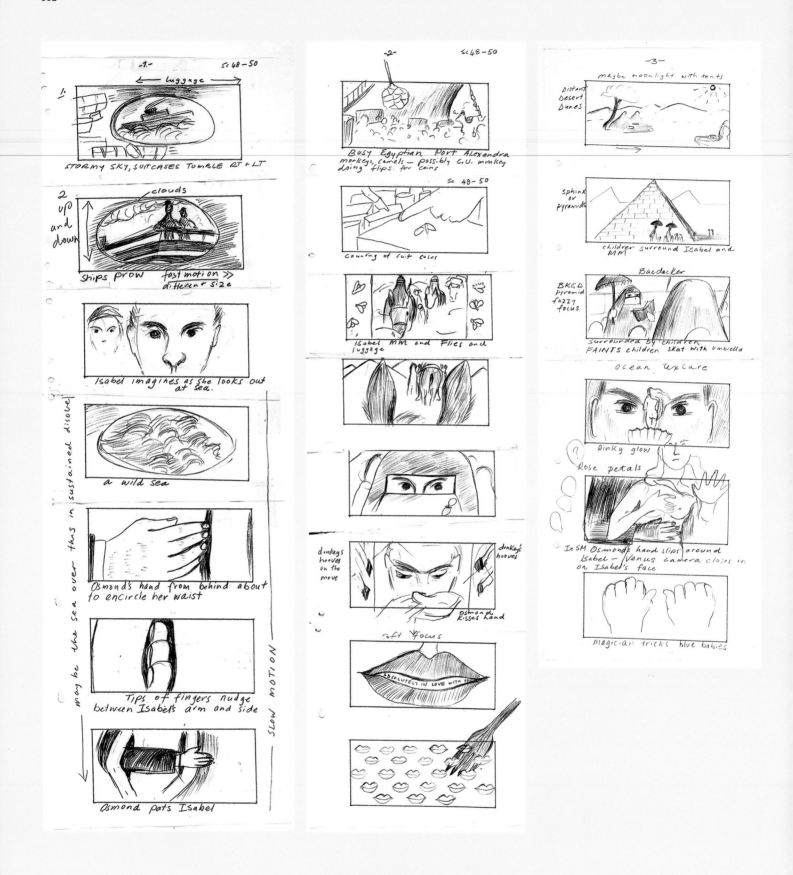

The storyboard of the trip Isabel takes to Greece
and the Middle East with Madame Merle.

*The trip sequence, shot in black and white,
pastiches Hollywood's orientalist films.*

*Agnes Ayres and Rudolph Valentino in
George Melford's* The Sheik *(1921).*

very quickly. She really is one of the princesses of our generation. In addition, she backed the project to the hilt—she was a real fan!

I have the feeling that New Zealanders and Australians are like turn-of-the-century Americans, who were less jaded, less superior than they are today, and who used to set off to explore Europe to gain experience.
Yes, we have a certain innocence. Our countries are younger than America. The United States is now very powerful, and the relationship has reversed. Europeans now cross the Atlantic to encounter the power that exists there. We don't have this power, we lack experience, and our heritage comes from Europe. That also brought me closer to James. I remember that when I saw Paris and Rome for the first time, I really was "elsewhere," overwhelmed.

You've brought out the melodramatic aspect of James's writing that resembles that of Balzac, whereas we see him more as a precursor of Proust. Like his novels, your film presents an intensified, "theatrical" reality.
We're using this dramatization to convey ideas about life and people. It's very useful! James understood people's taste for drama and used these recognized forms to explore humankind. That's what made me think that this could work in film, because it's basically a great story. I tried to discover the power of intimate relationships, to make them dynamic, cinematic, by filming encounters between the characters. I could have been more moderate and told the story with shot-reverse shots of people sitting in armchairs having conversations. That could have been interesting for a handful of people, but definitely not for the majority, and perhaps not for me either. I wanted to really throw myself into the story so that the audience, too, could share these emotions.

You use the architecture and background a lot to convey these emotions, such as in the scene with Henrietta and Isabel in front of the recumbent statues at the Victoria and Albert Museum in London, or that with Madame Merle and Isabel in front of the statues of the Capitol in Rome, places that are not in the novel.
I loved the fantastical, morbid aspect of these pairs of statues, and I felt that the setting of this museum, which I love, suited this conversation between two friends who had come to see the sights in London. For the second scene, I chose these statues at the Capitol because they've always greatly moved me. I don't know why they make such an impression on me. Perhaps because of their size and the fact that they're broken. There's an echo there of Isabel's emotional state. In James's novel, she was in the countryside among the ruins.

Why do you use tilted frames to show the Duomo in Florence and the Colosseum?
In the first case, to show the top of the cathedral. In the second, so that you don't see what shouldn't be seen: cars and other modern details. I don't have a problem with tilting the camera occasionally!

How did you and your cinematographer, Stuart Dryburgh, tackle the chromatic texture of the film?
We made two major decisions: to make the interiors in Italy as dark as possible and to almost overexpose the outside shots to get incredible contrasts. That corresponded with a reality I've seen in Italy, and also with the emotional realism of the story, with this opposition between darkness and light. We also wanted to avoid the intimate scenes looking glamorous, to get closer to the bodies.

You had never previously worked with composer Wojciech Kilar.
At the start, Michael Nyman was to write the music. In the end he turned it down, and I believe that was for the best, as he had a lot of reservations about the novel, which he didn't really like. However, that caused us some problems as we had to find a replacement quite late on. I knew a student in Sydney who had been recommended to me and who is completely obsessed with film music. He is very intelligent and very sensitive, works in a CD store, and has an incredible collection of soundtracks. He played me a huge amount of film music by Americans and Europeans, until he got to Kilar's score for Coppola's *Dracula*, which grabbed me immediately. I loved its completely unsentimental romanticism, its sense of mystery and its depth. We didn't know anything about him; we phoned him in Poland. He wasn't wanting to write music for film anymore but was happy to reconsider his position. He came to Australia, loved the film, and found it to have a romanticism he connected with, but he nevertheless turned us down. He felt blocked, and, as he's a true artist, there was no way to make him change his mind. A week later, he sent me a fax telling me that he believed he'd found solutions to the various problems we'd discussed. After that, I went to Poland and was amazed by his work and the way in which he'd understood the film.

It's a film where you really sense the passing of time and how much the main character has changed between the first and last images.
Obviously, there's no satisfactory outcome for Isabel. The man to whom she feels closest, Ralph, is dying. Her marriage with Osmond, likewise, is unsustainable. For me, *The Portrait of a Lady* speaks of the choices that we have to make in life, and also tells us that we can give sense to our destiny, even if it is as tragic as Isabel's—through love, honesty, and self-discovery. This, for me, is the sense of the journey that Isabel has undertaken. She had thought that this journey would be a battle against the elements, a purely external voyage, and she realizes, at the end, that she had undertaken an internal journey of self-discovery.

The Portrait of a Lady portrays alternately very dark
interiors and outside shots that are almost overexposed.

The final shot of The Portrait of a Lady.

Holy Smoke

(1999)

"Returning to the Age
in Which I Live."

P. J. Waters (Harvey Keitel) and Ruth (Kate Winslet) in Holy Smoke
<u>*Following pages:*</u> *Kate Winslet on the set of* Holy Smoke.
<u>*Pages 122–123:*</u> *This deprogramming treatment leads to a battle
of the sexes in which Ruth opens up to love.*

A cathartic work

An Unpopular Film

Holy Smoke marked Campion's return to Australia, ten years after making *Sweetie*. After three journeys into the past, *Holy Smoke*, like *Sweetie*, is a contemporary story, and, also like *Sweetie*, one of Campion's most eccentric and least popular films. Yet it is a work of great originality, and one that explores new territories. With the decline of traditional religions, it attests to the filmmaker's quest for a spirituality she had already touched on in *Sweetie*, with its references to tantrism and Kay's visit to a clairvoyant. Two film projects that Campion has mentioned in her interviews (see page 128)—*Ebb*, and more particularly *My Guru and His Disciple*, an adaptation of Christopher Isherwood's autobiographical account of his experiences in India—testify to these preoccupations. In 1939, while exiled in Los Angeles, Isherwood met Swami Prabhavananda, founder of the Vedanta Society of Southern California, which initiated inner conflict in him, torn as he was between a life of spiritual study and meditation that required him to remain celibate and a life of sexual pleasure with male partners. Campion was inevitably drawn to this theme, sexuality having always had a central role in her films. She herself had been practising meditation for several years, and in the late 1980s, had attended a seminar on personal fulfilment led by Anthony Robbins. She thus began working, together with her sister Anna, on the screenplay for *Holy Smoke*.

The Sacred and the Profane

During a trip to India, Ruth (Kate Winslet) falls under the influence of a religious guru, Chidaatma Baba (Dhritiman Chatterji), and decides to become his disciple. When her family becomes worried about her, her mother (Julie Hamilton) decides to go and bring her back on the pretext that her father (Tim Robertson) is in a critical state of health. On returning to Sydney, Ruth is handed over to an American exit counselor,

P. J. Waters (Harvey Keitel), who promises that in three days, he will have extricated her from the power of the sect. This deprograming treatment leads to a battle of the sexes in which Ruth opens up to love. As in the Indian tradition, the spiritual and the sexual are closely interconnected, and this alliance is at the heart of the conflict between Ruth and P. J.

The opening sequences in parallel montage bring Eastern spirituality and Western materialism into opposition. The first shots show an India of shimmering colours and teeming streets, where Ruth's face emerges amid a group of young women and dancing children. This introduction of the protagonist follows the same pattern that has been seen in Campion's other films. In contrast, a high-angle shot reveals the Sydney suburb, ironically named Sans Souci (meaning 'carefree'), where, in a distressingly banal red-brick environment, her family vegetates in an unattractively decorated house from which the only escape is a picture on the wall depicting a mountain scene that resembles more closely the green landscapes of New Zealand. It is this bleak existence that the heroine wanted to flee. Baba is viewed from a distance as a sexual and racial threat, confirmed by Ruth's mother on her trip to India, where she protects herself by spraying her mouth and covering her face to ward off the prevailing pollution.

Ruth, like the heroines of the previous films, is an intrepid young woman who is determined to break off all ties in her pursuit for personal fulfilment. She too has a need to be loved, and Baba appears to her as a father substitute. A subjective shot shows her surrounded by lights, lotus flowers, and butterflies, in an image from the world of Bollywood films, before she faints as though in a mystical rapture. Her lack of paternal affection leads her to turn to older men in a way that has already been seen in earlier works. When Ruth accuses her father of having deceived her by pretending to be ill to get her to come home, she publicly attacks him in front of the assembled family by reminding him of her half-sister born out of an affair he had with his secretary. Shortly before making

this film, Jane and Anna had themselves learned of the existence of a half-sister, their father's daughter from an adulterous affair.

The director takes an impartial view of the New Age philosophy and popular culture of her time, refusing to take on the role of either apologist or denigrator. While Baba might at first appear as a protective figure, we later learn that he had raped a thirteen-year-old girl and that he had had sexual relations with young boys. P. J. himself was once the victim of another guru, named Singh, when he took a trip to India. These mentors, paragons of wisdom, are perhaps just charlatans. Ruth's family watch videos of news bulletins about Charles Manson's 'family' and the murder of Sharon Tate, in addition to the hundreds of believers sacrificed by their sect. Meanwhile, in contrast to Ruth's frustrations, Yvonne (Sophie Lee), Ruth's sister-in-law, flaunts her hyper-sexuality (like a parallel to Sweetie): she admits that she has written passionate love letters to herself and that she can have sex with her husband, Bobby, only by looking at pictures of film stars—Tom Cruise or Brad Pitt—displayed beside their bed. Campion's ironic, one could even say grotesque, streak finds fertile ground for expression in mocking mass culture. The trip to India that has replaced that to Europe or the Antipodes of the three previous films opens with a song by Neil Diamond, 'Holly Holy', even the title of which connects the sacred and the profane. Later, another of Diamond's compositions, "I Am . . . I Said," is used to accompany the arrival in Sydney of P. J. and his triumphant individualism. Pop culture, that of Campion's youth, permeates the film—particularly its fascination for Indian philosophies (similarly evident in the reference to the Beatles in *A Girl's Own Story*).

A Mix of Genres

Many commentators have tried to classify Campion's work in terms of film genres. However, it seems, on the contrary, that her films (apart from *In the Cut*) have only the most tangential relationships with biopic, melodrama, or comedy, and that, in contrast to the Hollywood tradition, her ideas are much more idiosyncratic and driven by the pursuit of original forms. Dana Polan, in his fine study, relates *Holy Smoke* to screwball comedies of the 1930s, epitomized by Howard Hawks, Frank Capra, Leo McCarey, and Gregory La Cava.[1] These traits are not absent, far from it, in the relationship between Ruth and P. J., which is rich in moments of irony. However, overall this relationship is permeated by an emotional charge and a seriousness characteristic of the filmmaker, which can also be seen in confrontational relationships in her other films—between, for example, Ada and Baines or Stewart in *The Piano*, and between Isabel and Osmond in *The Portrait of a Lady*. Although the conflict between Ruth and P. J. does indeed constitute a battle of the sexes, it reaches a dramatic intensity that makes *Holy Smoke* one of her most moving films. The reason the film baffled audiences on its release is no doubt due to its often whimsical treatment, using a mix of genres—again, similarly to *Sweetie*—in dealing with a spiritual quest, for which a contemplative, serious tone would be more usual.

P. J. sees Ruth appear as a six-armed Indian goddess.

Top: Dressed in black, with a mustache, dark glasses, snakeskin boots, and tight-fitting pants,
P. J. Waters, an American exit counselor, embodies Western
rationality and technology.
Bottom: Ruth's family hands her over to P. J. Waters.

Ruthless

By, for the first and last time, entrusting a leading role to the same actor, Harvey Keitel, Campion suggests a comparison between these two roles, however different the two characters, Baines and P. J., might appear. In both cases, the heroine's transition from hostility to union is based on a feminization of the male character. To teach him to make love to her as she wants him to, and in the middle of one of their more brutal confrontations, Ruth makes up P. J. with red lipstick and dolls him up in a matching dress, as if to make him understand what a woman of his own age might look like. Dressed as a transvestite, he follows her, weeping, into the desert, so madly attached to this woman that, as he's lying on the ground, he sees her appear as a six-armed Indian goddess, to the sound of the Shirelles singing 'Baby It's You', thus linking the end of the film with the Bollywood imagery of the early scene. For *Holy Smoke* is not only a battle of the sexes, it's also an intergenerational conflict, with Ruth admitting she wants a young man and mocking P. J. for his taste for young flesh that makes him dye his hair. His first appearance portrays him effectively as a conquering macho, dressed in black, with a mustache, dark glasses, snakeskin boots, and tight-fitting pants. He embodies Western rationality and technology, sure of himself with the eight-nine subjects he has deprogrammed, bearing a recidivist rate of only 3.5 percent, and his three-day treatment program in a shack with the day-one goal of isolating the patient, getting her attention, and obtaining her respect. His desire for control fails, and his plan goes awry faced with Ruth's determination to derail his routine and to make him discover the intensity of passion. Gradually, by reversing the roles, she becomes dominant in the relationship, humiliating and denigrating him—he will speak of her in retrospect as 'his avenging angel'—until she begins to feel compassion for him. Each of them will drop their defences to be able to connect. In a particular scene, Ruth emerges naked from the darkness, and, when P. J. turns away from her, she lets urine flow from between her legs and begins to cry, physically expressing her emotional needs like a child wetting its bed while dreaming. Later, using a marker pen, he writes the words 'Be kind'—words spoken by the Dalai Lama—backward on her forehead, which she reads in a mirror. He abandons his cruelty and violence, and, in exchange, she accepts her name, Ruth, the woman who until that point has been *ruthless* with him.

When Ruth goes looking for P. J. in a truck with her two brothers and her sister-in-law and they pick him up, bleeding, on the roadside, she asks her brother to stop so that she can get in the back of the pickup with him and take him in her arms. She realizes then that he is the only person who has really loved her. It is with this surrogate paternal figure that she finds her identity. The conflict between nature and culture plays out in the fight between Ruth and P. J. When P. J. wants to assert himself in their discussions on philosophy and spirituality, he talks to her of the Upanishads, Socrates, Verdi, and the Gospel of John, and she denounces his aridity, advising him to go beyond quotations found in books. While P. J. accuses her of having imprisoned her soul in a fortress, he behaves no differently. They both need to accept each other: he by abandoning his cynicism and by recognizing the need for sensuality and emotion, she by experiencing feelings for the man who desires her. As Alistair Fox has shown, P. J. has torn down the strongholds that at an unconscious level she had erected by converting to a religion.[2] When her faith in this religion is destroyed by P. J., who has denounced the hypocrisy of the guru and his beliefs, the suffering caused by the trauma she was protecting herself from returns with force, and it is in turning to sex that she finds her truth. Just as *The Portrait of a Lady* was a criticism of the fallacious nature of the romantic impulse, so *Holy Smoke*, far from being an apology for New Age philosophy, questions its fundamental precepts. It is the convergence of the erotic impulse and the spiritual quest, or the search for the soul, that enables Ruth to break out of her identity crisis.

Campion concludes her film with an exchange of messages, correspondence being a leitmotif of her work, from the first of her short films, *Mishaps of Seduction and Conquest*, to *Bright Star*, via *Two Friends*. A year later, Ruth has returned to India, to Jaipur, now has a young boyfriend, and has allowed her mother to return to her job as a veterinarian. Both of them are caring for animals. She writes to P. J.: "I'm still chasing the truth. [...] I don't know why I love you. But I do . . . from afar." P. J. replies: he has married Carol (Pam Grier), his assistant, written a novel, and thinks of her, but asks her not to tell Carol. He is sitting facing his computer, in front of which is placed a picture of an Indian goddess. No doubt like Ruth, who admits to him that she has developed the ability to love and be loved. So ends, in appeasement and diversity, this cathartic work, one of the most violent and most original that Campion has made.

1 Dana Polan, *Jane Campion*, British Film Institute, London, 2001.
2 Alistair Fox, *Jane Campion: Authorship and Personal Cinema*, Indiana University Press, Bloomington, 2011.

*P. J.'s desire for control fails and Ruth gradually becomes
dominant in the relationship, humiliating and denigrating
him until she begins to feel compassion for him.*

Interview conducted in Paris, 14 September 1999

You have long had in mind a film adaptation of Christopher Isherwood's book *My Guru and His Disciple*, which has California as its background, and you've also spoken of your interest in Zen. Were these harbingers of *Holy Smoke*, which takes place in the East, more precisely in India?

Isherwood's book gives an account of his friendship with Swami Pravananda, one of the first Asian gurus to come to the West. I was fascinated to read in it about Isherwood's attempts to become a monk, until he renounced his vow of chastity because it was too difficult for him! What he was wanting, more than anything else in the world, was intimacy and love. He nevertheless continued his friendship with Pravananda because he admired his faith in his teachings; he was a man of great spirituality, who had devoted his life to spirituality. Today, California is famous for the New Age movement, which made its fortune there, but I like *My Guru and His Disciple* because it was written long before this fashion for feel-good, laissez-faire, and lack of discipline, which has been criticized, sometimes unjustly, sometimes with good cause. Isherwood's book, which it's difficult to address directly, has a lot of charm and realism. The problem is that I never managed to get a screenplay that I was really satisfied with, despite several attempts by writers. I felt I would have to write it myself, but I didn't really want to. That's when I started to develop in my head the idea of a film based on the spirituality of our time, while trying to incorporate seduction, complexity, misunderstandings, and the down-to-earth side, which, to my mind, are linked to all spiritual journeys. When the story of *Holy Smoke* came into my mind, I immediately realized that this was what I'd been looking for for some time. After three period films, I wanted to return to the age in which I live, because it's a relief for an artist not to have to dive again into a past he or she hasn't known. I was therefore attracted to the present. In addition, Harvey Keitel had told me that he'd like to work with me again. But first I needed a story, and I suppose that my interest in the sexual and other aspects of a relationship between two people led me to this story, which, of course, also had this spiritual dimension.

Did you know India beforehand?

I had made trips there, but they were different from Ruth's. I'd also taken part in workshops in Australia linked to Eastern devotional practice and beliefs. I also have friends who became disciples of Bhagwan Shree Rajneesh, now dead, whose ashram in the United States was very famous before it vanished in the wake of accusations of murder and corruption. The members of the sect called themselves the Orange People because of the colour they wore. Rajneesh's philosophical views were quite engaging, but it was difficult to reconcile them with his Rolls Royces and the power struggles generated by his bureaucracy.

For Ruth, isn't her trip to India above all the rite of passage that all young Australians take abroad, like the one you went on as a teenager, or that of the main character of *An Angel at My Table*?

Yes, it's what young people call 'backpacking cheap to Asia'. In Ruth's case, she doesn't really know what to expect. In the first sequence, we try to show that it's not that easy to travel. Ruth comes across other Westerners who seem very confident, strong, and happy to be there, while she feels a bit alienated. It's in order to better understand what she's up against that we have her visit an ashram.

Your attitude towards this spiritual community is neither satirical nor approving.

Obviously, we know there are false gurus and others who are misguided, because wielding spiritual power over others can lead to a lot of abuse. That's the whole problem with the spiritual life: meeting its demands and challenges. To some extent, this is the subject of the film, and I wanted to approach it from a young person's viewpoint. Young people insist on absolutes—when they've experienced something, they think that everyone else needs to experience the same thing, and that if people just opened their eyes and their hearts, they would understand that it's the only path to take. They don't accept shades of gray and believe, quite simply, that their parents are so narrow-minded that they're unable to understand. Opposite, there's Harvey Keitel's character, P. J. Waters, who claims that he, too, had experienced a cult, but that it turned out badly for him: he has reshaped himself negatively, like someone who, disappointed in love, believes that love is impossible and tries to put other people off.

Who exactly are these "exit counsellors" of which P. J. Waters is a representative?

They exist. They are eccentrics that have no legal status. In general, they themselves or someone in their family has had a bad experience in a sect and they attempt to help those who are part of one. It's a sort of reverse brainwashing. To prepare for the role, Harvey Keitel met one, spent time with him, and watched films where you see these exit counsellors at work. We built his character, of course: a former Marine, vain, of a certain age, and with a whole system of defense mechanisms against the outside world. It was important for the story. What interested me was how we construct our beliefs, how they change, and the way in which people take a "leap" when they fall in love or embrace a religion. There is also this idea—widely held—that the values of our society are the only ones that count, while in fact everything is relative.

All your heroines share a desire for self-fulfilment that takes them through a series of trials, sometimes at the cost of a temporary separation from their family. At the end, they are more mature, sexually and psychologically.

With slight differences. Ada isn't young; she's over thirty. Janet Frame doesn't rebel. The family for me is a metaphor of society. It's an important institution, but, like any institution, it must be appraised. We need to be both wary of and grateful for it. Like anything else, it mustn't become a sacred cow. Plus, our relationship to it changes as we get older. I've enjoyed being part of a family, but I'm not blinded by what it is. There is no perfect family, and I don't think having flaws is a crime—it's normal. Some people take umbrage when you point out some failing or other in a family, but, if we look at those close to us, we see as many tragedies as successes. It's difficult being a man or a woman, and no one manages it perfectly.

Ruth, like a lot of young people, is the victim of the lies and hypocrisies of adults, and that feeds her rebellion. Her family make her believe that her father is dying in order to get her to return home.

Her family is afraid it'll end in tragedy, and she herself is the victim of what we call in Australia a 'dobber', someone who spends their time telling tales on others because they don't have a life themselves. This type of person is often at the root of all the trouble. I find it amusing that, in the film, the person who takes on this role is Prue, whose 'imagination' is so stunted that she's frightened by the fantasies that Ruth fuels in her. I remember that one of my best friends with whom I lived at university became

Ruth, like the heroines of the previous films,
is an intrepid young woman who is determined to break
off all ties in her pursuit for personal fulfilment.

Later, using a marker pen, P. J. writes the words 'Be kind' on Ruth's forehead. He abandons his cruelty and violence, and, in exchange, she accepts her name, Ruth, the woman who until that point has been ruthless *with him.*

'Basically, I was asking Harvey and Kate
to express their true feelings, and my camera
just followed their movements.'

a disciple of Moon. She was unhappy, and when she discovered this sect, it was like an opening up to the world. She was very proselytizing and wanted me to follow her. With sadness, I saw her distance herself from me while believing it was her right to explore this path. Ruth's family could not have imagined this life for their daughter: drugs, illnesses, lack of contact. They rallied to the idea of her return as a cause. That has always interested me, that way that people have of embracing a cause to hide their own shortcomings.

As in *The Portrait of a Lady*, but in a very different way, you explore the relationship of a woman with an older man.

Except that Gilbert Osmond and Isabel Archer are closer in age and intelligence. The charm and self-possession of John Malkovich's character made him a much more obviously attractive proposition. P. J. Waters, on the other hand, is an obsessive seducer, unattractive at first glance, whose true human nature we have to discover beneath this external appearance.

For the first time, you wrote the screenplay with your elder sister, Anna, who is also a director.

I thought that Anna could help me, particularly with the intimate dialogue between Ruth and P. J. Waters. She has a lot of talent for that, and she's also very witty. She's someone who can be hilariously funny, so a good partner to have! In addition, I believe in goodness, in good, and that it's possible to be spiritually fulfilled if you make the effort, whereas Anna doesn't believe in that at all. I didn't realize, when we started out, how fruitful our friction on this subject would turn out to be. We personified these two opposite views, argued a lot, and, in the end, I believe I partially convinced her. The advantage of working as a pair is first and foremost that you can speed up the writing process if you have similar tastes. You can rave on about a new idea, but if you're not able to test it immediately with your co-writer, it can take you a week to realize you're going the wrong way. Writing is a continual moving from hope to despair. You have to consider each idea as brilliant and wonderful, and at the same time take a step back and evaluate it. Your co-writer is there to help you. Moreover, I'm very close to Anna, and we like to talk to each other about our family. It's a chance for us to get together, and, what's more, we're paid to do so!

How did the screenplay evolve?

We knew that, at heart, if would be the story of a reversal of fortune. P. J. Waters would try to deprogram Ruth and her beliefs, but, during this process, he would meet his exterminating angel and would have to reconsider his behaviour. The spiritual discussion ends up at the level at which people live; that is to say, it takes the form of a sexual power struggle. The result is a sort of armistice between the combatants, where neither any longer tries to dominate the other and a relationship is established like that between two wounded soldiers. They realize that they have more in common than the issue they're fighting over.

Was it necessary for P. J. Waters' machismo to lead him to a masochistic ordeal where he has to wear lipstick and a red dress?

It wasn't obligatory, but we thought it would be fun! You know, girls like to dress men up as women! More seriously, Waters is aware that Ruth is furious to see his girlfriend show up, and that she feels humiliated that she wasn't told of her existence. He realizes that the only way for him to pursue his sexual obsession with her is to let her express her anger as she sees fit, to invite her, so to speak, to realize the worst fantasies she's dreamed up. I don't believe that anyone imagined she could be so audacious. At the same time, it's a way of showing the level of intimacy and surrender they'd reached together. They have created a space for their privacy where they can tell each other the truth as they see it. Curiously, she feels then, more than ever before in her life, that she's secure with someone, and that allows her to express herself. She tries to make him understand that it's not flattering for her to be desired just because she's young and beautiful. Because, conversely, why would she then want him, given that he's neither young nor handsome. There's a double standard here that she wants to bring to light. She also thinks he's so strong he can take anything!

Was it difficult for Kate Winslet to surrender herself to that extent?

Believe me, it's easy for a young woman! During auditions, these were the scenes the candidates chose! They like being given the chance to laugh and tease. They completely lack the imagination to understand a man's emotions. However, they had trouble acknowledging their own vulnerability because they saw themselves as afraid of nothing. They considered themselves to be strong—it's a sort of mantra. Of course,

they're not—they have fears, like everyone. Except that the feeling of fear is alien to them because they've not had a lot of experience of this sort of thing, they've not encountered major disappointments. Undoubtedly, that was the most difficult thing for Kate to portray: her desire to hide her vulnerability, not to be caught really in love. I supposed we're all like that; the world isn't a very friendly place, it often even scares us and we want to be protected. Our personality provides that protection.

Their love scenes in the Halfway Hut are lit differently from those in *The Portrait of a Lady*, although shadow plays an important part there, too.

I wanted them to happen at night, but they're nevertheless very 'colourful'. In that sense, it's very different from *The Portrait of a Lady*, where it was much more somber, more blue. These are journeys into the dark continent of eroticism. Basically, I was asking Harvey and Kate to express their true feelings, and my camera just followed their movements. Even though the Steadicam's movements were sometimes complicated, I wanted to show their confrontation.

You were faced with a problem in mixing the family scenes, which were more farcical, with a passionate psychodrama.

It was a difficult balance. My choice of satire and burlesque was deliberate. I didn't want a BBC drama with an articulate message. On the contrary, we were wanting to ask questions. We weren't in the presence of a family with a correct view of life, rescuing their daughter. We opted for genuine anarchy. The family is supposed to be normal, but it's exactly this 'normality' that was questioned. They all wanted to save Ruth, but to reintegrate her into what sort of a world? In addition, I think her mother is sincere and the gay brother doesn't share the family's lifestyle. The father is vain and childish—which doesn't surprise me—so we are able to understand his behaviour at the end when he leaves his wife. As for her, she makes peace with her daughter and is no doubt going to live a more open life. It's a family like every other family, which has its problems. If we laugh at it, we'll do the same with Ruth, too, in the beginning, and with P. J. Waters. Everyone is treated with humour, but without condescension.

Yvonne Barron, the sister-in-law, spotlights Ruth because she herself is so one-dimensional.

What I like about her is that, in her own way, she tells the truth, she sees things as they are. She's fascinated by P. J. Waters's charisma, but she wants to draw the attention he's giving Ruth onto herself. She reckons she's got problems, too! She's a beautiful girl who got married young, had a child, and no longer knows what to do with her life.

This is the first time you've worked with Dion Beebe, your cinematographer.

He lives in Australia, and I wanted to work with him because he knows how to be economical. If you hire a famous director of photography, they demand to have a whole team around them; it's like a safety net. The same is true of renowned directors, who demand an increasing number of extra shooting weeks as their power grows. It gives you some breathing space! Dion Beebe has done some fine things, he has a poetic vision, and he's someone with whom you can talk about any aspect of the film, not just the photography. For me, he's like a friend. He has a lot of compassion and respect for the actors; he knows what they're doing. We were wanting to create a sense of reality and didn't want to use filters to make things look more beautiful. We were looking for a certain roughness, a living presence without unnecessary visual complications, because the story is enough. We had to constantly work in harmony with the emotional atmosphere of the sequence.

Where did you shoot?

In Sydney, and also in the Flinders Ranges in South Australia. That's where the farm and the Halfway Hut are, and it was also the landscape of *Walkabout*. It's the red heart of Australia, its spiritual centre and a region where little shooting is done. It's our equivalent of the mythic Arcadia.

On the other hand, you've always worked with the same editor, Veronika Jenet.

She's a wonderful, fearless person; she always tells me what she thinks, and that reassures me. She has a more common turn of mind than mine, so she's a good counterbalance! She also has a very fine narrative sense. As with my sister, I love her frankness. We're very different, but her directness is important to me because, when you've gained a reputation, it can play tricks on you. Sometimes your colleagues don't dare to speak up or contradict you because they assume you know what you're doing, when this isn't always the case! I like talking with people and them giving me their point of view. When I was starting out, they shared their opinions with me more easily.

Angelo Badalamenti said he wrote the music in two and a half days.

Angelo really did have that experience. For my part, I had a terrible bout of the flu, was dragging myself to recording sessions over the weekend, and wasn't even able to take him out for dinner. I'd met him a long time ago, and have always admired the music he composed for David Lynch, as well as for Paul Schrader's *The Comfort of Strangers*. He first watched the film in New York, then saw it again after several modifications and loved it. So he gave his consent. His understanding of the film was, of course, crucial. He got a piano in, told me he was going to look at the scenes where I wanted music and play, improvising as the inspiration took him. We began with the scene where Ruth is surrounded by her family. Angelo was originally a teacher and is comfortable with literature. He has a wonderful ability to emotionally understand the characters. He's a man full of passion and energy who loves his life, as well as his work. He wrote his score incredibly quickly, as the images were unfolding on screen, with perfect empathy. Strangely, the piece I like the best is the one that initially didn't have a place in the film but that we've used for the moment when the moon rises. What impresses me about Angelo is that he can work and have fun at the same time. Mixing concentration and pleasure is my style, too!

Did you rehearse with the actors?

Yes, for three weeks. It's what I always do, and we could have rehearsed for longer. It helps me see what might happen during shooting and thus to think about it in advance. Often the demands of shooting don't allow you to shoot in continuity. So these rehearsals give you the chance to see the story develop organically in your head. I was pleased to see Harvey again, happier, more open and more relaxed than on *The Piano*. He took this role as a challenge because it's a strong character; it's also an area of life that interests him a great deal. He loves talking about the mythical journey towards the heart, and, in a way, *Holy Smoke* reformulates this old story of a creative quest. I love the title from this point of view. 'Holy smoke!', while it's an exclamation like 'Good God!', also suggests the absence of substance to spirituality, which is smokelike. In the end, the answer to questions lies in ourselves. No reading of a text will do the work for us. The genuine spiritual journey isn't about following rules and regulations. On the contrary, it's a personal struggle against these rules.

You nevertheless decided, even though Ruth has "found" herself, to have her return to India.

She could have stayed in Australia, but we wanted her to return to India to live there differently. What has happened to her will turn her off wanting to join a sect there. She wants to be *in* life. The important thing is what both of them have said to each other. Living together or getting married wasn't part of their lives.

It must have been an unusual experience for Kate Winslet; different from anything else she's done. Have you discussed it with her?

She wanted to but I didn't wish to. She felt that these were extreme situations, but she was afraid of nothing, or at least so she claimed. I protected her a lot because it could have been very disturbing for her. The sex scenes with Harvey were quite difficult, even if the atmosphere was relaxed and they weren't as naked as they appear. They were, I admit, extreme moments, and I couldn't have played them—I'd have been too scared! I believe that the reason someone wants to become an actor is to feel powerful emotions by proxy, without danger. Most actors—even those who are hired above all for their looks—want to seriously, sincerely, and deeply explore what drives their characters.

Of all your films, *Holy Smoke* is the one that most resembles *Sweetie*.

It suits my 'Buñuelian' sense of humour, my lack of respect for respectable people. It also has something to do with my deeply childlike nature. I love being childlike!

Jane Campion and Kate Winslet
on the set of the film.

In the Cut
(2003)

"A Love Story."

138

Top to bottom: Frannie Avery (Meg Ryan) and her half-sister, Pauline (Jennifer Jason Leigh), followed by John Graham (Kevin Bacon); Cornelius Webb (Sharrieff Pugh); Pauline.

Top to bottom: Frannie with police detective Malloy (Mark Ruffalo); Frannie with John Graham; Malloy's Puerto Rican colleague Rodriguez (Nick Damici); Following pages: Frannie's dive into her unconscious.

The dizziness of physical desire

A Genre Film

The third literary adaptation, following on from those of works by Janet Frame and Henry James, *In the Cut*, based on the novel of the same name by Susanna Moore, is also, strictly speaking, the only one of Campion's films to belong to a genre—the erotic thriller, foreshadowed (even if they were not classified as such at the time) by films such as Roman Polanski's *Repulsion* (1965), Alan J. Pakula's *Klute* (1971), and Richard Brooks's *Looking for Mr. Goodbar* (1977). The genre, by then known by this name, reached its commercial peak with the hugely successful *Fatal Attraction* by Adrian Lyne (1987) and Paul Verhoeven's *Basic Instinct* (1992). Campion, while respecting the genre's key elements—sex and violence—and the structure of the narrative based on suspense, remains no less true to her usual preoccupations. Released in 2003, *In the Cut* is visually and verbally bold in its handling of sexual material, which contrasts sharply with the dominant puritanism of the Bush years against which it is set.

Frances Avery, known as Frannie, is a heroine seeking love while attempting to resolve her problems of strong inhibition. The fact that Campion was reading Moore's novel while preparing to shoot *Holy Smoke* doubtless explains the similarities between these two works, even though they belong to very different registers, both aesthetically and tonally. The relationship between Frannie and Detective Malloy is reminiscent of that between Ruth and P. J. Waters. There is the same relationship tinged with sadomasochism, the same attraction of a young woman for a virile man, the same discovery of passion and, above all, the same candor in Campion's handling of sexuality.

Doubles

In the Cut is also located, more so than any of Campion's other films, in an urban setting—the Manhattan of the early twenty-first century, devoid of its Twin Towers, which no longer feature on the skyscraper skyline of the opening credits. The only trips that Frannie (Meg Ryan) makes, unlike those of the long journeys to New Zealand, Europe or India taken by the protagonists of earlier films, are on the New York subway. The 'objective' narrator (there is no more voice-over),

Frannie is an English teacher who is fascinated by words, loves poetry, and is writing a dictionary of slang—is passionate, then, about both great literature and popular culture. The only people she sees are her half-sister, Pauline (Jennifer Jason Leigh), an Afro-Caribbean student called Cornelius Webb (Sharrieff Pugh), and a two-timing lover, John Graham (Kevin Bacon). Her encounter with a police detective, Malloy (Mark Ruffalo), who is investigating a murder committed by someone who turns out to be a serial killer, will change into a more intimate relationship that disturbs her, as she suspects the detective himself of being the killer.

The narrative revolves around two doubles. Firstly between Malloy and his Puerto Rican colleague Rodriguez (Nick Damici), following a classic pattern of detective films since John Huston's *The Maltese Falcon* (1941). Everything binds them—their job and friendship, even the way they keep women at a distance—but gradually, everything will bring them into opposition. Frannie, meanwhile, spends most of her time with Pauline, who has a promiscuous sex life (she has just had an affair with her doctor, who has ended it), and whose emancipation contrasts with Frannie's own inner frigidity, which leads the latter to envy her half-sister: "You live out of your unconscious. You're a poet of love," Frannie says to Pauline. This pattern, with variations, resembles some of the relationships between girls in earlier works: Kelly and Louise in *Two Friends*, Kay and Dawn in *Sweetie*, Ruth and Yvonne in *Holy Smoke*.

It is words rather than people that fascinate Frannie. She discovers them in the poems that adorn the subway cars and that are like an echo of her own mental state, such as these lines by Dante: "Midway along the journey of our life / I woke to find myself in a dark wood / For I had wandered off from the straight path."

In the Cut

It is in another dark place—the basement of a bar where she has come to have a drink with Cornelius—that Frannie's repressed sensuality will be thrown into disarray. She witnesses a woman with blue-painted nails giving fellatio to a man hidden in the shadows, of whom she sees only a three of spades tattooed on his wrist. It is a different experience,

*It is in a dark place—the basement of a bar where she has
come to have a drink with Cornelius—that Frannie's repressed
sensuality is thrown into disarray.*

Frannie and Malloy's bucolic retreat in the forest.
<u>*Following pages:*</u> *Malloy and Frannie in the bar.*

but one with the same connotation of sexual arousal that Isabel Archer has in the catacomb, another kingdom of darkness, where she hears Gilbert Osmond declare his love for her. Once again, Campion reverses the standard voyeuristic perspective: it is the woman who watches, fascinated, and who feels the thrill of physical desire.

Sex and violence are constantly intertwined here. So, while Frannie is making love to him, Malloy confesses "I like it in the cut" ("cut" being slang for vagina, and 'in the cut' slang for a place that is secluded or hard to find). Like the murderer who takes pleasure in cutting, in disarticulating his prey? *In the cut* or *in the cunt*? The women with the blue nails turns out to be the first victim of a serial killer, which triggers Malloy's investigation. The latter shares his name with the hero (played by Marlon Brando) of Elia Kazan's *On the Waterfront* (1954)—another New York film if ever there were one—and is played by Mark Ruffalo, whose voice and walk, a mix of virility and almost feminine gentleness, also evoke those of Brando. Separated from his wife, Malloy will uncover Frannie's repressed sensuality while discovering in himself loving feelings that he has been trying to defend himself against by taking refuge in purely sexual conquests. Initiated when he was fifteen years old by an older woman who taught him the art of giving his partner an orgasm, he will arouse Frannie's senses like Baines and P. J. did with Ada and Ruth in *The Piano* and *Holy Smoke*. In an astute study, Olivier De Bruyn has commented, not unjustifiably, that 'it is neither derisory nor provocative to consider *In the Cut* as a film about the revelation of clitoral pleasure'.[1] Like Isabel Archer, Frannie thinks for a long time that she has made a bad choice. A series of false clues—a tattoo, a charm, a key—lead her to believe that Malloy was the murderer, but without curbing the sexual attraction she feels towards him. Believing that he is her half-sister's assassin, she handcuffs him to a radiator, then makes love to him in a scene that is reminiscent, due to her dominance, of that where Ruth dresses P. J. up as a woman in *Holy Smoke*.

Journeys

Continuing the theme of doubles, the narrative makes use of two car journeys, the only escapes from Manhattan. The first sees Frannie and Malloy going to a forest near a lake. It's a bucolic retreat where, having made love in the city, they kiss at the lakeside, a kiss that seals, in a way that no other physical embrace does, the birth of their love. We are reminded of the importance of kisses and of water in the filmmaker's work by García Lorca's poem "Variations," displayed in the subway: "The still waters of the water / under a frond of stars. / The still waters of your mouth / under a thicket of kisses."

The second journey is the one that Rodriguez takes her on near Washington Bridge. This is a journey with the opposite destination: not an affirmation of love but an encounter with death. It is here, near the lighthouse, that Frannie confronts her nemesis and her sister's killer. The sight of the three of spades on his wrist confirms the twinning of two opposite men and drives her to kill him with the weapon that Malloy had shown her how to use in the countryside.

Flashbacks

In a classroom at the beginning of the film, Frannie, presciently, draws on the blackboard a red lighthouse, a phallic symbol, to illustrate her lesson on Virginia Woolf's novel *To the Lighthouse*. This establishes a significant connection between two great artists, the filmmaker, at many points in the film, visually reaffirming the stream of consciousness technique that Frannie is explaining to her students. In fact, *In the Cut* is characterized—like Campion's films in general—by a flowing narrative that seems to fit the subjective perception of the central character. By the recourse to uncertainty and to an almost impressionist

*The dreamlike ice-skating scene, one of the sepia
sequences that punctuate the film.*

Campion on the set of In the Cut,
for the ice-skating sequence.

technique, this narrative style enhances the virtually systematic use of a mobile camera that at no point neglects the precision of the framing. Nor does Campion abstain from using the sort of stylistic parentheses that had disturbed viewers and critics of *The Portrait of a Lady* and *Holy Smoke*. Here, four flashbacks in black and white and sepia punctuate the narrative and evoke the same scene from the past: a couple of ice skaters on a frozen lake, all Frannie's dreams about her parents meeting. Absent from Moore's book, they perpetuate the theme of family saga dear to the director and shed light on the present by reminiscing about a buried past. Shortly after the film opens, Frannie is lying down, petals are falling outside her window, and the white of her pillow becomes the ice on which a young woman is skating, while in the foreground, a man, his fist clenched in a leather glove, skates over to and around her, the camera then focusing in on the mark the blade of his skate has left in the ice (in the cut?). In a second sequence, Frannie is telling Pauline the story of their father. He was very handsome, an excellent skater, and already engaged when he met Frannie's mother. On a frozen lake in the middle of the forest, he offered her the engagement ring that his neglected fiancée had thrown back at him. Later, he abandoned Frannie's mother, who almost died of grief, unable to believe what had happened to her. Pauline tells Frannie that their father, who was married four times, never married her mother; Pauline asserts "I wanna get married once . . . just for my mom." The presented ring (like the one the serial killer offers to his future victims), the unfaithful father, the trauma of the betrayed wife, the frozen lake in the forest, the leather glove: these images and situations echo not only Campion's earlier films

(*A Girl's Own Story*, Bluebeard and the decapitated heads in *The Piano*, the womanizing father in *Holy Smoke*) but also certain autobiographical elements. A third flashback occurs after Pauline's death, when Frannie, drunk, has a nightmare. Finally, when Rodriguez is preparing to kill her, Frannie 'sees' her mother on the ice, crying out in fear, next to her father.

Que sera, sera

The weight of the past thus affects the characters' views of the present. When the film begins, Frannie, traumatized by her family history, has long since given up dating, aside from the odd fling, and has taken refuge in reading and writing while trying to resolve her inherited problems. Like Ada, Kay, and Ruth, she has felt her father's indifference to her need for affection. She felt abandoned, like Isabel, when her father left her on her own, age twelve, in Geneva to go to Washington. Like these other heroines, she will have to struggle to find psychological autonomy and her own identity. Lending the film a more personal note, Campion herself makes a brief appearance, Hitchcock style, as a waitress in the bar that Malloy takes Frannie to on their first date, and dances with Rodriguez. Another Hitchcockian touch is the song "Que Sera, Sera (Whatever Will Be, Will Be)," which accompanies Pauline walking in her sister's garden at the beginning of the film and which, with its fatalistic flavor, is resumed at the end—a leitmotif that was also used in Hitchcock's *The Man Who Knew Too Much* (1956):

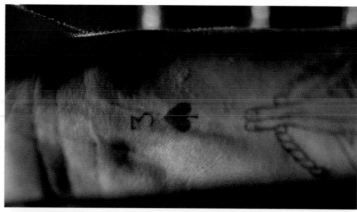

Now I have children of my own
They ask their mother
What will I be?
Will I be pretty?
Will I be rich?
I tell them tenderly
Que sera, sera
Whatever will be, will be
The future's not ours to see
Que sera, sera

The song evokes the relationship of a mother with her daughter: the
film is dedicated to Alice Allegra ("happiness") Englert, Campion's
daughter with Colin Englert, then aged nine. *In the Cut*, in its handling
of the family backstory, indirectly draws the portrait of a mother. In the
flashbacks, the mother is dressed in black, like Kay, Ada, and Isabel in
the earlier films. The character of Pauline has been changed to that of
a half-sister—rather than a friend as she is in the novel—which enables
her fate to be linked to that of her mother. As Alistair Fox has noted,
Pauline's desire is to rewrite the wrong that her mother suffered by
seducing men, but in fact, she relives her mother's rejection when she is
abandoned by the married men she has won over.[2] Meanwhile, Frannie
has never found what she's looking for in a man. Her relationships with
the four male characters in the story—John Graham, Cornelius Webb,

Malloy, and Rodriguez—echo the four suitors in *The Portrait of a Lady*:
Lord Warburton, Caspar Goodwood, Ralph Touchett, and Gilbert
Osmond. But unlike Isabel, Frannie makes the right choice. Cornelius
is a student who, in a moment of drunkenness and depression, she
kisses before pushing away; John Graham, with his panic attacks and his
brain that "practically explodes," bears too much resemblance to what
she could become if her inner demons prevail; and Rodriguez doesn't
attract her, as though she senses his true nature. In the novel, Frannie
dies; in the film, the door closes on her (in *The Portrait of a Lady*, it
didn't even open) after she has lain down beside Malloy. Campion has
always preferred the affirmation of life and open endings over the death
wish, whatever the trials faced by her heroines. Like Kay after Sweetie's
death, Frannie after Pauline's has perhaps, without knowing 'whatever
will be', found the right path with Malloy, who earlier in the film reads
a poem (Pablo Neruda's 'Poem XIV: Every Day You Play') stuck on
Frannie's apartment wall: 'I want to do with you what spring does with
the cherry trees.'

1   Olivier De Bruyn, '*In the Cut*: le secret derrière la porte', *Positif*, 514 (December
    2003).
2   Alistair Fox, *Jane Campion: Authorship and Personal Cinema*, Indiana University
    Press, Bloomington, 2011.

Trees in Snow:
The Watcher of the Meadows.

*Facing page: It is near the lighthouse that Frannie confronts
her nemesis and her sister's killer. The sight of the three
of spades on his wrist confirms the twinning of two opposite
men and drives her to kill him.*
*Above: Mood board with a postcard and one of the "Blondie Notes" that Campion
received from a psychopath when she was nineteen.*

*The design for the interior of Pauline's apartment
and a location-scouting photograph by production designer David Brisbin.*

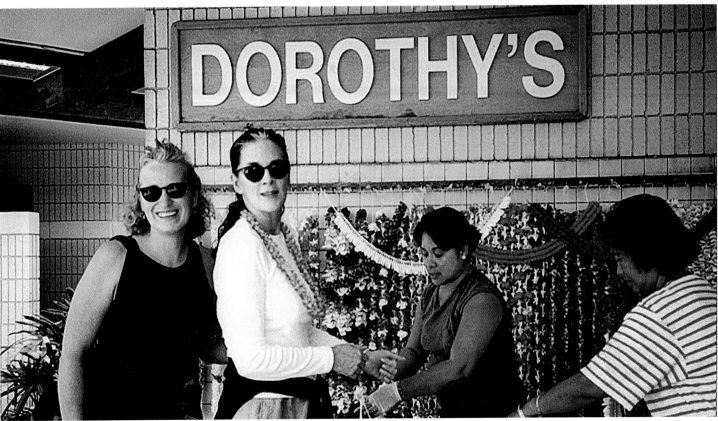

<u>*Top:*</u> *Meg Ryan, Mark Ruffalo, and Jane Campion*
on the set of the film.
<u>*Bottom:*</u> *Campion on a writing trip in Kauai*
with scriptwriter Susanna Moore, on whose novel the film is based.

Interview conducted in Paris, 19 September 2003

In the Cut is your first American film. It's also a genre film, which is new for you.
It's true that I'd never tackled this type of film, which, furthermore, isn't really to my taste as films go. That said, I love films that reflect on and challenge the conventions of this genre, like *Chinatown* or *Klute*. Simply making use of conventions seems to me a rather futile exercise.

Was the project one that was offered to you?
In fact, it began with my reading Susanna Moore's book *In the Cut* without having any thought of turning it into a film! Laura Jones, who wrote the screenplays for *An Angel at My Table* and *The Portrait of a Lady* for me, had suggested that I read it because she'd been impressed by its freshness and eroticism. It gripped me and affected me in a way that I had rarely been previously. It must have been its modernity and that mixture of genre conventions and a search for authenticity that you find, for example, in the language of detective novels. I liked the idea that Moore teaches creative writing, as well as that combination in the narrative of irony and the characteristic tone of a thriller. Aside from that, I found the conclusion both brilliant and devastating. For me, this novel spoke of the sacrifice a woman makes of herself. Even at the moment of her death, the heroine wonders what the man she loves is going to think of her. Moore shows great intelligence in grasping this kind of thing. She belongs to a generation before mine where women were more dependent on men.

I got in contact with my producer, Laurie Parker, and we discovered that the film rights for the book were available. I still didn't know whether this material was really for me and whether I'd be able to tell such a dark story. Then I met Susanna, a friendly, formidable woman—she's a very beautiful Hawaii-born American who was a model in her youth—and began to feel increasingly at ease with the idea of directing this story.

Nicole Kidman was originally going to play Frannie.
Initially it was she who had bought the rights to the book. She wanted to keep the title of co-producer, which her contract gave her the right to do, along with Laurie Parker, who had done the production work. Nicole had an extremely busy schedule; in addition, she was worn out by what was going on in her life

(her separation from Tom Cruise), and didn't feel strong enough to take on a role like this. That's what I understood when I heard about her divorce. We therefore had to find another actress.

The choice of Meg Ryan proved extraordinarily convincing. How do you get to know whether an actress can become the character?
First of all, there was, on Meg's part, this fierce desire to play the role: She loved the story and was absolutely determined to try it out. It seemed to me that she had the necessary energy to live this difficult story, plus, it didn't frighten her. I knew, too, that she was training with Sandra Seacat, one of the weapons in Harvey Keitel's armory, who was in possession of the screenplay; it was from her that I learned that Meg was working hard on the character in case Nicole should turn down the role. All of that was very encouraging news to me. I therefore organized an improvisation session with Mark Ruffalo in a hotel room in Los Angeles. I was totally convinced, especially because she managed to hide what her character was really thinking. She proved to be very strong and very intelligent in the way she fended off Mark, and I wanted to know more about her—which was a good sign. I hadn't recorded anything on video, so I had nothing to show others, but the memory I had of her performance was enough for me to believe in her, and as Mark shared my feelings... Other actresses that I'd auditioned could have given good performances, but she was the only Frannie with whom I could identify closely. There's a healthiness about Meg; she's a woman who's struggling to survive, and the viewer is prepared to follow her into the worst ordeals.

The theme of the sexual fulfilment that a woman finds with a particular man is found in most of your films, from The Piano to The Portrait of a Lady or Holy Smoke. Did you feel with these characters the need to explore a feminine sexuality that, in your opinion, films directed by men were ignoring?
It's difficult for me to talk of my films in terms of their similarity, because when I approach a story, it's always its uniqueness that attracts me, its newness. Of course, Frannie has had previous sexual experiences, but she's never met a man like Malloy, who not only awakens her sexually, but awakens her in a whole new way. When she meets him, she's going through

a period of depression and withdrawal. She is safe, but fatally safe! A man could, of course, have directed this story because he could imagine what a woman feels, but I *know*. Being a woman gives me the confidence to explore intimate territory. A male director could even reveal aspects of a feminine character, and do so as well as a female director, but, once again, a dog can imagine what a cat is doing, but the cat knows what cats think and feel.

How did the work of adaptation go with Susanna Moore?
We met in New York; she had expressed the desire to work on the adaptation, and I was in agreement. We discussed what we wanted to keep and discard, as well as the problem of the first-person narration. Susanna then wrote two first drafts and came back to me for my comments. We realized, at that point, that the process had been too simplistic, that there wasn't enough dialogue, and that the screenplay was too short. We weren't satisfied with the ending either, but I didn't want to tell her outright that I was wanting it to be different from that of the book. At this stage, she was wanting to write a new novel. I decided, after this work we'd done together, to return to New Zealand and to continue writing the screenplay on my own, which took me eight weeks. During the following eighteen months I continually went back to it, especially to give an organic structure to the new ending. It was, overall, one of the most difficult tasks I've ever faced. The novel is like a diary, with this very strong first-person narration that I'd decided to cut. I also wanted the character of Frannie to be less nihilistic, less sarcastic. All that seems obvious today, but it wasn't then! I had doubts about my new ideas. It was then that I brought in Stavros Kazantzidis, who was great. He knows everything about the cinema, is obsessed by genre films and watches all sorts of films, so he brought a new energy to the project; he was extremely helpful, and I was at last able to see the light at the end of the tunnel. But this screenplay had been through more versions that any other that I'd worked on up to that point.

Were there films that inspired you in your making of In the Cut?
One of the reasons that I was prepared to work so hard on the screenplay was the lukewarm reception that *The Portrait of a Lady* and *Holy Smoke* had received. Thinking about

<u>Top:</u> *Pauline and Frannie are both close and different.*
<u>Bottom:</u> *Frannie discovers her sister dead.*
<u>Following pages:</u> *When Frannie meets Malloy, she's going
through a period of depression and withdrawal.*

it, I had the feeling that Laura Jones and I could have further refined the Henry James adaptation. I was more inclined to be sensitive to feedback that I would get on this project and to incorporate suggestions that would be given. That has not often been the case in the past. From that point of view, this process of talking things over was important. In terms of the references you were asking about, the film I felt closest to was certainly *Klute*. I've always liked that film, and I think that Jane Fonda went through a similar transformation to Meg in playing a more dramatic, serious character than the frivolous roles she'd previously been offered. That encouraged us in our choice of Meg.

It's your first film set in a big city, and you've managed to capture its atmosphere, thanks, in particular, to Dion Beebe's very mobile camera.
Laurie Parker and I spent a week talking with Dion Beebe and the production designer, David Brisbin. We had numerous films on video at our disposition, and David suggested the idea of using a wide range of colours to make the half-darkness, using warm colours rather than limiting ourselves to green, blue, and dark tones, as the story was dark enough in itself. Dion and I planned how the camera could contribute to the story and what we could do within the constraints of the budget, which allowed us nine weeks of shooting. We talked about the direction of the actors: I didn't want to be too prescriptive, but, on the contrary, relaxed: I needed to allow them some freedom so that would be very present on screen, like in Coppola's *The Godfather*.

We also recalled the opening sequence of *Holy Smoke* and decided that it would be good to film the whole of *In the Cut* in that register, allowing the actors to perform the scenes and only afterwards looking to structure what we'd filmed. This was our modus operandi: the actors, particularly Meg, would develop their way of acting a scene and their movements, and the camera—with a few necessary adjustments on their part—would adapt to their ideas. Dion is very sensitive visually; intelligent and deep. Most of the motifs in the opening sequence come from him. We understand each other perfectly, and this way of filming—where we basically trusted our instincts—was invigorating because nothing was really established before shooting, even though Dion had made storyboards, which he later abandoned! I should say, however, that we did make use of

them for some sequences—for example, the intimate scenes, where the choice of angle was important.

At the beginning, the scene where she descends the stairs in the bar is like diving into her unconscious.
That's exactly what I wanted to suggest. In the story, this scene represents a sort of mythical underworld, which is also the start of a voyage. She enters into the world of the detective film, like Alice in Wonderland, but a darker version! It's the story of renewal, and at the same time a love story, which wasn't exactly the theme of the novel, which was more focused on sexual encounters.

The last shot, of the door closing on the couple's intimacy, confirms that it's a love story.
Susanna defined her novel for me in this way, but not without a touch of irony in her voice. I told her that I was taking her at her word and that it was like that that I would shoot her story. It wasn't so easy—the story is anti-romantic—but ultimately, that's what it's about.

Although there are elements of suspense and characteristics of the thriller with the four suspects—the inspector, his colleague, the Black student, and the former lover—it seems clear that it's first and foremost the story of the relationship between Frannie and Malloy that interests you.
I don't believe I have the talent for detective stories of someone like Hitchcock, nor, moreover, his interest in them. What attracts me is studying these characters and the relationships between them. But, of course, these two plots, love story and thriller, are intertwined and have both love and fear in common. The noir genre is characterized by paranoia, but love can be there, too. In a crime story, protagonists who are vulnerable, who are open, are more at risk.

In *In the Cut*, we find again, in the relationship between Frannie and her half-sister, Pauline (Jennifer Jason Leigh), a motif that's common to nearly all your films: an intimate, deep, and affectionate bond between two women.
The friendship between these two women is very important. This is even more visible in young girls: it's like a love that they share, or a camaraderie. It has something tender and

deep about it, a feeling that they look for, and often fail to find, in men. That's not exactly how it is between Pauline and Frannie because they're adult women. Together, they face the disappointments that life has dealt them. Men are always very curious about what goes on when women get together; what they say to each other, what they share. They can, of course, question them about it, but they can never be sure. And when they join the women, their very presence means that the situation is no longer the same. As a woman, I've often known this sort of intimacy with other women. And there's something wonderful in sharing your hopes and troubles in this way.

Pauline and Frannie are both close and different.
Pauline is very sex-orientated, as is shown in her conversation in the café. She's like a veteran of Vietnam, but in the field of sex! She's been hurt and is aware of her problem, but she can't control her obsessions. I think she no longer believes that—at the stage of life she's reached—she could live as half of a couple, but she thinks Frannie could. It's an idea that's dear to her, that her half-sister could meet a man, fall in love, and have a child with him.

Did you choose Jason Leigh after having given the role of Frannie to Meg Ryan?
Yes, it happened in that order. Once we'd engaged Meg, I though Jennifer would be perfect for the role. She's an incredibly experienced actress, intelligent and smart. I had the feeling that, during the whole rehearsal process, she would help Meg reach another register in her performance. She's a warm, kind woman who's full of enthusiasm, very different from most of the characters she's been able to portray. She believes in other people and trusts them; she has her feet on the ground, and her way of appreciating things and people is always original and fruitful.

With such a short shooting time, how did you prepare your actors?
I find it hard to grasp how directors get everything in place before shooting. This time, I didn't emphasize the scenes by defining the role of each one and how they lead to a conclusion. I wanted to invest in the characters as much as possible. Sometimes one of them would lie or wouldn't want the other one to know what he or she was thinking. That seemed to me to be part of life and something that happens quite often.

Top to bottom, left to right: A drawing by Campion to illustrate Cornelius's essay; Jane Fonda in Alan J. Pakula's Klute; *a photograph of Pauline used in the film; a sketch quoting Philip Larkin.*

*The passion that binds Frannie and Malloy
disrupts their well-ordered existence.*

We had lots of discussions with the actors to establish their true feelings, and we tried to fill the missing links in their personalities. You notice with good actors that their unconscious takes over and they manage to construct their character. It's a mystery to me; I don't understand how they do it. Of course, the narrative had been worked on at length, but nevertheless, I had the feeling that we were letting it happen. Also, if the actors adopted a tone for a sequence, I was able to follow them, even if it didn't match exactly what was written. The most important thing was that it would benefit the film. On the other hand, if I felt that what was happening on set wasn't working in the film's favor, I encouraged them to go in a different direction. The main part of my job was to help them construct their characters. After that, it was plain sailing—they were able to provide what was needed.

Did you do much research on the world of the police and where the characters were coming from?
We decided, for example, that although Malloy's father was Irish, like in the novel, his mother would be Italian, because of Mark Ruffalo's origins. Mark worked hard on his background and environment; he spent time with a lot of the policemen we'd already met when writing the screenplay. Laurie Parker and I spent time researching the forces of law and order. And, of course, Susanna Moore had spent a year with some detectives, and even lived with one of them! I love this kind of work because you get to unearth things you could never imagine; that gives you confidence to go in a particular direction. You discover, for example, that policemen have a pretty low opinion of each other, and that although they're capable of affection for their colleagues, they can also be very hard and cruel with each other. We also thought a lot about the image that inspectors have in American society, their relationship with the truth they're supposed to be seeking and the filth that surrounds them, the problem of corruption and bribes. It's not unknown for them to arrest the wrong man, and that makes them bitter. From there they sink into alcohol, sex, and drugs, which are supposed to help them forget the dangerous world they have to confront. At the same time, this position they find themselves in, this proximity to everything that's going wrong in society, makes them attractive, sexy even!

Malloy's character is similar to Frannie's. The passion that binds them disrupts their well-ordered existence: in her case, her job as a teacher, and in his, a sex life of brief affairs with no emotional involvement.
Falling in love is a challenge that's much more difficult to deal with than having purely sexual encounters. He has the feeling that his obsession with her is making him lose the concentration he needs to do his job, and that troubles him.

Kevin Bacon [who plays the ex-lover] isn't listed in the credits.
That was by mutual agreement. He loved the character and wanted to film with me, but as he usually plays more important roles, he didn't want to create a precedent and preferred not to be credited. I love his performance. Kevin can scare you because you never really know what he's thinking; he reveals very little of himself.

Bright Star
(2009)

"From the Point of View
of the Rebel in Love."

<u>Top:</u> *The poet John Keats (Ben Whishaw).*
<u>Bottom:</u> *Fanny Brawne (Abbie Cornish)*
and her sister Toots (Edie Martin).

The domestic and the sublime

Drought

Before undertaking *Bright Star*, her seventh full-length film, Campion returned to her first love with some short films. *The Lady Bug* is a mischievous three-minute sketch that is part of a collective film entitled *Chacun son cinéma*, commissioned by Gilles Jacob, president of the Cannes Film Festival, where it was shown in 2007. In it, the filmmaker satirizes the attitude of men towards women in the film world. Much more ambitious is *The Water Diary*, which was made in 2005 under the auspices of the United Nations, in connection with the Millennium Development Goals, and which has as its theme water and global warming. Having taken on this particular topic, Campion has made a work that is eminently personal, not only because her daughter, Alice Englert, plays the main part in it, but also because it echoes autobiographical elements and recurring themes in her other films.

As with *The Lady Bug*, drought is at the heart of the narrative, the story of the grief experienced by a young girl, Ziggy (Alice Englert), and her cousin Sam (Tintin Marova Kelly) after the death their much-loved horses, which Ziggy's father (Russell Dykstra) had to sacrifice, being unable to feed them after a long period of drought and famine. A woman dreams that the way to bring about a saving downpour is to ask the prettiest girl in the area to play her viola on the top of Bob's Hill. Having invited the children from the neighbourhood to meet her there, the young viola player performs standing on top of a water tank. Campion's mother, Edith, was always passionate about horses, and Jane had a mare when she went to live in the country when she was thirteen, the same age as Ziggy. Like Kay in *Sweetie*, Ziggy has a collection of porcelain horses that she arranges on the windowsill in her bedroom. In an early scene, the young girls are looking for bodies buried in the now dried-up dam and Sam finds a wedding ring, which she decides to wear on a string around her neck while waiting for her dream man. Such a ring was also present in *The Piano* and *In the Cut*, and will be seen again in *Bright Star*. Once again, Alistair Fox has unveiled some of the autobiographical foundations to this story.[1] He symbolically associates the destruction of the horses by the father with the destruction of Richard and Edith's marriage and of a girl's chance to obtain an ideal of masculinity that she can devote herself to. The pursuit of rain becomes the quest for an emotionally fulfilled life, which links this and some of the director's other films, with their lyrical portrayals of nature, to those of Terrence Malick.

Getting to the Heart of Romanticism

Quoted in *An Angel at My Table*, John Keats's poetry is heard again in *In the Cut* when Frannie is walking beside a lake with Malloy and recites 'La Belle Dame sans Merci'. However, the depiction of love in *Bright Star* could not be further from the violently sexual relationships of the previous two films, *Holy Smoke* and *In the Cut*. From Frannie to Fanny, the heroine of this new film has passed from physical desire to a vision of life where sensitivity, tenderness, and the beauty of feelings and emotions prevail, which is portrayed without any hint of blandness but, on the contrary, with great energy. In deciding to focus on the last two years of Keats's life, from October 1818 to September 1820, and his loving relationship with Fanny Brawne, Campion rejects the conventions of the biopic and chooses, as is her wont, to tell the story from the heroine's perspective. For her third foray into the nineteenth century, after *The Piano* and *The Portrait of a Lady*, she again chose the nineteenth century, this time the early part, at the peak of the Romantic period. She also revisited, nearly twenty years after *An Angel at My Table*, the theme of literary creation. While distant from each other in terms of both time and space, Janet Frame and John Keats both came from modest social backgrounds that gave no inkling of an artistic future, and both were marked in childhood by family tragedies (the New Zealand writer successively lost two sisters in drowning accidents, while the poet's father died in a riding accident when Keats was eight years old, and his mother from tuberculosis five years later).

From the very first images, it is clear that Campion will reject the sentimentality and decorative style so often associated with depictions of Romanticism. In close-up, a needle forcefully pierces a piece of fabric that is being embroidered with the same violence with which the skate blade cut Frannie's mother's legs in *In the Cut* or the axe chopped off Ada's finger in *The Piano*. This scene introduces the domestic motif that, throughout the film, Campion will intertwine with that of the sublime. *Bright Star* takes place amid the daily life and work of a household near London, surrounded by gardens and fields. Fanny (Abbie Cornish) is besotted with fashion: She creates hats and garments (she was related to Beau Brummell, the arbiter of Regency elegance) and, as she points out to them with irony, she makes a better living from doing so than the two poets, Keats (Ben Whishaw) and Brown (Paul Schneider), who live in the adjoining house. John and Fanny are only twenty-three and eighteen

The opening sequence of Bright Star:
a needle forcefully pierces a piece of fabric
that is being embroidered.

when they meet—and Campion films them in the present, without putting into perspective the fame the poet would acquire posthumously.

An ephemeral bliss

Keats is vulnerable and overflowing with imagination—he dances a Scottish jig for the Brawnes when he dines with them at Christmas. Like Andrei Tarkovsky, who in his *Andrei Rublev* (1966) never shows the icon painter at work, Campion avoids filming the poet composing his odes in the way that many biographies of artists do. Nevertheless, her film is without doubt the most beautiful one ever devoted to the work of poetry, and for two reasons. Firstly, she lets us hear the poetry itself, either in voice-over ("Ode to a Nightingale"), or read on-screen by the writer, or, even more movingly, by having the two protagonists recite "La Belle Dame sans Merci" to each other as though making love verbally. Secondly, she gives her shots an intense beauty without disrupting the flow of the narrative. Keats is the poet of the present moment; he wants to capture the moment that is passing in order to fully savor it. According to Albert Laffay, one of the most renowned French scholars on Keats, for the poet, objects formed a world full of sensations, bursting with retained energy, which his poetry attempts to charm, to hypnotize: 'If Shelley's favourite bird is the lark that rises vertically, Keats's is the nightingale that lives in the leaves.'

This is why nature—the Romantics' favourite companion—plays such an important role in the film: Fanny reads a letter from Keats among the bluebells, Keats walks to the Brawne's house through a field of daffodils, Fanny presents Keats with a spray of blossom, Keats lies in a tree in flower. Similarly with butterflies: Fanny wears earrings in the form of butterflies, her brother Samuel (Thomas Brodie-Sangster) and sister Toots (Edie Martin) chase them in a meadow and they keep them in Fanny's bedroom until they die for lack of air. The sequence is like an echo of one of Keats's letters where he dreams that they are

both butterflies with only three summer days to live: '...three such days with you I could fill with more delight than fifty common years could ever contain'.

That this love is constantly threatened, and ephemeral, lends intensity to the moments lived. Jeopardized by the social constraints that Mrs. Brawne (Kerry Fox), while accepting her daughter's feelings, reminds Fanny of, and above all by the poet's fatal illness, this idyll sees its end in sight. The setting for their effusions is a life in the countryside brimming with sensations. The film evokes the domestic bliss of the interiors of Dutch paintings as well as the landscapes of the Impressionists (and of Constable, who was also a source of inspiration). By contrast, the scenes in London and later the shot of the funeral at the Piazza di Spagna in Rome, are tinged with a dim, crepuscular light. In the final shot, Fanny in mourning dress recalls the black clothes of Ada (*The Piano*) and Isabel (*The Portrait of a Lady*); she walks alone in a winter landscape reciting 'Bright Star', the poem Keats had dedicated to her:

> Still, still to hear her tender-taken breath,
> And so live ever—or else swoon to death.

Thus the cold invades the end of the story like it does in *The Portrait of a Lady* and *A Girl's Own Story*, and in the dream sequences of *In the Cut*.

The Yearning for Life

However, tragedy is not the dominant note of *Bright Star*, even if Keats is haunted by the spectre of his own death, as he declares in a letter to Fanny on July 25, 1819: "I have two luxuries to brood over in my walk, your Loveliness and the hour of my death. O that I could have possession of them both in the same minute." The yearning for life is personified in Fanny, the passionate and elated heroine, like many of the director's heroines, with her desire to break free of established rules, to swim

Nature plays an important role in the film, notably butterflies, which Fanny's brother Samuel (Thomas Brodie-Sangster) and sister Toots chase in a meadow, then keep in Fanny's bedroom until they die for lack of air.

Following pages: Fanny, in the company of Toots, reads a letter from Keats among the bluebells.
Pages 168–169: Keats lies in a tree in flower.

*Top: Brown (Paul Schneider), Keats's protector, and Keats (Ben
Whishaw) make a complementary pair: one bearded and rough;
the other thin and fragile, almost feminine.
Bottom left: Bright Star evokes the domestic bliss of the interiors
depicted in Dutch paintings.
Bottom right: 'There is a holiness to the heart's affections.
You know nothing of that.'*

The shot of the funeral at the Piazza di Spagna
in Rome, is tinged with a dim, crepuscular light.

against the tide, and her liking for the out of the ordinary. What a difference from the protagonists of Jane Austen, whose last novel, *Persuasion*, was written two years before Fanny and Keats met, and in which reason and propriety govern behaviour. It is this fierce independence of Fanny's, her desire even more than her wit, that offends Brown, Keats's protector, with whom he makes a complementary pair, one thin and fragile, almost feminine (played by Ben Whishaw, who was also one of the Bob Dylans in Todd Haynes's *I'm Not There* in 2007), the other bearded and rough (powerfully portrayed by Paul Schneider), who mimics the ape to which Fanny compares him. Brown, while not actually resembling them, is like Stewart in *The Piano* and Osmond in *The Portrait of a Lady* in understanding nothing of the female psyche. His behaviour towards Abigail in getting her pregnant, for which Keats rebukes him, contrasts with Keats's sensitive conduct. The only moment when the latter shows his aggression is, significantly, when, in the woods, while Fanny has withdrawn, he pushes his friend against a tree and tells him: "There is a holiness to the heart's affections. You know nothing of that." But it would be to ignore the complexity of Campion's view of human behaviour, her rejection of Manichaeism, to dismiss the confession Brown makes to Fanny shortly before the poet's death, where he declares three times, "I failed John Keats," trying to erase at the same time, perhaps, the slights to which he had previously subjected the young woman.

"The Substance Which Rises to the Surface"

Like the climax of great classical art, *Bright Star* continually amazes us in the unfolding of its action, gestures and words before finally allowing us to appreciate the perfection of its development, like a work by Mozart, such as his Serenade No. 10 in B Flat Major, which accompanies the lovers in the Hampstead springtime. Campion seems to have appropriated the last lines of 'Ode on a Grecian Urn':

> Beauty is truth, truth beauty,—that is all
> Ye know on earth, and all ye need to know.

The filmmaker refuses to believe that a painting (or a poem or a film) is essentially, according to Maurice Denis's simplistic definition, too often quoted favourably, 'a flat surface covered with colours assembled in a certain order'. According to Victor Hugo, 'form is the substance which rises to the surface'. This would seem to be a better definition of artistic creation, particularly that of Campion, for whom substance and form are inextricably linked. A film helps you see everything by offering a perspective on the world, images reflecting ideas.

A wood-paneled dividing wall separates two beds that are pushed up against it. On one side is Fanny (the admirable Abbie Cornish, trembling with sensitivity), on the other, Keats. She places her hand against the wall, he does the same, and their two hands caress without being able to touch each other. The viewer is stirred more powerfully than by many a scene that is more explicitly erotic.

Masses of white cotton sheets fluttering in the wind; Fanny offering Keats a pillowcase on which to lay the head of his deceased brother; washing hanging on the line; Keats suddenly opening a door and almost causing Fanny to drop a tray she is carrying; the cat associated with poetry present when Keats holds it on his lap and when Fanny reads his poems or one of his letters; the mischievous looks of Toots and Samuel (the recurring presence of children in the filmmaker's work); Fanny lying on her bed yearning for a letter from her lover, the curtains blowing into the room; Keats putting a ring on Fanny's finger, telling her that it belonged to his mother; a winter landscape with bare trees: so many epiphanies, so many beautiful and significant moments that have become characteristic, over the twenty-six years since *Passionless Moments*, of Campion's art and yet that fit into a flowing narrative, as though echoing the inscription, chosen by Keats, on his tomb in Rome: 'Here lies One Whose Name was writ in Water.'

1 Alistair Fox, *Jane Campion: Authorship and Personal Cinema*, Indiana University Press, Bloomington, 2011.

172

Interview conducted in Paris, 3 June 2009

How did you come to decide to make a film about the love between John Keats and Fanny Brawne?

It was almost by accident. I was in the process of writing the screenplay of *In the Cut* with Susanna Moore, the novelist whose work I was adapting and who also taught creative writing. We were working, notably, on the character of the heroine: for us, there needed to be something romantic about what made her tick. I realized that I didn't know much about poetry and, by chance, I had in my hands the biography of Keats by Andrew Motion. Halfway through the book I discovered a Keats that wasn't interested in women, who was resolutely unromantic, and mocked those of his friends who allowed themselves to get ensnared in love's trap. It was then that Fanny Brawne appeared in his life: He gives a very detailed description of her in a letter he sent to his brother, who had left for the United States. That drew my attention, because his attitude was really perverse. Clearly he was captivated by her—her temperament, her shape, her movements; he describes her in the minutest detail, focusing, for example, on her nostrils and making very critical comments. Then there is no further mention of Fanny Brawne in his correspondence until he begins to send her extraordinary love letters. In his biography, Andrew Motion fills in the gaps and suggests what might have taken place. I was moved and struck by the intense and extreme nature of this amorous passion. These two people were living in two houses that were so close to each other that they seemed to be a single one, and that created a special intimacy where everything, even health problems, was immediately noticed. I was touched by the personality of Keats, who, so young, could be so conscious of the purity of his feelings and appreciate their worth. It seemed to me that this story contained everything I needed to know about life. Having said that, although I felt strong emotions when reading this book, I had no thought at all about making a film out of it. After filming *In the Cut,* I took a four-year break to look after my daughter, who needed me as a teenager, and to discover who I was when I wasn't working, what interested or affected me without me having to produce anything. I started to think about the stories I wanted to tell, and I immersed myself in Keats's letters and poems: I said to myself that I could evoke their passion

from Fanny's point of view. That enabled me to lay down some boundaries for my story. I was also enchanted by her embroidery work. I had no intention of making a biopic, and what better way to approach Keats than to see him through the eyes of his beloved, who herself would change, mature, and develop! I really wanted to attempt this project, but I had doubts about the possibility of realizing it given the state of the film industry. I had taken four years out. I'm someone who likes tranquillity, to keep company with mystery, rather than having perpetual distractions. I was worried about the logistical hurdles I would have to overcome.

You decided to write the screenplay by yourself, a first for you.

Yes, though I did wonder whether I was capable of capturing the spirit, the playfulness of a young woman. As for Keats, he was of course a genius, but also a man. I could feel his energy and the tone of his voice in his letters. There was something clear in the way he wrote to his brother, which must have been close to his way of speaking.

The shyness of the lovers, the restrictions that were placed on their movements and the codes of conduct, make the lyricism of *Bright Star* less direct than that of *The Piano.* There's a sort of distillation taking place.

The film is extremely emotional, even if the emotion is held at more of a distance. To get to the place where my story ends, I needed to lead it there with some caution. It was important not to force anything, because I didn't want the viewers who were willing to take this journey with me to feel manipulated. Andrew Motion's book had had a great impact on me; I was hoping to share this experience with the audience, but I hate feeling that a director wants me to feel an emotion at all costs. Let him tell his story and I'll feel what I like! Going back to *The Piano,* the emotion there was sexual. Here, it's more subtle, it's about the feeling of love. I don't mean to say that Keats and Fanny were uninterested in each other sexually (they kissed and touched), but imagination and spirituality intervened in their relationship. *The Piano* was a much more feverish film.

The first six months of 1819 was a time of intense poetic creativity for Keats; he wrote, in quick succession, "Ode to a Nightingale,"

"Ode on Melancholy," "Ode on a Grecian Urn" . . . then wrote his first love letter to Fanny in July, as though his first declarations had been in the form of poems.

I don't think any letters were lost, because it was at this time that Keats left the house next door to go and live on the Isle of Wight. I wondered, while reading Motion's book, why he hadn't fallen in love sooner. Perhaps it was due to a lack of self-confidence on Keats's part. He had experienced a lot of disappointment, and the great shock of his brother Tom's death. The spectacular failure of *Endymion* and the two famous negative reviews he received must also have affected him. He wasn't expecting much more of life and wrote his great odes not to be appreciated by others but for himself. In addition, he didn't think these poems were of the sort to make his reputation, unlike *Hyperion* or *Endymion,* in which he had placed so much hope. I think his brother's death had a positive influence on his poetry; it gave him access to a greater depth and maturity. And his friend Charles Armitage Brown helped him financially, which meant he wasn't obliged to earn a living. Finally, spring came. All this went to his head and he declared his love for Fanny.

In contrast to lots of costume dramas, your characters are unaware of their place in history. Pierre Henri Cami, a French humorist, had one of his protagonists pronounce an anachronism: "We, the people of the Middle Ages, are leaving for the Hundred Years' War." Keats didn't see himself as a representative of Romanticism; he was a young man in love with poetry and a woman.

Exactly, they didn't know that they were Romantics. With hindsight, we associate these poets (Byron, Shelley, Keats) with a short lifespan. They all died young, but of the three, Keats has an angelic halo: he was the purist and the youngest of them. I didn't want to fall into romantic clichés by making him sickly, weak, and melancholic. He was an active, charming, funny, incredibly honest and passionate man. Fanny Brawne, too, has been misunderstood by history. When I was in India, for example, lots of people told me that she avoided Keats, that she fled from him! Nothing could be further from the truth, even though that's what's sometimes written in textbooks. She was someone very honest. When she made some negative remarks about *Endymion,* she of course aroused his interest, but her judgement

Such a 'YES' coming thru'

8/01/08 43.

KEATS
They may have been yours. *(shall I see)*   *F - Yes*

Keats closes his eyes and presents his lips for Fanny to
kiss. Fanny gently places her lips on his.

Keats waits and Fanny kisses him again. Keats pulls Fanny on
top of him and kisses her and she him and he her. They lie
down together lip to lip. *or sit-*

KEATS (cont'd)
"Pale were the lips I kiss'd."

Keats kisses her again. *Fanny could gasp*

KEATS (cont'd)
**"- and fair the form. I floated with about
that melancholy storm."**

Margaret comes calling up the hill. Keats makes sound
effects of wild flowers squealing as Margaret stops. *or snapping twigs*

KEATS (cont'd)
"Help." "Ahhh."

Keats slows her to a halt. To her chagrin she cannot step
without crushing something.

MARGARET
Stop it! *could do without*

64   **EXT.   HAMPSTEAD HEATH - EVENING**   64

The three make their way across the Heath home. Keats and
Fanny follow behind Margaret who plays a game of catching
them touching, kissing. *FREEZE*

65   **EXT.   STREET WENTWORTH HOUSE - EVENING**   65

A glowing Keats walks backwards along the road next to
Wentworth House looking at Fanny.

going into
Back door
Sun-
extended
Keats close
to her —

Keats lets Fanny pass and watches her from behind. Keats
opens the gate to Wentworth House and narrows the opening so
she must pass close to him. Fanny smiles and slyly touches
hands.

In the garden Samuel has climbed onto the HEDGE. Mr Brown
stands underneath, disconcerted by Keats's attention to
Fanny. Fanny walks in a cloud up to her room. *Brown notices*

A page from the screenplay of Bright Star, *annotated
by Jane Campion.*
*Following pages: A wood-paneled dividing wall sepa-
rates Keats's bedroom from the one occupied by Fanny.*

*Campion intertwines the domestic and the sublime
throughout the film: the daily life and work
of a household near London is surrounded
by gardens and fields.*

was a long way from being erroneous: it's a difficult poem, but not one of his better ones. I think he appreciated nothing but the truth; we see that in his letters to Fanny, in which he hides nothing, including about his illness. I admire the ability of such a young woman to sincerely value the worth of everything he said to her.

In your seven films, the main character has always been a woman, and often a very strong, very tough one.

I suppose that's true, but I've never thought about it. Even Janet Frame, who was fragile, was in her way very strong. When we showed *Bright Star* to the staff of Keats House in London, several of the viewers told us that they'd never imagined this story from Fanny's point of view. It's natural for me as a woman to take this position. I'm attracted by each of the protagonists of my films for different reasons, without ever really knowing why. I see Fanny, now, as a rebel in love. She needed courage to make the choice she made. Keats had no money, his health was getting worse and worse, and if their love affair were to end (which seemed inevitable), she would remain single without being able to marry.

In your staging, and even in the film's design, you're constantly mixing familiar, everyday things (dances, embroidery, pets, walks) with the sublime.

The scope of the story was initially domestic. Keats's poetic impulse was to ascend to the heights, reach a climactic note, then fall, as though the ecstasy could not last. Hence, the resultant feeling of sadness, as in 'Ode to a Nightingale'. It seems to me to be a completely natural instinct for an artist to want to create a solid world and to fear its dissolution. Keats and Fanny feel something similar in the love that they feel at their first kiss in the spring, which they then, separately, try to relive to retain its ardor.

There have been very few films made about poets, but none has give the poetry centre stage in the story, with the verses being recited at length by the characters or a voice-over.

From the outset, it was my ambition to find a way of bringing the poetry into the film, to share it with the viewer. It was without doubt my most daring decision. I also wanted, when Keats falls ill again, for the two of them to form

a duo, and for Fanny, reciting the poem, to make him understand how brilliant it is and that he'd never do better. He uses the same poem to say to her, "Listen, we are an illusion, a fantasy, our story is without hope." Perhaps at that moment neither of them was conscious of that, but later they would understand that they knew, without knowing it, that there was no future for them because they would not continue to live.

By avoiding filming a biopic, you allow yourself to go into more detail.

Absolutely. In choosing to relate two years of his life, and especially his relationship with Fanny, I could re-create the highs and lows of this love, although, despite everything, I had to sacrifice many episodes. When Keats's illness worsened, he suffered from bouts of paranoia, where he imagined Fanny with other men.

You don't mention the last months of his life in Rome, except for transporting the coffin across the Piazza di Spagna, shown in one shot.

I've never been able to explain rationally why I needed this shot: by using it I was breaking my own rule, which was to show their story through Fanny's eyes, thus making an ellipsis of Keats's last days in Rome. I had read this detail about the coffin in Andrew Motion's biography, it had stuck in my memory, and I suppose I can say that the shot occurs in the young woman's imagination.

There's an aspect of Keats that you don't tackle: his progressive ideas, his interest in the French Revolution, a political stance that comes, perhaps, from his feeling that he belongs to an inferior social class, an aspect that is, on the other hand, very present in *Bright Star,* with the economic factor that intrudes in his relationship with the Brawne family.

There were, of course, other possible approaches. I've chosen, I believe, the one that opened up the most perspectives and that gave a majority of viewers access to his personality.

You have stated that you conceived *Bright Star* as a ballad.

I thought of lots of different structures with regard to this film. But it's true that if you read a ballad like *The Eve of St. Agnes*, it's a story in the form of a poem that develops in stanzas. In *Bright Star,* it's about their increasingly

deep attachment and their increasingly large problems. I was also thinking of Bob Dylan's ballads.

If Keats were alive today, do you think he would be more like Bob Dylan or Leonard Cohen than a traditional poet?

You could see him like that. He had an intuitive sensuality in his language, an instinct for a flowing prosody. His reflections on poetry were very mature and remain relevant today.

How did you choose Abbie Cornish and Ben Whishaw, and what was their relationship to Keats's poetry?

I was very surprised, but they fell in love with the poems and loved entering this world. I was a little scared, as neither of them really knew Keats. But then neither did I until I began this project! It was a very gratifying journey for all of us. Abbie had both a clear and an instinctive understanding of the poems and felt very confident. Andrew Motion, who is also a renowned poet, came onto the set to discuss *The Eve of St. Agnes* and "Ode to a Nightingale" with the team. I chose Abbie after an audition in which she performed a scene from the film and read the poem "Bright Star." You could feel that she desperately wanted to play the role. She proved to be very capable, with a wide emotional register and a lightness in her performance that contrasted with the roles of unstable girls she had previously portrayed. Fanny, on the contrary, is very well adjusted. Ben Whishaw wrote to me to say that he'd loved the screenplay. People had spoken to me about him, as he'd portrayed a memorable Hamlet, and I'd seen him in *Perfume*, a film that held little interest for me, but it's difficult to judge an actor based on a role that's so different. I looked at some photos of him, in which he looked very handsome, and, auditioning him, I realized that he had a perfect accent, neither affected nor London (he comes from the north of England), and a fantastic ability to recite poetry.

Since you mention his accent, you had all varieties of English in your cast: Paul Schneider is American, Kerry Fox from New Zealand, and Abbie Cornish, who's Australian.

Abbie Cornish had insisted on having with her an acting coach, Gerry Grennell, who proved to be a great help to all the other actors. He gave them confidence and studied their perfor-mances in depth. He is brilliant, and stayed with us for the whole of the shoot. He was a support for Abbie: she had a lot of lines to speak, and he helped her get her accent right.

The character of Brown, played by Paul Schneider, is a counterpoint to Keats. He personifies a certain type of machismo, which is revealed in his relationship towards women. Paul marvelously re-created the idea that I had of Brown with his boorishness and his big doglike appearance. What is beautiful, and tragic, in his character, is that he can't be Keats, but at the same time, he was able to gauge his talent and love and support him. He wasn't a bad guy, as he was motivated only by Keats's happiness and success. The problem is that he didn't have the intelligence to see that Fanny represented a help rather than a hindrance to his friend. But we can't brush aside the terms of the conflict. Can love be a distraction from creative activity, or does it inspire it? It brings us back to the classical idea: Can an artist outlive his muse? One must, I suppose, allow oneself to be exposed, to be revealed in all one's vulnerability, in order to be a fully developed human being.

How did you work with your cinematographer to avoid the beautiful, contrived image that spoils so many period dramas and to rediscover the freshness of a past captured in the present?
We chose to ignore the imagined preciosity of this period. Greig Fraser and I discussed this at length. It seemed to us that the intimacy of the story should be preserved at all costs, and that our framing should never "freeze" the story. The camera movements that surround Fanny and Keats, as much as 360 degrees, were essentially in order to maintain a necessary fluidity. They should go unnoticed, as though we were sharing the same space as the two lovers. Greig is an intelligent and sensitive director of photography. As regards the lighting, I trusted him completely in our combined research for a natural effect, although we often made use of supplementary lighting.

Were you inspired by certain painters?
One of my great sources of inspiration was Monet's haystacks paintings. I like their domestic nature, their tranquillity and their depth. I love them. There is life there, air that moves around them. These paintings helped us develop our sensitivity to the humble, simple,

everyday things that we sometimes neglect, and that created the setting of our film.

Nature is always very present in your films. *Bright Star* is no exception, with, among other things, the presence of flowers.
We were very lucky, as we were filming in natural settings. Without us really having been aware of the fact at the outset, we had fields, a wood, and a garden nearby. Gradually, over the eight weeks of shooting, they informed our work. I have always found nature to be reassuring, but for Keats, the moors, in particular, had a therapeutic value, helping him live and, of course, richly inspiring him. But you have to be careful how you film nature: it can overwhelm you with an excess of beauty. I'm thinking of the shot of Fanny surrounded by the deep blue of the bluebells. When I saw them, it was like an acid trip: their beauty was so exquisite it was shocking. We knew that nature would bring an authenticity to our story's setting, as we didn't have an urban setting from the 1820s, just a few houses. The landscapes, on the other hand, were those that Keats could have contemplated. And the costumes, which were made by hand, were similar to those that people were wearing at that time. We were helped by a book, *Mrs Hurst Dancing & Other Scenes from Regency Life*, which contains a series of paintings by a young woman of her life at that time. What struck us was how empty the living rooms were. That prompted us to do the opposite of what you see in period dramas, which are overladen with objects and furniture. We used a single property composed of several houses, and another for the sequences of the lake in summertime. We were lucky with the weather during this shoot near Luton in Bedfordshire, north of London. By a curious coincidence, the local pub was called Bright Star!

The choice of music was tricky, because poetry is also music.
For me, this film is above all a love story. Quentin Tarantino, who detests period dramas, told me he loved this one for that very reason. Mark Bradshaw, who had already written the music for my short film *The Water Diary*, is a very young composer, twenty-four or twenty-five years old. I wanted to surround myself with young people of the same age as my characters; it you trust them, they can create astonishing things. Mark is very gifted with voices. We knew that Keats's circle got

together to organize musical evenings in Hampstead Heath, where they imitated musical instruments. When they sing, Mark performed 80 percent of the voices! We also developed the duet at the beginning and end—where he is singing with my niece, in fact. He also wrote other pieces, but sparingly, so as not to interfere with the poetry.

Keats developed a theory of "negative capability," according to which human beings must be capable of living with uncertainty and mystery. Your approach to cinema is not far from this idea, because you don't like explaining and rationalizing.
I think this idea of Keats's is a good guide for innovation and for addressing poetry. It's like creating a space in your life and your thinking that enables you to accept not knowing. It helps make your mind more mature.

SPRING/SUMMER

Spencer Gore
The Icknield Way (...)

John Singer Sargent *Dorothy Barnard 1885–6 Tate*

— tender vulnerable view

Robert Bevan
Maples at Cuckfield (1914)

Top: Mood boards with, notably, a portrait of John Keats
by Charles Brown (1819).
Bottom left: Monet's White Frost, Sunrise, 1888—1889,
Hill-Stead Museum, Farmington, Connecticut.
Bottom right: Abbie Cornish and Jane Campion
on the set of Bright Star.

Following pages: A vision of life where sensitivity,
tenderness, and the beauty of feelings and emotions prevail,
which is portrayed without any hint of blandness but, on
the contrary, with great energy.

Top of the Lake
(2013 and 2017)

"Everything About This
Project Was a Risk."

Top: Robin Griffin (Elisabeth Moss) and detective Al Parker (David Wenham).
Centre left: G. J. (Holly Hunter), half-guru, half-witch, surrounded by women seeking her counsel: Anne-Marie (Alison Bruce), Bunny (Genevieve Lemon), Anita (Robyn Malcolm), Melissa (Georgi Kay), Prue (Sarah Valentine), and Grishina (Skye Wansey).

An auteur film

Without visible seams

Top of the Lake wasn't Campion's first foray into television. Her first feature-length film, *Two Friends*, had been made for television, and there were two versions of *An Angel at My Table*, for the small screen and the cinema. But she was without doubt undertaking a project on a whole new scale in proposing to several international partners, and in first place to BBC2, a TV series of six episodes, written by her and Gerard Lee, her collaborator on *Sweetie*. Media fascination with American film is such that it is easy to overlook the fact that, since the 1970s, the greatest European directors have been making films for television composed of six to thirteen episodes and that they were, indeed, the pioneers of such series: Maurice Pialat (*La Maison des bois*, 1970–1), Luigi Comencini (*The Adventures of Pinocchio*, 1972), Ingmar Bergman (*Scenes from a Marriage*, 1973), and Reiner Werner Fassbinder (*Berlin Alexanderplatz*, 1979). It was an auteur film of this genre that Campion decided to make, and she insisted, moreover, that it should be based on an original screenplay.

In fact, in Hollywood, series (with a few isolated exceptions, such as *Twin Peaks* by David Lynch and Mark Frost, 1990–1) had long been considered as works by screenwriters, who by this means got their own back on directors, who were often interchangeable and little known (who, for example, directed the long-running series *The Sopranos*, created by David Chase?). The person in charge was the show's creator, who ensured that the basic principles were adhered to, participated in the scriptwriting, managed a team of scriptwriters, and was the executive producer of the series. It wasn't until the new millennium that renowned filmmakers—including Martin Scorsese (*Boardwalk Empire*, 2010), Michael Mann (*Luck*, 2011), Todd Haynes (*Mildred Pierce*, 2011), and David Fincher (*House of Cards*, 2013)—made their mark on television series, often directing the pilot episode without necessarily having written the screenplay.

In the case of *Top of the Lake*, Campion found substantial resources (the budget was twice that of an average series), which the cinema would probably not have offered her, to satisfy her love of multilayered stories with lots of characters. *The Portrait of a Lady* was already evidence of this interest in the large-scale forms of the nineteenth-century narrative. This was also the opportunity for Campion to return to film in her native country, twenty years after *The Piano*. But this unique experience cannot conceal the fact that *Top of the Lake* is profoundly linked to Campion's world.

Four Groups

Yet again, there is a female protagonist at the centre of the story, this time played by Elisabeth Moss, a remarkable actress who has something of Jodie Foster about her. She plays Robin Griffin, a detective specializing in crimes against children. She goes looking for a twelve-year-old girl, Tui Mitcham (Jacqueline Joe), who, after it has been discovered that she is pregnant, has gone missing. During her inquiry, Robin's own traumatic past comes back to haunt her.

There is an element of the sexual thriller in *Top of the Lake* that is not dissimilar to *In the Cut*. The young people, Tui and Jamie (Luke Buchanan), walled up in silence, trying to protect themselves from the outside world and facing adolescence with difficulty, are reminiscent of teenagers in Campion's other films, from *Sweetie* to *Holy Smoke* via *An Angel at My Table*. G. J. (Holly Hunter), half-guru, half-witch, is a new version of the eccentric characters of the nonrational world—fortune teller, Eastern sage, psychotherapist—that populate her other films, and is the symbol of matriarchy (even though she has no children) around which most of the other female characters in the film congregate. Meanwhile, Matt Mitcham (Peter Mullan), Tui's father, represents the father's law, the patriarchal authority figure that most of Campion's female characters are driven to confront.

Although the story revolves around Robin's quest, it is formed of four groups of characters that, while geographically autonomous, are constantly being exposed to each other. As in *Twin Peaks*, Laketop is the type of small town that is full of secrets that everyone knows.

The first group is that of the police squad led by Al Parker (David Wenham) and his subordinate Robin, whom he leaves, halfway through the series, to continue the inquiry by her own means, considering, for his part, that the case is closed.

Opposite page, centre right: The schoolfriends of Tui, the girl who has gone missing: Gemma (Alice Ward), Kayla (Connor Olivia Moore), Daniel (Layne Opetaia), Jase (Sam Dickson) and Tegan (Sydney Telfer).
Opposite page, bottom: The Mitcham clan: Matt, the father (Peter Mullan, on the right), and his two sons, Luke (Kip Chapman) and Mark (Jay Ryan).

Pages 186–187: Tui Mitcham (Jacqueline Joe), the young pregnant girl
who mysteriously disappears in the first episode of the series.
Pages 188–189: The camp of the women who have been damaged
and disillusioned by life is ironically called Paradise.

Jamie (Luke Buchanan) refuses to talk.

The second is the camp of middle-aged women who have been damaged
and disillusioned by life. At the head of this tribe, located near the
lake and ironically called Paradise, is G. J. (with long grey hair, like the
director's). Beneath her veneer of kindness and her detached air, she
dismisses sham and dispenses harsh advice. These women have based
themselves here, in this wild and apparently liberating place, to flee the
world, but they remind us that the rot has already set in; the serpent and
the fall are not far off, even in the middle of paradise. They are looking
for happiness, peace, and love but don't find it.

The third group is formed by Matt, with his shady schemes and drug-
making operation, and his two sons, Mark (Jay Ryan) and Luke (Kip
Chapman), to whom should be added another son, Johnno (Thomas
M. Wright), who has moved away from his father and spent several years
in a Thai prison for drug trafficking, and Tui, the young missing girl,
whom Matt fathered by his third wife, a Thai woman. Matt lives on a
property surrounded by barbed wire and guarded by dogs and seems so
bound to the community that Al Parker, the policeman, appears to give
him special treatment. Matt also makes claim to the land on which the
women, who scoff at him, have set up camp.

The last group, that of the children who surround Tui, reflects one of the
filmmaker's favourite themes: She has made children the protagonists
of her stories, from _Sweetie_ to _Bright Star_ via _An Angel at My Table_ and
The Piano.

These adjoining worlds are like planets that are searching for one
another to form a complex web of human relationships. For example,
Johnno renews contact with Robin, a childhood sweetheart, bringing
to the surface old and painful memories that make her even more

determined to save Tui, with whom she identifies. A reflection on sexual
violence (like _In the Cut_), the film also examines the concessions people
make to maintain relationships with those who have betrayed them. The
past that Robin has denied and tried to forget makes her vulnerable
beneath her carapace of strength and invincibility. Also, Robin has been
engaged for five years in Australia to a man that she cannot bring herself
to marry and has come back to New Zealand to be with her mother,
who is dying of cancer and who reproaches her for not settling down.
This difficult mother–daughter relationship, with its sometimes violent
clashes born of a deep attachment, is a recurring theme in the director's
work, and is reflected in the complex relationship that the narcissistic
Matt has with his deceased mother when he flagellates himself at
her grave.

Vices and Splendour

Hidden vices, latent corruption, and the darkest undercurrents of the
human psyche are constantly juxtaposed with the splendour of nature.
With _An Angel at My Table_ and _The Piano,_ Campion had established
herself as one of the great landscape artists of contemporary cinema,
alongside John Boorman and Terrence Malick. She is particularly
inspired by her homeland, although the domestic nature of the English
countryside in _Bright Star_ also brought out the inspired painter in
her. In the case of _Top of the Lake_ it is a giant lake, Moke Lake near
Queenstown, and the high mountains surrounding it, along with the
green forests of the southernmost tip of New Zealand's South Island,
that serve as the setting for human tragedies. Beautifully intensified
by the photography of cinematographer Adam Arkapaw (_Animal
Kingdom_ by David Michôd, 2010; _Snowtown_ by Justin Kurzel, 2011), the

In season 2, China Girl, *Robin investigates the murder of a young woman, assisted by Miranda Hilmarson (Gwendoline Christie) ...*

... and seeks to meet her daughter Mary (Alice Englert), who is hostile towards her adoptive mother (Nicole Kidman).

natural world depicted here is no less harsh than in *The Piano*, with its dark undergrowth and torrential rain. In *Top of the Lake*, the water is calmer and the skies brighter, but the landscape can be dangerous and threatening, and the mountains oppressive after sunset when darkness falls. The confrontation between an often-idyllic natural setting and the most sordid schemes generates an intriguing tension.

Campion is a moralist who ponders the mysteries of existence, the world in which we live, good and evil and the dual faces of human beings, without, however, judging her characters. Like her other films, *Top of the Lake* is the story of a journey, that of Robin—bold and sensitive, stubborn and full of doubts—who is driven by an inner anger and whose descent into hell—like that of Isabel and Frannie, the heroines of *The Portrait of a Lady* and *In the Cut*—is represented by a dark, underground place. This is the home of Wolfgang Zanic (Jacek Koman), suspected of pedophilia, or that of Matt Mitcham, with its labyrinthine passages and hidden recesses. When G. J. says to Robin's dying mother, 'The body knows what to do. Just go with the body', it is as though we are hearing the voice of Campion herself, so physical are her films with their concise dialogue, which is aligned with the movements, look, and impulses of her characters. This is seen, for example, in the behaviour of Robin, attracted, though not really sexually, to her colleague Al Parker, a sort of mentor, and to Johnno, the former lover with whom she has met up again and to whom she is irresistibly drawn.

Top of the Lake would not be a Campion film without the special place given to humour. The women's camp, for instance, the treatment of which has something of Robert Altman's sardonic look about it, is viewed with an ironic distance that transforms this battle of the sexes into a delicious comedy of manners. The specifications inherent in any

television project in no way curb the eloquence of the filmmaker, who remains true to her sense of incongruity and the bizarre (shared with her co-screenwriter Gerard Lee since *Passionless Moments*), from the spontaneous depictions of nudity, to the character of Bunny (Genevieve Lemon, one of Campion's favourite actresses since *Sweetie*), who, at the Laketop bar, offers a hundred dollars to the first man who will agree to sleep with her—with the alarm on her mobile phone set for seven minutes so that she avoids any risk of emotional attachment!

One of the most remarkable achievements of *Top of the Lake* is the symbiotic nature of its realization. Not only does Campion, as in her previous films, manage to mix American, Scottish, Australian, and New Zealand actors by varying the voices and accents, but she also succeeds in creating a seamless texture between the episodes that she directed (1: "Paradise Sold," 4: "A Rainbow Above Us," and 6: "No Goodbyes, Thanks") and those directed by Garth Davis (2: "Searchers Search," 3: "The Edge of Universe" and 5: "The Dark Creator"). Mark Bradshaw's music, with its melancholic accents, is in harmony with this disenchanted story, in which Campion has succeeded, through observation of reality and the work of the imagination, in creating a world that reflects all the complexity and all the nuances inherent in human nature.

The second series of *Top of the Lake* continues, four years later, with six new episodes in the same vein as those of the first series.

Interview conducted in Berlin, February 2013

How did *Top of the Lake* originate? Was it a commission, or was this a story you particularly wanted to tell?

It was me that took the initiative. Even before I shot *Bright Star*, I had been wanting to make a very modern film that would take place in the south of New Zealand, where I have a cabin and live for part of the time. I'd been thinking about it for five years; I'd even considered writing a novel on the theme of *Top of the Lake*. Finally, I decided to make a film of six hours, a detective story, because I like this genre, which provides, in my view, a driving force for the story. At that stage I talked about it to Ben Stephenson of the BBC's drama section. I had in my mind the idea of a girl who goes into a lake. Then, there was the character of a female detective from Australia, visiting her mother, who finds herself involved in a case of a mysterious disappearance that throws her world upside down. There was also a colony of women, and, of course, the family of the young girl who had gone into the lake, her mother, who is the third wife of Matt Mitcham, and the suspicion of criminal activity that surrounds these characters. Then there was the battle for land in this local paradise.

Why did you decide to resume your collaboration with Gerard Lee? More than twenty years had elapsed since you worked together on *Passionless Moments* and *Sweetie*.

From the beginning, I knew that the screenplay would combine a situation that is close to the edge with funny moments. Gerard is the only person I know that shares that sense of humour with me. It had been a while since I'd seen him, but I knew he was in Sydney, and it's true that the work of writing a film of six hours is a huge challenge. Gerard suffers from feeling he has been somewhat mistreated by the film world; he is disappointed; he's a sensitive man. He is wary of people in the industry but we discussed it at length and we were on an equal footing with regard to the conditions. As for the subject, that interested him too, particularly the women's colony and the presence of a strange woman, that is to say G. J. I knew the story would strike a chord with him as he has been practising Transcendental Meditation since he was seventeen years old, so for quite some time. I wanted to know what had happened to him at that time of his life. Of course, it is not our story, but I wanted to include this experience of a particular age of innocence, because it helps you understand how these things work, this way of seeing the world and of behaving.

How did your collaboration go?

In fact, once we'd decided to go for it, we worked together every day. Then, after an interruption of two years, due to filming *Bright Star*, I learned that the BBC was interested in the project, and they asked us to provide them with a synopsis. We received the funds to write both the first episode and a résumé of the other five. From then on, the money for the production was at our disposal. So the financial situation was favorable.

As for the way we wrote together, we used to meet up in the morning for a coffee, which is a very important moment! Then we would discuss our dreams and talk about the sequence we were working on. We would take it in turns to criticize each other's ideas, quite severely, which didn't upset us in the least. Gerard can tell me that an idea I have is rubbish, and I'm grateful to him for that because it prevents me heading off down a dead-end track. That saves me quite a lot of time. The gain is twofold: it's twice as fast, and twice as much fun, because of our mutual trust and affection. Both of us prefer what the other one does to what we do ourselves individually. Sometimes there are surprises, but generally not. We would also often act out the roles of the different characters in the series ourselves. If a role was posing a problem, this role-play helped us to see the aspects of the dynamics of the situation that it would be worth us exploring. For example, if we had an episode to write that the BBC had decided to finance, we had to be quite attentive to the tone to adopt. For me, this aspect is fundamental, and Gerard and I knew perfectly how to arrive at the required tone. So, with the résumé to hand, we would draw up a list, more or less in order, of the various stages in the episode. That said, sometimes one of us would say that we'd like to try something with that part while the other one might have liked to do it. On the whole, the original structures were mine, but occasionally Gerard would get enthusiastic about experimenting with different ideas, sometimes to the point that he would ask me not to speak to him for three hours. That was how we worked. Which didn't stop Gerard from coming back and declaring, "OK, I'm going to read what I've done." And me from saying: "But it's rubbish!" To which, he would reply: "Oh, really?!" He tends to get more surprised than me; he finds it difficult to judge beforehand whether something will work or not. Despite that, he's always ready to go back to the drawing board with an idea.

Were there characters that you particularly enjoyed developing? For example, were you more inclined to work on the female characters while he was happy to work on the characterization of the men?

No, not at all. In fact, I was rather better at finding the voice of the guys. In terms of the writing, we both needed to be able to do both. I imagine it's the case for most miniseries because people are working on a single episode. But it was not uncommon for us to rework the other one's part, he mine and I his, if we thought we could improve it. But we both understood the voices of all the characters. To the point where it seemed to me that the voices and dialogue of the Mitcham sons, Mark and Luke, were not sufficiently developed. Even so, the two actors, Jay Ryan and Kip Chapman, were so good that they improved their characters and restored what might have been missing in their characterization.

In addition to his sense of humour, what are the qualities you find in Gerard Lee as a scriptwriter?

Gerard's style as a scriptwriter is unusual. He has exceptional powers of observation; he is compassionate, surprising, and funny. Moreover, the structural aspect fascinates him. I'm more intuitive, while he really contributed ideas in terms of the structure.

How do you explain the fact that so many excellent directors are interested in series and serials: Todd Haynes with *Mildred Pierce* and David Lynch with *Twin Peaks*? Do you think the cinema today no longer provides the same opportunities to build characters and create stories?

No, I believe that cinema can do some great things and provides the same opportunities as before. I think the reason for it is the financial environment of the film industry, particularly in the independent sector. There is a struggle to find an audience. When I saw *Deadwood*, for example, I was dismayed that HBO had been able to produce a film with such a demanding subject. I said to myself: There you are, things are changing, it's great. It seems that this series has found its audience. Certainly not a huge one, but significant nonetheless. The artistic license of the cinema is not an absolute ideal. Independent cinema is always very concerned about finding an audience. At home, people sit in front of their television and search through the programmes to find an interesting and well-made film. A large part of our audience is probably made up of middle-class families. It

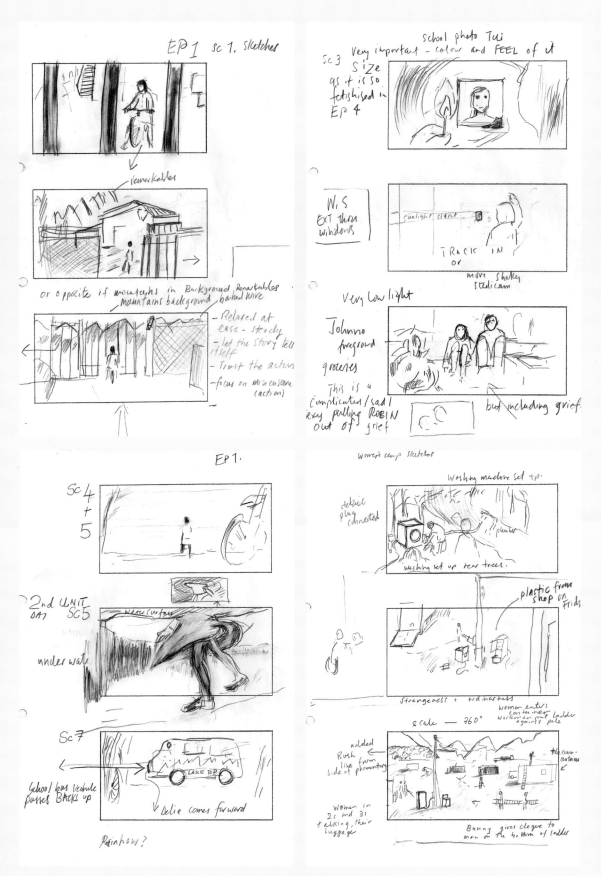

Storyboards for Top of the Lake
drawn by Campion.

Mood board with visual references.

Elisabeth Moss and Jane Campion during the shoot.

can be compared to reading novels. It's a sort of weekend activity, when you refuel by indulging in a TV series. Don't get me wrong, I'm not aiming to change the world; I try to observe how it is and come to terms with the way things are.

Because I love novels, and because we live in the world at a given time, I love delving deeper into characters. I believe that, for most people, characters are much more interesting than plot. Also, with series, there is the opportunity to digress, like when Mitcham has that relationship with Anita. When you have six hours for a film, you can introduce more diversions of this sort.

Yet at the same time, it's like when you produce a film, you need three or four partners. With this series, you had not only BBC2, but also Sundance Channel and BBC UKTV, an Australian channel.
We were very fortunate in having producers who were working with partners. They could see that the budget wasn't sufficient to achieve what we wanted to film.

I'd also like to talk about the landscapes. It seems to me that when you film New Zealand landscapes—I don't know whether it's due to your childhood or adolescence—it's very different from when you shoot in Australia, like for *Holy Smoke* and *Sweetie*, where it's arid, whereas in *An Angel at My Table*, *The Piano*, or this film, nature has a beauty, a sensual side that affects us more deeply. What is your relationship to the landscape, particularly to this region of New Zealand?
In fact, I discovered the south of New Zealand quite late. For *The Piano*, we explored a lot to find the location. It was a huge, open, desolate, and very powerful place. I am very moved by this landscape. It has a certain something, a special, liberating atmosphere; I love being swept away by it; I feel it in my soul. I've found a region that I love, that's at the end of a lake, with mountain rivers flowing into it. It is, in a manner of speaking, the end of the road. Beyond that it's wilderness. In summertime, the days are really long (at ten o'clock in the evening, it's still day), there are shrubs, moss… you feel powerful forces. At the same time, it's a very safe place; there are no snakes or anything like that. And, you know, I love the feeling of being away from people, of being isolated. I'd rather be there than anywhere else in New Zealand.

There is also a contrast between the beauty of the environment and the tormented, corrupt, and cruel world of the characters.
I know that there are harmful humans, and I know, too, that the place is very beautiful. You know, I got to hear stories about some difficult characters. And Gerard Lee has lived in a very isolated community on an island off the coast of Brisbane, a community of men. He saw and got to know these people and was inspired by them. You know the kind. People who go off and settle there in the hope of recovering, while in fact, often their condition worsens. And in my own region, I've had dealings with a few eccentric people I haven't liked. The series doesn't describe a family exactly like that. It was more a sort of germ of an idea. But Australia has a macho man culture. Everyone knows that. Personally, I know how they think, these men, and what they think. Quentin Tarantino also describes similar characters in his films. In my view they are almost poetic characters because they are flamboyant and have a way of speaking, a vernacular language, that is fascinating. They each have their own originality.

Why did you decide to shoot only three episodes and to have Garth Davis direct the others?
It's too much work.

But you were present during the filming?
Yes, but it's very different simply being there, without shooting!

The cohesion is remarkable. Of course, we know that episodes 1, 4, and 6 are by you, and analysing them more closely, there are doubtless some revealing nuances, while Garth Davis has more action scenes. The flow is impressive, despite the risk.
Yes, it was a risk. Everything about this project was a risk.

You and Gerard Lee ensured the unity of the writing, but the directing was another story.
There, too, Garth was happy to answer to me. From the start, he told me that he would do whatever I wanted, that I was the boss. There was also the important element of the constant presence of cinematographer Adam Arkapaw, which ensured the continuity. At the beginning, we organized a big meeting to talk about the way that the whole series would need to be shot, and for me to explain how I saw the project. The guidelines were as follows: I wanted to avoid a sentimental approach and excessive dramatization; I wanted the story to tell itself,

right to the end, becoming more and more powerful and convincing, because we trusted it! In terms of the photography, my main recommendation was: no frills. In any case, Garth, whose background is in commercials, is excellent. Moreover, he's really good with people. I was in charge of casting. It was me that would take them to task!

Did you do the location scouting together?
Yes, he's better at that than me, better at judging the dimensions and the landscapes. A case in point was when we visited the A-frame house, which appeared perfect for us for the home of Mitcham and his sons. At the beginning, the idea was that access to the cellar, where the drugs were being made, would be via a cupboard. However, in this place that wasn't possible, and what we did in the end was better, thanks to Garth, who had the idea of taking out the shower and making a false one that would hide the entrance. He's quick, and he's a lovely man. When it's a collaboration, my method is to choose the people and study their projects. I wasn't at ease about the helicopter sequence, which was going to cost a lot of money and thus frighten the producers, and I said to Garth that perhaps we didn't need two helicopters. But he explained to me what he had in mind, and it was great!

Do you work with a storyboard?
He doesn't, but I do, though not as much as I used to. We had around four weeks and two days, something like that, to shoot an hour and a half of film.

How long did the filming take?
Eighteen weeks. The work was very, very hard; it wasn't at all like doing something just for television.

And you also had two editors?
There, too, everything was monitored closely. Garth was working in Melbourne, where he lives, with his editor, Scott Gray, and I was working with mine, Alexandre de Franceschi. In addition, every four weeks, we would meet up to organize screenings and finish the work together. You know, I have great powers of concentration. I can start over and over again until I achieve the desired result.

What I like, too, about the series, is the juxtaposition of groups: the women from Paradise, the policemen, the macho family, and Tui's friends, the children. Of course, since *An Angel at My Table*, you are familiar

with that sort of work, all these different communities, in particular the women and the Mitchams.

It's the fact that they're fighting over the same land that puts them in opposition. I also believe that a film of this kind needs a very specific approach, a way of handling the actors and the world created. Otherwise, in the end, you're left with nothing. Therefore, it seemed to me essential that we organize working groups, workshops, for the police, the women, and the Mitcham family, and that we keep the actors in their respective groups. We needed to find ways of getting them to open up to each other. Even the minor characters came, and it was intense. Everyone was convinced they had ideas to contribute. We invented scenes. David Wenham became comfortable in his role as chief, and his style of leadership imposed itself on the policemen. Because of that, they were able to drop the stereotypes and the clichés to feel the real texture of human relationships. The Laketop had its own working group. Of course, the women's workshop was the most important one.

Of course, it's no accident that you have the same hair as G. J.!

Except that my hair is silver! Her hair is 'bum-length', that's the word used in the screenplay. Yes, I had a very clear, a very specific picture of her, including her way of dressing in tan-coloured clothes, men's clothes. All that helped me; I was convinced she should be like that.

She is the guru character. There's also a guru in *Holy Smoke*, and there's a woman who reads coffee grounds in *Sweetie*. Were you inspired by Krishnamurti?

I haven't read U. G. Krishnamurti, but I have met him. He came to the Theosophical Society. Basically, he's an Indian, a gentleman who apparently went through a period of change. He had, as we say, 'lived differently'. He's one of those people who are not bound by reality. His vision could be described as nondualist thinking, where phenomena are not perceived as being in opposition. I met him quite by chance.

Was that in India?

No, in Australia. He's probably the only really free person I've ever met in my life. He made a huge impression on me. Later, we became friends. It's rare to get to know someone like

that; these things take time. I had a daughter, I couldn't leave, but I went to see him two or three times, and then he came to Australia for a few days. He doesn't travel with a whole band of disciples; he doesn't like that sort of thing. His way of commenting on the dualistic world is very aggressive. He doesn't try to be gentle and conciliatory, but there's a harsh sense of truth about him.

This community is looking for love, peace, and the like, but there's a sort of sterility there, isn't there?

[She laughs.] I think the members of the community are trying hard to pretend, as though they are what they aspire to be. In reality, the series doesn't provide any answers, there's no resolution. At the same time, there are some signs of healing. All the women know what it's like to suffer. One of the things that interests me about these women, who are said to be invisible and are believed to hold no sexual attraction for men, is that they know what the root of sadness is because they've spent their whole lives looking for love. These women exist is real life. I find them sad and affecting, and some of them never manage to get free, to move on. But others do.

One of the characters that stand out from the others, after G. J., is Bunny.

Bunny is the one with the money. The irony is that her money comes from her husband, who is very wealthy.

She pays for seven minutes of sex.

Yes, but even if it wouldn't really happen like that, I understand in a way why I was determined to include that scene. In fact, I made this series because it gave me those sorts of opportunities.

Do you know how many times you've worked with Genevieve Lemon? There was *Sweetie*…

I've worked with her as often as I could!

She's also in *The Piano* and *Holy Smoke*. So this is the fourth time.

I thought she'd be good in the role. And then she performs with Robyn Malcolm, who plays Anita, the one who had a chimpanzee. You see, the stories we chose for these women were all inspired by stories we'd been told about or had read about or had heard on the news. Everything, or nearly everything, has its counterpart in real life.

Robert Altman would have loved this community of women! I also wanted to mention Robin Griffin's character, particularly from the perspective of her relationship with her mother, and, possibly your relationship with your own mother. She also lived in Australia, and you used to go and see her.

Yes, my relationship with my mother was passionate and difficult. She wanted more from me than I could give her, as I understand it. [She laughs.] From my point of view, I saw her as a manipulative woman, while she thought I was cold. To my mind, this situation is not unusual.

She wants her daughter to get married.

Yes, she wants her daughter to be happy. In a way, she understands, and moreover, in this particular case, the mother carries a heavy secret. She doesn't tell her the truth; she's incapable of doing so. Certainly, she warns her daughter off Johnno.

There's also the parallel with Matt, who has a bizarre relationship with his mother who has died, and there's the scene at the grave where he flagellates himself.

Yes, that's something we explored, trying to understand, to see why this guy is so crazy. I think that in fact he, and other big bullies like him, are obsessed by the idea of their mother. I talked about it with Peter Mullan, who grew up around aggressive guys, drunks, and I believe that his sister works with serious criminals. And the things you discover, like when these men put on rubber gloves and choose a detergent to wash the dishes, are bizarre, absurd. They are people to be pitied. By contrast, there are lots of strong characters in the film. G. J. is one, and Robin Griffin has strength, too, of a much quieter sort.

At the same time, she's fragile.

Certainly, but I believe that in life we like these strengths, these people who, regardless of others, try to anticipate what they will do and have a go, give it a try.

In Top of the Lake, *Campion worked again with two*
of her favourite actresses: Genevieve Lemon, who
plays Bunny (top), and Holly Hunter, who portrays
G. J. (bottom).

The Power of the Dog
(2021)

"The Essence Comes Not From the Brain
but From Much Deeper."

Phil Burbank (Benedict Cumberbatch) and George Burbank (Jesse Plemons) in The Power of the Dog.
Following pages: Peter Gordon (Kodi Smit-McPhee) and Phil Burbank gradually open up to each other.

Three men, a woman, and a ghost

A Definitive Work

Following the two series of *Top of the Lake*, and twelve years after her last film, *Bright Star*, Jane Campion has completed her tenth film, which she discreetly admits could be her last. True to herself, and in the line with the anti-modernists admired by French literary critic Antoine Compagnon, she continues, as Resnais, Kubrick, and Polanski have done, to dialogue with tradition while reconstructing rather than destroying it. Her film thus belongs to a genre that she describes as 'post-Western', just as *An Angel at My Table* was linked to the biopic, *In the Cut* to the erotic thriller, and *The Portrait of a Lady* to the romantic drama. It is also, like many of her works, a study of family; in this case, the relationship between two brothers, just as *Sweetie* and *In the Cut* explored that between two sisters, and *An Angel at My Table*, *Holy Smoke,* and *Bright Star* involved a parental one. It is also, like half of her filmography, a film set in the past: in 1925, so less distant than the nineteenth century that Campion, as a brooding romantic, has so far favoured (*Bright Star, The Piano, The Portrait of a Lady*). Finally, like *An Angel at My Table, The Portrait of a Lady,* and *In the Cut*, it is a literary adaptation, based on a novel by Thomas Savage published in 1967 (*The Power of the Dog*). We can therefore consider *The Power of the Dog* as a film that consolidates her earlier work while also proposing new avenues. In this respect, commentators have focused on the appearance, for the first time, of a male protagonist at the centre of the story. While it is true that, in past films, a woman was the reverberator in the stories, in *Bright Star*, an equal share had already been given to the young poet John Keats, even if he was seen through the eyes of his great love, Fanny Brawne. And let us not forget the memorable roles played by Harvey Keitel in *The Piano* and *Holy Smoke,* and by Mark Ruffalo in *In the Cut*, because Jane Campion, while acknowledging her debt to the #MeToo movement, films men with compassion and an awareness of their vulnerability.

Two Brothers in Opposition

This is the central theme of *The Power of the Dog*, in which Campion examines the masculinity of her protagonist, Phil Burbank. We are almost at the start of the twentieth century, in the American West, where cars are gradually replacing horses, Indians are now dirt-poor wretches, and two brothers are herding cattle on the vast plains surrounding a ranch they have inherited from their parents, who have moved to live in the city. Everything sets apart the two brothers: Phil, the eldest (Benedict Cumberbatch), is violent and unkempt, while George (Jesse Plemons) is courteous, staid, and under the thumb of his brother, with whom he still shares a bedroom.

When, without telling his brother, George marries Rose Gordon (Kirsten Dunst), a widow and the owner of the Red Mill Hotel, and she comes to live on their property with her son, Peter (Kodi Smit-McPhee), the tension erupts. Phil first lays into the skinny and secretive boy, who differs from him in every way, then the mother, who gradually turns to drink. But this summary does not do the film justice, in that each sequence surprises and reveals a new aspect of the characters. Phil is a former university student, and the constant emphasis on his virility is actually a cover for his latent homosexuality. Peter, whom he victimizes, before adopting a more ambiguous attitude, finds in him a mentor, as was for Phil Bronco Henry, a ghostly character who haunts the story, and whose memory Phil recalls by polishing his saddle and bathing naked in the lake they used to visit together. He also throws himself into a musical duet, playing his banjo, with Rose at the piano. He later takes Peter horseback riding in the sumptuous landscape.

From Montana to New Zealand

These sequences confirm Campion as one of the great landscape architects of contemporary cinema. What inspires her above all are the open spaces of her native New Zealand, which represent those of Montana in the original novel. They are the same ones that were celebrated in *An Angel at My Table*, *The Piano*, and *Top of the Lake*. As a young girl, Campion enjoyed horseriding, and she told Thomas Baurez a revealing story:

> Before making this film, I had a strange dream [...] I was on a dark horse, which I didn't know at all—a rather nervous animal. We were on a steep path that was climbing to the top of a rock. Right at the top, there was a huge precipice. The path we were travelling on was getting narrower and narrower, and we could no longer see the route behind us. Our only solution was therefore to advance towards death. I didn't interpret it negatively, but rather as a warning: 'Jane, focus on the essentials!' The important thing to note here is that I didn't know this horse I was riding; yet if there's no relationship of trust between you and the animal,

you'll get nowhere. This black horse was a bit like my film. I needed to take ownership of the story and the characters.[2]

The filmmaker thus sums up, through a dream, the work of fusion that is involved in any adaptation.

Dreams and Tragedy

The place of the dreamlike is established even in the title, which is also that of the novel: the dog's open mouth, which is like a monstrous threat to the mountain itself. As a counterpoint to the story, Jonny Greenwood's score—grating, haunting, like that composed by Michel Legrand for *The Go-Between* (1971)—echoes the conflicts at work in the characters, who, each in their own way, are seeking to emancipate themselves. From this point of view, Rose's inner turmoil, with her suffering and her silences, is undoubtedly the most moving, expressing all the things that are left unsaid about her son.

The beauty of *The Power of the Dog* lies also in the way that Campion reframes her story by constantly changing the way in which we view its protagonists. She develops the relationship between Phil and Peter, who reveal themselves to each other even though they are different in every way, the first refusing to wear gloves despite the extreme cold, the second remaining fragile and withdrawn. With this drama—both visceral and sophisticated—Campion brilliantly concludes a body of work that is all about beauty and truth, as extolled by Keats, her favourite poet: 'Beauty is truth, truth beauty'.

1 See the photograph of Jane Campion on horseback, reproduced on page 15.
2 Thomas Baurez, "Jane Campion au pays de Lumière," *Première*, October 2021 (interview), p.84.

Above and facing page: Phil's manly demeanour crumbles to reveal a more ambiguous personality.

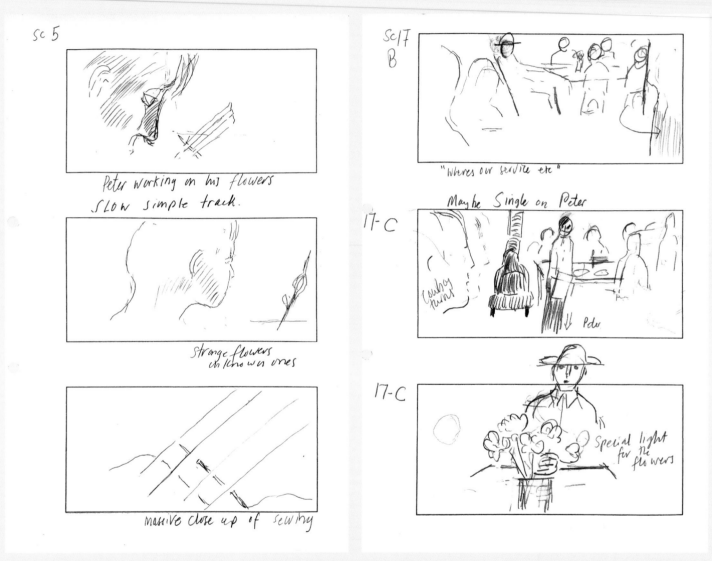

sc 5

Peter working on his flowers
slow simple track.

Strange flowers
unknown ones

massive close up of sewing

Sc 17
B

"Wheres our service etc"

17-C

Maybe Single on Peter

Cowboy hand

Pdv

17-C

Special light
for the
flowers

*Storyboards by Jane Campion: scenes of Peter creating
paper flowers and Phil disparaging them.*

The paper-flower sequences in The Power of the Dog.

Interview conducted in Lyon, October 15, 2021

After finishing the first season of *Top of the Lake*, you acquired the rights to the novel *The Flamethrowers* by Rachel Kushner, for an adaptation you abandoned in favour of *The Power of the Dog*.

I admired the writing in *The Flamethrowers*, but at the same time, I was very busy shooting the series. It was difficult for me to read the novel properly. I thought I could figure it out, but when I'd finished filming, I starting having a lot of doubts. I couldn't see how to do it.

What was the story about?

That was the problem! The writing was remarkable, and there were some wonderful parts with some great scenes, but I couldn't see how to tie them together to build a narrative. The story is set in the 1970s, and there was something French about it—a touch of *Jules and Jim* (1962) by François Truffaut, but not as good. There were also a lot of subversive passages evoking the Red October movement in Italy. *The Flamethrowers* touched on some very varied subjects, including biker gangs and tire manufacturers. At the heart of the book is a young girl who is trying to find her way. I certainly don't wish to diminish the quality of the novel, which is remarkable, but I didn't know how to adapt it and find a narrative thread.

So then you read *The Power of the Dog* by Thomas Savage . . .

I started reading it for pleasure, with no thought of adapting it. I remember immediately thinking it was excellent. It had been sent to me by my father's second wife, who's an English teacher and a great reader. I was immersed in the story right to the end, which isn't always the case. A week later, I was still thinking about the scenes and the character of Peter; I remembered everything. And I loved how it was all falling into place. A good story has that ability to continue to open itself inside you. After that, I asked my agent to find out if anyone held the rights, and the answer was "yes." So the book was not available; Roger Frappier, a producer from Quebec, held the rights and was already in negotiations. As it happened, I was going to Cannes for the second series of *Top of the Lake,* and I met him there, at the Carlton. We

talked together about the scenes from the book we loved, and when I commented to him that he was lucky to hold the rights, he just told me I could have them! He had lots of adaptation projects hadn't come to anything, including one that he'd commissioned but that wasn't right for him. What was certain was that I wanted to make this film immediately. But straight away, I started worrying, because I'd abandoned *The Flamethrowers* project, and this film, *The Power of the Dog*, contained a ghost: Bronco Henry, one of the main characters. I had to work hard to portray Bronco Henry in a tangible way when he wasn't in the book. I did this through the depiction of a small tomb, a scarf, and a stable. I found a way to reveal him and to show how important he was in understanding Phil's suffering.

Half of your films—*An Angel at My Table, The Portrait of a Lady, In the Cut,* and this one—are adaptions; the others are original screenplays. Do they present different sorts of problems?

The screenplays for the first two were actually written by Laura Jones. I was very involved and made suggestions, but she was responsible for writing them. I adapted *In the Cut*, and it was a difficult experience. This time I felt more at ease, and it went faster. I think it was due to all the writing I'd been doing on the twelve hours of *Top of the Lake* with Gerard Lee, and also on *Bright Star* with the assistance of Tanya Seghatchian. Tanya developed the project for *The Power of the Dog* with me, too. She has a great sense of structure and shape. Working on *Bright Star* with her was pure joy. I loved writing at length late into the night, sorting through my research until the story began to take shape, digging deep inside myself for the energy and emotions. The essence comes not from the brain but from much deeper. Once the connection is made, writing becomes easier. Otherwise, there's a block that causes anxiety for the author.

How did you approach working on the two brothers?

They're very well described in Thomas Savage's novel. There are lots of mentions of their past that helped me to understand why these brothers are so different. Phil is depicted as a

character who has had a rise in fortunes, then a fall, but George has his own story, too. He approaches Rose, a widow, to comfort her, without Phil's approval for once. He pulls away from him as the story progresses, while Phil tries to rein him back in by drawing him to the ranch and going riding with him in the hills. In the book, Phil likes playing chess and reading, while George is keen on comics. He's a nice guy, while his brother believes that he himself is cruel because he doesn't like people who pretend to be more than they are, and he considers that it's his place to say so! Basically, we have two opposing characters, with George, who has submitted himself his entire life to this power balance, and Phil, who, deep down, is fragile. Even though they're adults, George still shares a bedroom with his brother. I love the dynamic of this story, as well as the relationships between the characters. It seems that Phil is having a sensual memory of Bronco Henry when he's bathing naked in the river. The two brothers are, indeed, very different. When we were casting, we were unanimous in thinking that Jesse Plemons was an obvious choice for the role of George. But he saw himself playing Phil! Talking with him in a café, he confessed to me that he was sick of playing characters that other people thought were made for him, and I can understand that he wanted to extend his range, but I wanted someone who wasn't going to be reluctant about playing this role. I drew his attention to the fact that we were going to develop his character in such a way that it would be different from anything he had yet played.

How did you go about casting?

We needed to start with Phil, the main character. We needed a great actor, but also someone who could help me obtain funding. There were a few actors we could have considered. Cumberbatch's agent told us that Benedict had read the screenplay and was ready to play the part. He was on my list, despite the fact that he's not American. He's an astonishing actor, with lots of charisma and panache. He also has the ability to express the character's vulnerability. This is key to ensuring that viewers remain caught up in the story; you don't want them seeing him as a bastard and rejoicing in his death. I wanted to draw attention to the wounded man, to his complexity, to someone

In marrying Rose Gordon (Kirsten Dunst),
George gradually distances himself from his brother.

Sc 81

everyone moves from the table leaving Rose

*Storyboard by Jane Campion, and the scene at the end of the dinner
where Rose's despair becomes evident.*

who represses his emotions. Benedict was up for the challenge.

How did you choose the young Australian actor, Kodi Smit-McPhee, who's a revelation in the role of Peter?

He was such a gift for the film! We were living in the United States, desperately looking for boys interested in acting. But we were getting nowhere. We even organized workshops to try to find people who might have the qualities needed for the role, but in vain. No one really convinced me, but the process did help me realize how Peter could be. Researching actors remotely without being in direct contact with candidates was complicated and boring. I had a real struggle to find the right person for this story. Then I remembered having seen Kodi Smit-McPhee in the *Gallipoli* series (2015) and in other films. And I realized that, my God, he was perfect for me! We tried to call him, then met up with him where he lives in the States, and I was thinking that he was my main asset. When he arrived at the front door, he was already in character, happy to engage with this interview as though he'd already got the role, telling us about his relationship with his mother, the death of his father, how he'd suffered, improvising all of it. He already had some interesting theories and strange ideas that revealed Peter's world. He was even better than the character in the book! During filming, Kodi told me that the previous year, he'd been diagnosed with an immune deficiency that prevented him from bending down. He struggles with paralysis but never complained of his illness, despite his age. I really love him. He's a great person: elegant, cautious and very funny!

The female lead is played by Kirsten Dunst, who you directed for the first time …

Initially, I was wanting to give the role of Rose Gordon to Elisabeth Moss, who I like a lot and who's very intelligent. But she wasn't available because of other projects, and then the pandemic hit. We were both of us disappointed not to be able to work together again after *Top of the Lake*. But then I immediately thought of offering the role to Kirsten Dunst, who was interested. She was extraordinary in *Melancholia* (2011) by Lars von Trier and in *Virgin Suicides* (1999) by Sofia Coppola. I'm a really big fan of her moods; every time I think of these films, I'm captivated. I really enjoyed talking to her on Zoom and then meeting her, but once again, there was a problem with planning, because she was playing in a series, which meant she was unavailable for several months. But we managed to get her, thanks to Jesse Plemons, who's her partner in life and who had accepted the role of George. It was a big advantage to have a couple on set, because it's never easy to bring someone to New Zealand when it means they'll be separated from their family. Kirsten Dunst has developed an acting method with her coach that enables her to integrate memories physically. This made her very confident playing Rose on a psychic level.

You're an artist and not a judge or a prosecutor, which enables you to show, in Phil, a character full of contradictions and yet who remains misogynist, racist, and homophobic . . .

He's also lonely, sad, and grieving. He's a sensual person, capable of admiring the beauty of life, and he can also love. Before I started writing, I reread *Death in Venice* by Thomas Mann. Even though it's obviously not the same story, there's something similar there about late love.

Why did you decide to shoot in New Zealand a story that takes place in Montana?

We shot it right in the south of New Zealand, a place that I'd never previously been to, but in a region where I've spent a lot of time over the past twenty years. Initially, I thought that it would be much more authentic if we shot the film in Montana; it would have been a true American film. Emile Sherman, the producer, started talking about the costs, wondering what we could get from Netflix or elsewhere, and there were limits. Montana was very expensive; there was no state aid, no tax relief. So we turned to the idea of making the film in New Zealand, hiring as many American actors as possible, even for supporting roles. We did some scouting, and we found, in particular, a building that I already knew from a painting by Grahame Sydney, who paints landscapes of almost photographic realism in the region where we shot the film, the Hawkdun Range in Otago. It was surrounded on all sides by a landscape of nothingness: a total void, apart from a few small things that had to be removed here and there. At that moment, I knew I'd found the location. It was prairie, earth, devoid of vegetation. Then we visited some other places before returning to Montana, where we met O. Alan Weltzien, the author of a biography on Thomas Savage *(Savage West: The Life and Fiction of Thomas Savage)*. He teaches at the university near where the writer lived. We took a tour of his region and visited his ranch and the house where he used to live, and that has been moved. During the whole time we were there, I had the feeling that it wouldn't work for us to shoot the film in that place; that it just didn't compare to the landscapes we'd found in New Zealand. I felt distant from it. And I still hadn't seen the dog. Did it exist? Then, suddenly, just as we were driving away in the car, I saw it, on a cliff. I stopped. It looked like a sculpture of a crouching dog. The vision was like a sort of welcome. I'd seen the dog; I could do the film! That reassured me, because I'm not American and I'm not a man, although that wouldn't have been a problem for Savage. You have this sense that you need to grasp a project in its true context to do it justice. I wanted to be sure that I was the right person.

Your Australian films, like *Sweetie* and *Holy Smoke*, feel gloomy in their urban sequences, where the landscape plays a less important role than in your New Zealand films. They match those of your youth, your childhood. There's a photo where we see you on a horse dressed as a very young cowgirl. Your relationship to the landscape remains very sentimental . . .

The landscape has always inspired me. That began in New Zealand, of course. I love the feeling of being inhabited by the landscape; you get out of your head and just feel the air, and you feel part of everything around you. For me, that relationship is very important.

Your film looks like a Western, but it's not really one. It begins, true to the genre, with two brothers on horseback herding cattle. As a film lover, do you like Westerns in general?

I think everyone has a romance with the idea of the Western. When I was a child, I used to love this genre, being on a horse, pretending to be a cowgirl. But Thomas Savage doesn't describe a romantic vision of the Western, because he was himself a man of the West; so he had a very different perspective. He was even hostile towards these cowboys. I imagine he had to support characters like Phil, while also analysing their type of masculinity, which was pretty coarse. There was nothing romantic about it; it was horrible, even. I think it's wonderful that he managed to see beyond the myth of the Western. He talks about it in his biography. In fact, he detested Montana, which he found quite oppressive.

Today, lots of female directors, including Mona Fastvold with *The World to Come* (2020) and Kelly Reichardt with *Meek's Cutoff* (2010), are making Westerns. Is this a genre that you dreamed of directing?
Not particularly, but I was interested in the end of the conquest of the American West and the way in which it had been won by the pioneers, when ranches were built and the Indians were suppressed and moved onto reservations. In most Westerns, the character of the cowboy doesn't mention these events and is at pains not to resemble real cowboys.

How did you work with Ari Wagner, the cinematographer? It was the first time you'd worked together . . .
Ari Wegner is a young cinematographer. I chose her because she's got a wonderful eye, as she showed us in *Lady Macbeth* (2016) by William Oldroyd, but she hadn't yet worked on a film on the scale of *The Power of the Dog*. And I wanted to work with a woman to give her the opportunity to be supported and develop her skills. It's important to me to help women in this industry.

Just as you filmed your first full-length film, *Sweetie*, with Sally Bongers . . .
Absolutely, and she has remained my best friend. I asked Ari Wegner to accept the idea of a long preparation and joint reflection, as she had little experience. She was involved with me in all of the development and was really dedicated and responsive to the screenplay. She wasn't looking to create sensational images, but she stayed deeply connected to the story. Together, we studied how other films had been lit by great cinematographers such as Harris Savides. Ari and I discussed a lot and watched him talk on YouTube about his theory of cinematography, which is based on an economy of means to light as simply as possible. Of course, he translated

that in words that could disguise his knowledge, but we understood what he was doing nonetheless. To tell the story of *The Power of the Dog*, we thought a great deal about how the camera should approach the scene, holding the shots as long as was could while preventing its movements becoming acrobatic.

It was also the first time you'd worked with the composer Jonny Greenwood, who wrote the original soundtrack for *There Will Be Blood* (2007) by Paul Thomas Anderson, which could also be called a Western of another genre . . .
I'm not sure that we could call it a Western. It's more a film about capitalism, the American West and oil. It's a magnificent work, but it's not comparable to *The Power of the Dog*, even though it deals with a similar period. The reason I chose Jonny Greenwood was first of all because I love his work, in particular with Paul Thomas Anderson. But the decision to work with him was also taken to meet the financial obligations of the New Zealand production structure, which required me to work with a New Zealand composer. So I listened to recordings of the extraordinary Australian Chamber Orchestra, which is led by violinist and composer Richard Tognetti. I was particularly interested in the piece 'Water', and I discovered that it had been written by British composer Jonny Greenwood. The score had been commissioned by the Australian Chamber Orchestra. I wanted to use this piece of music, despite the restrictions imposed by the financial plan, and I asked the investors to make an exception, because the choice of composer is so important to me. The fact that I had previously worked with the British composer Michael Nyman on *The Piano* also helped my case, because of its success. These artists are irreplaceable; they have a unique voice. Jonny Greenwood loved the screenplay of *The Power of the Dog*. He really is a genius.

His score is wonderful . . .
Yes, thank you on his behalf! In the booklet for the soundtrack record that Netflix is publishing, I added the emails I'd exchanged with Jonny Greenwood to show how talented he is, how he heard the film through his different instruments and gave them a unique power, so recreating a whole world. He presented me

with a whole range of musical sounds that he wanted to interpret using a mechanical piano, which is a strange instrument that can play music faster than any human! I was astonished by the unusual way he was proceeding with this piano and the brass and string sections. He'd already imagined the score for the brass for the end of the film as the sound of a passage, an abandoned track—very beautiful in this landscape. Jonny composed thirty-four sketch-like pieces. My editor, Peter Sciberras, and I began to try to fit them into the editing. That took some time, because there was so much material, and we wanted to insert it all before presenting our work to Jonny. He was very cooperative: he didn't want us to insert a piece just to make sure it was used, and insisted that we let him know if we felt we needed him to write another piece of music. We had a lot of conversations about certain complex scenes, such as the one with Phil and the scarf. We also took the time to find the right combination with the tambourine. Jonny has a real talent for using harmonics. It's not easy for me, because I don't play a musical instrument. I can hear it and I can feel it, but I won't remember it tomorrow. I believe it's important, when you're working with a composer, not to try to find a key to ensure you're understood. I just talked to him about my own personal experiences with music so that he could write what I was feeling. I didn't expect anything else from him.

The dialogue between Rose's piano and Phil's banjo is reminiscent of the musical duel in *Deliverance* (1972) by John Boorman . . .
Yes, and the scene in John Boorman's film with the guitar and the banjo is incredibly brilliant. You're reminding me of it now, and it remains unforgettable for everyone.

The theme of the family is one you return to regularly in your films . . .
It's difficult to escape! Each of us has a family. I can't imagine anything else.

Nevertheless, other film directors show no interest in it, yet, without being autobiographical, this family theme can reveal the director's personality through their fictional characters . . .
Perhaps, but I don't have a brother like in the film. How we hide ourselves is indeed a real

mystery. Over the years, I've come to better understand the importance of what I need to protect about myself in relation to the content of my stories.

The close-ups of Phil's face gradually appear ambivalent. At first, they show his strength, his power, but later we understand that he's increasingly beleaguered.

Actually, Peter becomes a deadly weapon. In fact, this change of perspective came from what we discovered on set. It also came from the fact that we had to stop filming in New Zealand for three months because of the pandemic, which gave us the chance to review all the shots we'd filmed. I was able to analyse what we were missing, what we needed to select, and what we needed to focus on. These close-ups were part of that, revealing the moment when Phil becomes really vulnerable. In Thomas Savage's book, the relationship between Phil and Peter turns out differently. At the end, he makes them friends, but Peter's motivations seem to me to be more complex than that. He knows that he should be by his mother's side, but at the same time, he risks losing a new friend, Phil, who's paying attention to him, making him feel important and helping him. So I changed the end of the film by abandoning the return to making paper flowers and choosing the leather rope, which conveys the whole problem of the story. This becomes apparent when Phil is looking to give the rope to Peter but can't find him and understands that something has happened. We then grasp his emotional pain at the absence of Peter, his friend. And I believe that Peter becomes aware, with sadness, that Phil's life is marked by his love for a ghost. At the same time, he realizes that he will come to hold the same memories of Phil, who, with the rope, the horse rides and their conversations, has been a great teacher. He will probably remember Phil in the same way that Phil remembers Bronco Henry. Thomas Savage was able to write a story that is singularly strong, dealing with all the characters together while maintaining the perspective of each of them and their interaction. I really like the shapes in the narrative. And I love this story because it demonstrates a different masculinity in Phil and in George.

Interview with Pierre Eisenreich

Phil becomes Peter's mentor, teaching him how to braid a rope,
like Bronco Henry had done with him.

Above: Ari Wegner and Jane Campion on the set of The Power of the Dog.
Facing page: Notes from Jane Campion to explain to her team her vision of the rope in The Power of the Dog.

As the director it's my job to enter the story deeply, to make sure it is enlivened from the blood, the guts, the bones up; to bring my imagination to each character individually and to look beyond the present moment of the story to where in each character's life, their pain, yearning, humanity their character was formed and what it figures now in the life of the story.

I start with my curiosity but this is not enough, a story like POWER OF THE DOG demands everything — I must meet my characters where they live. I cannot peer, poke or pred from the outside or they will not yield to me and the work will be flat and shallow. I have to meet them with my own grief, love, pain, with everything that I am and that they are.

Our story is set amidst extraordinary space, an ocean of space, in the sky and on the land, between the Ranch and the towns, between one person and another.

Amidst this space there is the unusual togetherness of the brothers, Phil and George. Why, where there is so much space, in the house, on the land do they still cleave together? What makes George after all this time seperate from Phil?

It's not known. But what we do know is that by the time George brings Rose home as his wife, the trouble has begun and the story is set in motion.

The story, it's shape, the way it unfolds and travels through time is THE CONTAINER.

"The transcendental will come of it's own accord when the container is strong enough" Marion Woodman

So what is the transcendant? It's that which surpasses the normal or physical human experience It's the great, deep, high reach of the story beyond the sum of it's parts. It's the capacity to awaken the psyche, to stimulate and enliven the soul. "When in doubt strengthen the Container"

The container is the story structure but I also see it as the world building of the film. By in large, the choice of locations, the designs of the building, and rooms within the buildings, to make one believable world. The story, the animals and every living being in the story, the animals and what they are wearing everyone wears where this story takes place.

A world that will be memorable and whole. With a cast costumed to define and illuminate them—

Within the container I look for the images the symbols that need to be noticed, pulled out, paid attention to.

the POWER OF THE DOG grows itself like a rope, a plaited, rawhide rope or the rope with which Peter's father hung himself and he, Peter the son, cut him down.

Rope can make all sorts of shapes, lasso's, hang men nooses, figures of eight. It can tie things together like calves to the horn of a saddle when it's time to brand or castrate or both. It can help you escape save your life like the thick fire rope with the knots tied in it at the Red Mill so you can let yourself down from the top floor to the ground in case of fire.

The lariat, the rope that Phil crafts with his clever hands at the haymaking and decides to give to Peter is rich with consequence and meaning. A lariat is a rope designed for lassoing. Catching calves or horses or perhaps in Phil's case a boy.

This rope, Phil's rope is made in front of us though we barely notice! The cow that is hung and skinned (as George drives off, yet again, to his suicide widow) this hide is stripped from an animal grown and raised on their land.

ground them. The skin heavy with fat is hung over the corral fence to dry and later be processed. Magpies land on it picking the flesh off it!

Next the skin is stretched, nailed up on the barn wall and later the hair scraped and soaked off it.

Once the skins are clean Phil cuts the skins strips, a process I want us to see when George talks to Phil about 'washing' for the Governors dinner. These strips are cut in a circular pattern around the outside edge of the skin and create the threads that the rope will be plaited from.

The weave of the rope is like the braiding of the story, the threads of Rose, George, Phil, Peter bending in and out of the story they, old lady and old Gent are fiber threads added in for colour and punctuation.

But 'rope' in Peter's world has a darkness. It did not save his father's life but ended it this darker message is already inside him when Peter collects an infected skin—in case, in case he needs it, in case he can use it. Rose has given away the other skins needed for finishing the rope. The rope is now literally tieing itself into the story.

miraculously the moment comes.

The skin Peter offers Phil is found far out on the ranch from a dead cow bleeding from it's nose, an animal Phil would never normally touch. But in the heat of the moment, a very hot moment when Peter puts his hand on Phil's arm, Phil's guard is down, he believes the boy cares for him as he has come to care for the boy.

The making of the last metre of the rope is the climatic ending of the film. A love scene, a sex scene and a poisoning. The rope, the snake growing between Phil's legs is charged for sex and death.

The mood in the barn that night is tense with anticipation, their goals could not be more different. Phil wants love Peter to kill.

All the while the cut, the broken rope of Peter's father's suicide is being made whole.

The next day feverish with Anthrax poisoning Phil leaves for the hospital. Where is the boy, Phil is waiting for Peter to come, perhaps even drive to the hospital. Phil, the finished rope in hand, finally asks George "where's the boy? George reassures Phil he will give him the rope. Now the cycle of the rope is almost complete. It means everything, but nothing as well. It's a talisman that winds us back to the

beginning of the story. Made from this land, from a cow, but plaited and woven into a sophisticated object mirroring all the complexity and cleverness of the human heart and mind. It's what humans do, craft things like the rope then the rope things. The rope do things back like hang them or in Phil's case poison him.

Death by antrax is not at all certain of the book would have it. It must have been a nail biting moment for Peter. If Phil survives Peter and Rose's time at the ranch will be over, Phil will have put 2 + 2 together and Peter and his mother will be back to poverty.

As Phil's remains are lowered into the ground, (Rose ropes again) Peter who did not go to the funeral plays like a kid with Phil's dog. Later he reads psalm 22 one Peter expects they might have read at Phil's graveside.

JANE CAMPION'S WRITINGS

THE DENT
(1988)

BIG SHELL
(1991)

BLUE SKY
(2002)

MY JOHN KEATS
(2009)

Jane Campion, April 1992.

THE DENT

(1988)

At Heathrow airport you have to move slowly up and down, up and down, through a maze of royal-blue roped corridors before you get to the end of the rope and a white line on the floor, which has written on it,

STAND BEHIND THIS LINE

People probably didn't read it, because there was also a blonde, bee-hived Customs Officer and an Indian one with a turban. The blonde woman said, "Behind the line" in an East-End voice. She had a special make-up-conserving way of speaking that kept her face still.

I was travelling to London to see my boyfriend Tim, whom I hadn't seen for five months. I really like Tim, but in the past I've had a problem keeping attracted to my boyfriends, and I was nervous that the same thing would happen with him. Lately, when I've been thinking about seeing him, I've conjured up his face and it always began with the dent between his eyebrows and filled out from there. I felt concerned that this might be the beginning of my case against him and the dent might be a sign of real dissatisfaction.

In dealing with this, I felt right out on the edge. The image of his face was probably my intuition speaking, but my intuition had its blind spots too. I was feeling in the dark and I didn't know how to interpret the dent. I know I had a pattern of becoming unattracted so this could be part of that, or it also occurred to me that it might be my real feelings, which the optimistic part of me was trying to disguise.

When I got through Customs, I went out the arrival door into another roped pen where Tim could spot me. He wasn't up against the rope like I would have been, but standing up against the back wall with a newspaper. We both felt very shy and happy. I realise now that I didn't even notice his dent.

On the Underground into London we held hands.
"Your hair has grown. It's nice."
"I've lost weight too."
"You look good."
"You look so lovely," I said, "I can't believe you're so lovely." My eyes started to fill.
"Why are you crying?"
"I don't know; because you're lovely."

His flat was one of those rented ones where absolutely everything comes with it. His wasn't the best bedroom in the house; it was the basement one and he'd made his foam day couch into a double bed. On top of the bed was a leopard-skin-patterned blanket. Everything in the room was like that but it didn't matter. The walls were white so it was quite light. I got under the leopard-skin blanket to try and sleep off the aeroplane trip. He pulled the curtains and got in beside me to keep me company. We kissed and held on to each other and I kept saying "I'm very happy," and he said, "I've missed you so much Julie, I'm so pleased you're here."

Later on he had to go to his office in Haymarket. I went with him and hung about Piccadilly until it was time to meet up.
"Do you like these glasses?" I asked. He frowned a little and looked at them. They were round and had mirrors on them.
"I don't know why I got them, I must be jet-lagged."
We both laughed; they were pretty bad. Outside the coffee shop it was still light so I put them on. He said,
"Are you going to wear them?"
There was an edge of concern in his voice.
"Well, no, not normally; it's just a bit glarey."
Anyway, I took them off. We walked along a bit, not talking, then I said,
"You hurt my feelings about those glasses."
"I think they look a bit odd. I can't see your eyes."
"You think they're ugly don't you? That's what it really is."
"Julie, honestly, wear them; I don't want to argue."
We stopped and kissed. In a way the quarrel made me feel it was real, that we weren't just playing at being in love.

On the bus home I explained to Tim how I thought the quarrel was a good sign. While I was talking he pushed the side of my hair back from my face and put his cheek there. From the surface of my cheek a strong divine warmth began to radiate. It travelled through my body as literally as a rug being slowly pulled up over me, until the whole of my body tingled, and my cheek was burning. I started to cry.
"I can't believe I feel this way. I really do love you."
I was very surprised by the tenderness I felt. It was more than I imagined I could feel and this was strange to me because I thought that things could never be more than what you'd already imagined.

On the third or fourth day, I'm not sure which now, Tim took the afternoon off work because he wanted to show me his favourite London park. I found it hard to believe that a park could ever be really interesting. It seemed to me they were ideas of nature rather than nature itself, like someone strolled along and said, "Yes, let's have a big oak here. That would be nice, a big oak," and then they'd plant it and after that other people would come along and believe it was there in a more divine way. Like the tree itself had chosen to spring up in that spot, and if they were given to making metaphors from nature, they could get the whole world very wrong.

Despite all that, I liked Holland Park a lot. First he took me around the formal part, then we went into the wood bit, which had pockets of meadow and, in one spot, rabbits hopping about. The rabbits were a shock; it was like seeing my baby plate coming alive. Tim and I held hands and while we walked I noticed that we were intuitively able to know when each other wanted to pause, and just as intuitively we knew when the other was going to move off. This impressed me as it suggested I was developing a deeper type of sympathy than had been normal for me before.

At the Park Café we bought some food and sat at a white metal table. I said, "Tim, this is really good. I feel so comfortable in my love for you." Sitting at the other tables in groups were young foreign nannies with their babies. One baby had a miniature Rolls-Royce car with a real little motor. He wasn't able to speak but he could manoeuvre it pretty well. When he climbed out of his Rolls to sit with his nanny and sip his milk, other toddlers came to look at it. The Rolls-Royce baby didn't like this. He got down from his chair and chased them off, one arm held threateningly up behind his head like he was going to hit them. By the time he had got off his seat for the fourth time to chase the children away, his Nanny pushed her thick, unbrushed hair behind her shoulder and said, "Alfie, vy don't you get in your own carr is you don't vant to let ozer tchildren play vis it."

Alfie got in his car and turned the key on its small dashboard. The baby Rolls-Royce engine made a lot of noise because it was stuck up beside a table and made all the cups clatter. 'Go forvard, go forvard', said his nanny. She roughly pushed Alfie's gear stick upwards and Alfie jolted forwards and drove right over a man's foot. The man was shabbily dressed and apologised to Alfie, pulling his foot back under the table. Alfie drove on, his hands in the ten-to-two position.

"It's like the middle ages here," I said. "There's a class of people who aren't just privileged, they're allowed to run people over. Everyone just lets them like, 'Oh there's one of those special people who drive over other people . . .' "
"Julie, he's just a baby."
"In Australia he wouldn't be allowed to get away with it. He ought to be smacked."
Tim was looking at me with a pleading expression. The sun was hitting his face from the side and complicated shadows from his hair made his face difficult for me to look at.
'Can you move; I can't see you with the sun like that.'
He moved his back to the sun and his face became clear again. I watched him as he ate, dusting sausage roll delicately from his fingertips. I had forgotten Alfie and remembered my old theme, a theme that was soon to turn about and hurt us both.
"Don't you think we're getting on well?"
Tim nodded and kept on eating. I said,
"I feel really comfortable about us; I think we are stronger for being apart, and more in love."
I waited for him to stop chewing so he could speak. When he did he said, "I'm really starving."
I said, "I feel very happy about us and I really look forward to you coming to Australia."
I smiled at Tim, but somehow I didn't feel satisfied.
"Do you feel happy about us?"
"Yes I do."
"Well, do you think it's true?"
"What?"
"I just want you to say something about it."
Tim looked at me puzzled and then went glum. For a while I thought he wasn't going to say anything, he took so long to speak.
"All right," he spoke flatly, "I think we're getting on well."
I tried to tell him he didn't look very convinced, but before I'd finished he waved his hand in front of my face and said,
"Julie I don't want to go on with this. Can't we leave it at that?"

On the way home to his flat I bought a packet of dry roasted nuts. He tried to hold my hand, but I had to keep letting go of it to eat the nuts. Anyway, I didn't like him 'waving his hand in my face' but I hadn't wanted to say so because it didn't fit with the conversation about getting on. As we continued to walk back I began to feel a prickly, hot feeling deep inside and I noticed my mouth getting tight, as if to keep the heat in. When Tim asked me if anything was wrong, I said, 'No', and I noticed the feeling got even stronger.

That night, when we went to bed I took a pile of *Face* and *Tatler* magazines from the upstairs coffee table to read. Tim was already in bed, curled up and trying to sleep. I said, "Do you mind, I want to read for a bit?" He didn't answer, he just turned over away from the light. I felt a woozy, hot feeling inside when he turned away, and kept reading my magazine. It was a father's account of his daughter's murder trial. The daughter's boyfriend had strangled her. He was a chef at a Los Angeles restaurant and she was an actress. Suddenly Tim got up.
"I'm sleeping in the lounge."
"Tim, why?"

"Try and guess."
The door did a London City Council regulation slam. 'Jesus', I said to myself. I kept looking through the magazine as if nothing had happened, but my mind was pretty worried about Tim. Why shouldn't I read in bed? We'd had enough sex already hadn't we? Why can't I look at magazines?

When I went upstairs to the lounge he was lying underneath one of the leopard-patterned blankets. He opened his eyes and watched me with an injured expression on his face. A part of me knew that if I gave him a hug it would all be over, but I didn't. Instead I sat in the opposite armchair and brought my legs up against my chest. We looked at each other coldly. There was the dent, a strange deep furrow, right between his eyebrows. It was amazing I hadn't noticed it again till now. It really was a prominent facial feature, the kind of feature that makes you wonder if the person hasn't had some sort of brain surgery, or even if the person might have had some childhood skull deformity that meant the front section never joined and they were excused from sport because they had this vulnerable soft channel that led straight to their brain. One bad knock with a bat and their brains might ooze out.

I moved from my armchair next to Tim on the couch. He blinked and his dent seemed to pulse like there was a tiny artery underneath it.
"Tim, why are you being like this?"
Tim looked at me.
"Why were you reading magazines?"
"Aren't I allowed to read?"
"It's the way you did it, you didn't even touch me."
He sat up and wrapped the blanket around him.
"I don't think you love me as much as I love you."
"Yes I do, I tell you all the time."
"That's what you *say*, but you didn't want to hold hands with me on the way back from the park. Twice you pulled your hand away."
"I was eating peanuts."
"So you preferred to eat peanuts."
"Jesus, aren't I allowed to eat or read?"

His feet were poking out from under the blanket and I noticed that his toe nails were very dirty and long. They looked like they hadn't been cleaned or cut for months.
"Don't you clip your toes?"
He held his right foot up in the air and laughed.
"Nice eh?"
"I think you should cut them, it might be why your socks smell."
"They don't smell."
"Well something smells down there… it's disturbing me."
When I said this last bit, a quaver came into my voice that surprised me, I sounded so upset.
"Okay, it's living by myself. I'm dirty. I'll clip them tomorrow."
I was crying now, and for some reason, even though I'd been mean about his feet, Tim seemed cheered up. He hugged me in a fatherly way.
"Come on Julie, I'm sorry about making a big fuss about the magazines, I just feel so in love with you and so attracted, I don't know how to behave."
"Okay," I said, still sniffling.
"Do you forgive me?" he asked.
"Alright."

We went back down to his bedroom and pushed the two half couches back together. He straightened the sheet between the two couches, tucking them firmly around the sides so as to stop them separating and leaving a gap. We got into bed and started to cuddle. He puts his lips on mine and licked them with his tongue. It didn't feel good and I realised

220

I was still thinking about his toes. I thought, "I'll just go to sleep and everything will be how it was at the park."

"Hi," he said in the morning. I turned over and stroked his arm. He smiled. There was the dent again. My eyes just couldn't stop themselves being pulled into it, like it was the only thing on his face.

"What is it?" he said, putting his hand over his eyebrows and smiling. "What's there?" He looked at me, then felt with his fingers along the dent furrow and up above it. "What's there?"

"It's nothing," I said, snuggling up to him so I couldn't see it. I felt worried: why was I making such a thing of his furrow? It's just a facial characteristic, nothing else. When I first met him, I loved burying my little finger in it. I remember telling him it was a finger warmer.

"What's the matter, Julie?"
I was standing looking up at the street from his basement room. The day was grey and I was shivering.
"I just feel so depressed. I've got all the wrong things with me."
"Borrow my black jumper, it's dry-cleaned."
I watched him take it off the hanger, out from under the plastic. His hands didn't seem to be made right, like only two of the fingers worked separately and the rest seemed to be stuck together like a cleft hoof.
"Can't you move all your fingers?"
"Yes."
He looked at me very puzzled and I thought, "He can't; he's got odd hands."
"Look, mine move like this," I said, stretching my fingers out wide and back in again. "See."
He tried the same with his, moving them in and out.
"So?"
"So yours don't move much, that's what, they're constricted."
His face was still, he was looking at his hand.
"What are you on about?"
"Don't get het up, I'm just pointing out a difference."
"No you're not, you're trying to make me feel bad about my hands."
"I don't think we should carry on with this conversation."
I got up and started dressing in my summer-weight trousers and t-shirt; over that I put his black jumper. Tim was back again with the covers pulled over his head.
"He can't face the truth," I thought. "We won't get anywhere like this."

Outside I felt much better. Looking out of the window of the Underground, I felt a strong memory of Tim come back. I remembered him wearing a suit to the beach in Perth and surfies clapping him as he walked along, in big brown fashionably orthopaedic shoes. He sat on the beach and watched me swim, holding my towel just the way I wish my father would have done, and he called me things like 'Fearless Amazon', even though the waves were not very big.

When I got back Tim was still in bed. He hadn't got up. He hadn't gone to work. He was turned away, his body in a guitar shape under the cover. The shape suggested a deep indolence, a hopelessly ingrained sensual laziness. The kind of shape you see in girlie magazines with shiny sheets over them. And all about were dirty clothes, just dropped where they were taken off. I looked at his barred, awful window and felt like I was sharing a zoo cage. Even the lake-side scene, a painting done in fuzzy airbrush style and screwed onto the wall, reminded me of the icebergs painted on the polar bear pit at the zoo.

"Did you have a good time?"
"Yeah, it was good. I found the photography gallery and bought some cards."

He nodded and turned back. I stood and watched him for a bit.
"Are you doing this because of me?"
"No, I'm just depressed." I went to the toilet and came back.
"Shall we go out for an Indian meal?" he asked.
I was standing holding onto the door looking down at him.
"No, I want to tidy up."
Tim looked disappointed. His face fell and his skin seemed to be sucked further back into the furrow.
"Are you going to wash your hair?" I asked, not looking. I was picking up dirty clothes and throwing them into two piles, his and mine.
"You don't like me, do you?" Tim got up and stood creased and naked in front of me.
"Of course I do."
"Well you act like you don't."

What does it mean that I don't like things about him? I lay in the bath, my legs floating up to the surface. When I got out of the bath, I wiped off the mirror, and noticed my face looked stiff and sullen. I was thinking, "I must stop criticizing Tim . . . Perhaps if I tell him, admit my feelings about his dent, his feet and his hands, I'll be able to get over it." As I said this, I realised that my criticisms had begun at the extremities of his body, and I felt an awful ache; a ghastly premonition had occurred to me. Somehow I had become a kind of critical virus that would not be stopped. Surely and deliberately, I could see myself working inwards, from his hands, criticizing his forearms, then his calves, knees, and down from his dent, his eyes, nose, mouth, neck. In this way I would continue until it all met somewhere in the middle and then his whole body would be finally loved dead.

At the laundromat I ate from a small packet of special corn kernels, something I imagined the West Indians ate. I started a conversation with a black guy who was doing his drying. He said London was hard. He said it was hard to make money, because only money made money. He asked if I was visiting long. "No, I've come for three weeks, really to see my boyfriend. He's going to immigrate."
"Lucky guy."
On the way back I thought, "Yes, he is lucky." I walked on a bit more and thought, "Yeah, he doesn't appreciate that."

When I got in, Tim said, "I want to show you something."
I followed him downstairs. There was something in his voice that made me a little nervous and my face went hard and solemn. He opened the door to his bedroom.
"Look at this."
He pointed to the black jumper I'd borrowed. It was lying on the bed.
"What?"
"That was cleaned when I lent it to you."
He picked it up and shook it out.
"I'm astonished at the way you treated it; it's not only creased, it's got carpet fluff all over it."

I was mad. I walked over to the far corner of his room and tapped my foot on a grey sweater he'd been wearing that was unfolded and strewn on the ground. I told him I couldn't believe he was making something of what I'd done, when I had at least folded his pullover and he hadn't even done that to his own! He said it wasn't the same thing. For one thing, the grey pullover didn't show fluff, and anyway, as far as he was concerned, it wasn't a pullover. It was such a light wool mix and had buttons that it was more of a shirt, and furthermore I had put other things on top of the pullover I'd folded, so that any good effect of the folding was ruined because the other things had pressed strange creases into it.
I shook my head.

"I can't believe all this going on about the jumpers. Jesus Christ, I'll dry clean it!"
"It's not the dry cleaning, it's what it means that concerns me."

I looked down at the two jumpers at far ends of the room, empty and formless, the arms twisted about at impossible angles. A huge wave of terrible pity washed up through me. Pity for the jumpers, pity to be in this awful London flat, pity for my cold, cruel heart. I turned away from Tim and sank on the bed, my face pressed up on his leopard-skin blanket. I started to cry. Tim left the room.

That night Tim told me he couldn't go on like this. He said he felt undermined by me, unhappy and unconfident. He was sitting at the kitchen table with a big neon light glaring down. I didn't look at him but nodded.
"Well?" he said.
"I don't know what to say. You're right, I've been really critical."
"Maybe you don't want the relationship anymore."
"No, I do want it."
"Well why don't you stop?"
"I wish it were that easy. I don't like being like this either."
"Well stop!" He yelled this.
We both looked at each other, blinking.
"Can't you try to be sympathetic to me, I'm not in control, if I could stop, I would."
"No, I can't. You just stop."

In bed we slept on far sides of the mattress, but by morning we had both rolled into the gap between the two couch pieces and were squashed together in a foam ditch. It reminded me of the big furrow between his brows, like the whole bed was his forehead and this was the dent.

I closed my eyes and bit Tim on the arm. He woke up.
"Ouch, shit Julie!"
I bit him again on the shoulder.
"Julie!"
I rolled him over and said something like, "I hate you," all the time kissing and attacking and biting him and saying other things like, "I'm going to get you now." Tim started laughing. I didn't care, I just went on biting and being very aggressive. We had sex this way and Tim got angry too and acted like he wanted whatever happened to hurt. I just thought, "Good, I don't care, it won't hurt me," but not deadly seriously; like an act, like I was acting thinking that.

The sex went on a long time, much longer than normal. When we stopped, I was really sweaty. He rolled up the sheet in a ball and mopped my back with it. 'Look at the couches,' he said. I sat up. They were about two yards apart. It was all chaos: clothes, sheets, shoes, all confused with one another. I don't really like untidy rooms, but right then I felt happy and, it seemed strange to say, even proud, like I wouldn't have minded the other people in the flat looking and seeing it.

Tim said I had probably been under a lot of stress, a lot more than I had realised and that's why I had acted strangely. We were at Holland Park again, leaning on the fence looking at the bunnies in the little enclosure. I agreed that it was probably a factor. I looked at his neck as he leant forward and thought the curvy shape of his hairline to be the sweetest, most innocent and darling sight I had ever seen. He held my hand as we walked across to the coffee shop. At the entrance we saw Alfie's Rolls-Royce, parked outside the brick wall next to the cafe. Alfie was sitting in it all alone drinking a paper cup of milk.
"There's Little Rolls-Royce'" said Tim. "Shall I spank him?"

We went on into the café, which, like last time, was full of foreign nannies and pale-faced English babies. Alfie's nanny was in there too, reading a magazine while twisting her fist-thick hair into a giant coil. While I sipped my cappuccino, I kept thinking of solemn-cheeked Alfie sitting behind the brick wall.

When we left, Alfie's nanny was still there; she'd been joined by a friend and they were talking together in French. Outside the brick wall, Alfie had gone to sleep. He'd slumped across the steering wheel like he'd had a car accident. Tim bent down next to him and shouted, "Look out!" Alfie woke up, he blinked and his top lip curled up. He got out of his car and, crying in a bleating kind of way, ran off down a path away from the café.
"Tim, he doesn't know where he is!"
"Watch this, he'll come back."
Tim tooted the little horn on Alfie's car. Alfie stopped and turned; his face went red with anger. The little spotted handkerchief around his neck stuck out in a hopeless, jaunty way.
"I'm getting his nanny."
His nanny came out around the wall with me, she saw Alfie and marched up to him. She took his hand and roughly took him back to his Rolls-Royce, so that his feet were not properly touching the ground.
"Get in, go on! Now you vait zehr and don't move."
She turned to us and shook her head in an exasperated manner. Alfie sat in his car whimpering. I bent down to him.
"Are you okay Alfie?"
I looked into his face. It was solemn and stiff, his cheeks puffed out soft and full but I didn't dare touch them. He didn't speak, maybe because he was too little to talk.

When we were walking out I said to Tim,
"What came over you, you don't do things like that?"
"I know. I don't know why I did it."

On my last night we went to an Indian Restaurant for dinner. It was Nepalese and there was a tiny Nepalese waiter who wore black flared pants, shiny from so much pressing. He must've been almost forty and when I looked over in his direction, he came running as if I had fallen over and hurt myself.
"Could I have some water please?"
"Certainly. Wiff ice?"
"No thank you."
I watched him go.
"That's who I want to be like."
"Like who?"
"Like that waiter; he's a really good, humble man."
Tim started laughing.
"Don't laugh, what's wrong with that?"

He kissed me and looked at me in a knowing way, pulling an 'ask yourself' face. As he did this, his forehead screwed up into folds and the dent between his eyebrows deepened into a deep, dark ditch. I closed my eyes but not quickly enough. The dent was there, it was back again and coming out at me like that's all there was, like it was all I could see. I could feel my face getting stiff.

We didn't make love, even though it was our last night together. Tim looked at me and said,
"What's the matter with you?"
I thought, "What is the matter with me?" and I said,
"Don't worry, I'm going to live by myself in some hut in the bush."
"Julie," said Tim, "I really love you, but I can't take this. Can't you try and be friendly?"

On the train out to Heathrow Tim said, "You know why I did that to Alfie?"

"Why?"

"Because he's got the same sort of face as you."

We looked at each other. We came out of the Underground and we were passing muddy backyards and bare trees.

"I'll get better, you'll see. It's being in London, I feel depressed here."

While we had tea at the airport cafeteria, I smiled at Tim and told him I loved him and I'd really miss him. All the time I was very careful to de-focus my eyes so they couldn't be sucked into his dent. I thought "If I can get through this, I'll have some sort of therapy when I get home. I'll get to the bottom of it and it'll be alright."

The noise and smoke in the cafeteria made me feel sick. I went very pale and my head felt dizzy. In the ladies I put my head between my legs, but I still felt sick and my head was singing. I told Tim I must be upset about leaving.

He carried my bag over to the Customs and there he held me and said, "Well, goodbye Alfie"

"Alfie?"

"Yes poor little Alfie, in her big Rolls-Royce Jumbo Jet."

As I carried my hand luggage up the rubber walkway to the aeroplane door, I thought of Alfie's Rolls-Royce and of the wheel running over the old man's foot and the way the man pulled his foot back under the table. While I thought all this, I stepped over the small crack of daylight between the articulated airport gangplank and my 747 Rolls-Royce engined jumbo jet to Australia.

BIG SHELL

(1991)

I worked at a souvenir shop during the Christmas break that sold shells. In this shop was the biggest shell I had ever seen. It would have come up to my knee and it wasn't for sale. The owner had fitted a light inside it and it sat in the front window and glowed. The colours were all colours of pink, purple-pink, cream-pink and where the shape curled inside itself the pinks became very dark, almost black.

I got this job because I didn't have any money and I didn't have the confidence to go and sell myself as an art director, especially before Christmas when everything was jolly.

A month or so ago I'd finally finished with my boyfriend. I only got the strength to do that because of this course I did. At the time, I realised all these things about myself and him, and I was very clear that the relationship was not 'an opening for possibility'. I realised that he had 'a negative conversation' about me, and my relationship with him was 'based on complaint'.

John was gone and he took his mirror. It was a door off a wardrobe that used to lean up against the wall in my room, so I could always check myself before I came in or went out. That's what got me; looking to see myself and my not being there. That's when I realised he'd gone. I went right down in a big spiral. Once I felt I was going down, I stopped trying to be bright or happy; I decided to go right on down, as down as down could go.

My buddy from the course rang me up one evening.

"Hello, this is Fran Basset, your buddy."

"Oh, you must be looking for Lou, she's not here," I lied.

"Oh right. Well could you tell Lou I just rang to find out how she was going with her commitments."

In a journal I wrote: "John, oh God, I miss you." Then I divided the page into two separate columns and wrote at the top of one column "positive aspects of being alone," and on the other "negative aspect of being alone." Under positive I wrote 'no arguments about housework.'"Then I rang up a friend.

"Hello Kay."

"Oh Lou, how are you? Still high from that thing you did?"

"Not really, I'm a bit depressed."

"Oh why?"

"Oh, you know, everything, no John, being alone. No work right now . . ."

'You've got to pull yourself out of this . . .'

"Hmmmm . . ."

"It's self indulgent . . . hold on . . ."

I listened to the sounds of her baby screaming. It seemed very distant as if it was coming from across a big green glade.

"Pull yourself together." "Shit," I thought. "I'm always doing that. No, I'm not going to this time. I'm going to fall apart."

Anyhow, I ran out of money and got this job selling shells, mostly to tourists. One American came in with slacks and runners. He looked right at me and said,

"So she-sells-seashells. You know what I want? I want that damn giant."

"Well I can't sell you that seashell, it's not for sale."

"It's good though. Huh, I bet it gets them in here."

"I don't know really. I haven't been here so long."

That afternoon a guy in a wheelchair came into the shop; he was pretty young and I guessed from the States. I like people in chairs because they remind me of my brother, though this guy was nothing like Trevor: he was a Yankee tourist with a nylon money belt and a whole pile of badges stuck to his chair.

He said, "Hi there, how ya doin'?"

After he'd looked at both sides of the shop, he said,

"That's some shell you got in yer window. Hey, you been to Bris-Bane?"

I said that I had once.

"Yeah I'm doin' some tour of the Gold Coast. I've been to Perth and Cairns. It's more economic to do Bris-Bane from Sydney, so I'm doin' it that-a-way."

"Great," I said. "Have fun."

"Yeah I hope so."

As he wheeled out I followed him and gave him my phone number. I offered to show him something of Sydney.

He said, "That's fine, 'cause I got four days in Sydney before I fly to Papua New Guinea. They got big shells there too," he added.

"I didn't know."

"Yeah I read it. They swap them for wives and things. Have a good day."

My brother Trevor was disabled from birth. He didn't like other disabled people; he called them cripples, frothers and half-wits. My brother played lead guitar in his school rock group. Beautiful, intelligent girls took turns to wheel him to school.

He's dead now. He got into drugs when he left home. First his girlfriend Vivian overdosed, then after that when he came home to live, Mum found him with a blue plastic bag over his head, tied around his neck. Mum thought he was joking at first. But Trevor was dead.

Trevor told me he was a great fuck because he was very still. He said stillness is what the 'rooters' never learn. He said sensitive girls appreciate the aesthetics of still sex, it made them feel powerful and it was much more subtle and erotic.

Vivian and I went shoe shopping one Saturday. She told me that once Trevor peed on her by mistake, and because she laughed, he won't let her near him, not ever again. She was pretty far gone by then, very thin. I'm not sure, but I believe it's possible she got their dope from prostitution. When I did the course, I stood up and shared about Trevor. I put my hand up and the leader read out my name tag.
"Yes Louise."
I stood up and an assistant ran crouching towards the edge of my row. He passed the microphone along the row until I could take it.
"I'm very said because I never told my brother how much I loved him."
"Is your brother dead?"
"Yes."
"And you didn't tell him."
"No."
"Good, I got it. Are you complete about that?"
"Yes."
"Thank you Louise."
Everybody clapped and I handed the microphone back along the row until the crouching assistant took it and ran crouching back.

"Lou, guess who this is."
I had no idea, but I could hear lots of noise in the background.
"Sorry, who is it?"
"You gotta guess."
"I can't. Who is it?"
"Now come on try . . ."

I put the phone down and went back to watching my television set, which I have to keep my toe on to get a good picture. The phone rang again with the same long-distance peeps.
"Hello Lou, it's me, Dale, remember? I'm up in Surfer's Paradise."
"Oh right, why didn't you say?"
"I was just playing about. I guess you weren't in the mood, huh?"
"Not really. How is it?"
"It's O.K. No I'm kiddin', it's wild! I get back tomorrow afternoon; so Lou, you wanna go sight-see?"

Dale arranged to meet me outside the shell shop. He was late, so I amused myself by looking at our big shell. I tried to imagine the size of the creature that lived inside it. It must have been very, very big. A huge, boneless, slug with grey snail-like skin that could contract and expand as it moved itself along.

When Dale wheeled up, he was wearing a t-shirt that had a shapely woman's bottom drawn on it and underneath in black letters:
WHAT A BUMM-ER Gold Coast.
"Hi there, how yer doin'?"
I couldn't take my eyes off the t-shirt.

"That t-shirt, Dale, is horrible."
"Yeah, it's bad taste, huh'"
"Yes it is."
"I tell you, there's worse."

I was starting to feel depressed about being with someone in a t-shirt like that. Dale started to look depressed too.
"It's a joke t-shirt, Lou, a joke."

It was after our Opera House tour, after Dale had put a jersey over his t-shirt, (despite the heat and his sweating), that I realised I was in love with him. I decided he was the most courageous man I had ever met. My love eyes focused in on his brown eyes, carefully avoiding his hair, which wasn't washed and anyway, didn't have any style and slid down to his lips, which were very young looking. He was sipping a cappuccino and, while he told me about his South American tour, I started to imagine him undressed. I thought about his legs and how I could gently lift them white and thin onto the bed. He'd probably have a colostomy bag and I'd slip that lower down in the bed under the sheet. Then I'd touch him slowly all over, possibly the first person to ever do that, and he'd lie there and maybe even cry. Then we'd maybe make the slow still sex that Trevor had talked about. That was if he could have erections; otherwise maybe we'd just kiss. I wasn't asleep to the idea that this might be some sex ode to my dead brother. But Dale was not Trevor.

Dale didn't seem to know self-pity. When I told him I'd been depressed because my boyfriend and I had broken up, he looked sad because I looked sad, but mostly puzzled.
I said, "You've never been depressed?"
"Nope."
"Are you sure? Not ever? What about when you were a teenager?"
"Nope."
"What about school sports day?"
"Nope, I just stayed home an' watched the box."
"You can't ever remember being depressed?"
"Nope."

Dale said he had to go because his hostel had a curfew. I said I'd drive him. In the car I said,
"Why don't you come home and have a look at my flat?"
"Gee I'd like that, but I'll miss the curfew."
"Well you could stay the night. I've got a sofa bed."
He took a while to answer.
"I guess you're a bit lonely."
"Yes, I am a bit," I said, irritated, "but that's not why I asked you."
By the time I got to my place Dale seemed tired.

"Lou, what floor are you on?"
"Oh shit. Oh Dale I can't believe I didn't think of it."

The challenge of the steps seemed to cheer Dale up. He gave precise and encouraging instructions to me. He kept on saying. "I'm not heavy," and laughing. I thought of Robert de Niro in *The Mission* dragging all those things up the waterfall and I started to believe I'd get my salvation out of this. I didn't know why Dale wasn't worried. I honestly, twice nearly lost him. He said, "Oh, oh, close."

When we both had a glass of wine in our hands and I'd had a shower, I decided to tell Dale I loved him.
'Really?' He looked puzzled, then raised his eyebrows and said,
"Gee."
I said he could sleep on the sofa if he liked but I'd love it if we could sleep together.

"Lou I'm not sure."

"Well, do you like me?"

"Yes, I do, but you're quite a bit older than me."

"Yes, I know that. Nine years"

"Let me think about it a moment."

"Are you scared about something?"

"No."

"O.K."

I moved a bit closer to him and said, "Well Dale, I'm going to bed now, so I'll put down the sofa. You'll have to move back because it fills this space here, and then you can choose where you'd prefer to sleep."

Dale wheeled into the toilet, where I guess he was emptying his bag. I heard the toilet flush, so I supposed that's what he was up to. When he came out he wheeled into my bedroom.

"Wow, dim lights, satin cover and everything, Lou."

By the time I got to the doorway he was looking up at the wall reading one of my affirmations.

"Dale, I feel a lot of love for you, but it's quite okay by me that you don't. What's not okay is that you treat me, my love and my bedroom as a joke. So out you go to the sofa-bed; go on, you and your horrible t-shirt."

"Hey Louise, can't I sleep in here?"

"Not like that. No."

"Well. I'm sorry. You know Lou it would be a real adventure to sleep here with you and, what the heck, that's what I'm here for."

"You're a jerk Dale. I don't know why I said I love you."

"Lou, I love you, too. It's just not how I was expecting it."

I calmed down and sat on the bed looking at my toes. He wheeled close and put a hand on my leg. He didn't just leave it there he kept parting it in a nervous way, until it started to grate and I held it still.

"I don't mean to hurt yer feelings Lou, but I never thought my first girl would . . . well, have wrinkles." Then he started laughing like it was really hilarious.

 "Oh, what did you expect?"

"Nothing really. Heck, I'm a regular guy. I just wanted some girl with smooth long hair, brown or blonde, who looks hot in jeans . . . Hey, what are yer doin'?"

I had taken hold of his chair and was wheeling it out to the sofa bed.

"Lou, don't!" He was mad. Then he put the brakes on and I couldn't shift it at all.

"Well wheel yourself."

"Thank you, I will!"

I went back to my bedroom, closed the door and turned out the light. I lay on the bed stiff with anger. I must have fallen asleep because I woke up to Dale, in his chair, already parked next to the bed. He spoke in a soft, almost little boy's voice.

"Lift me into your bed, Lou.

He had taken his clothes off and just had on his BUMM-ER t-shirt. His legs were white and very thin. Not so much legs, more like a tadpole's tail, or the see-through legs they first develop before they become frogs. They felt dead because they were so cold and lifeless. He was heavy, but I could hold him, and when he put his arms around my neck to help me, I kissed him on the cheek. I laid him down on the bed and asked him where he wanted to put the bag.

"Oh, just down beside me thanks."

I kissed him on the lips this time, and he kissed back so hard I couldn't really feel a thing.

"Softly Dale."

He softened up and we kissed for a bit more, then he started crying; big, gulpy, painful tears.

"Dale, let's stop. Just relax and go to sleep."

I cradled him in my arms and, half sobbing, he snuggled his head up towards my chest and hungrily, like an animal, he started to suck.

"Ouch, Dale, gently!"

He was in a kind of animal over-drive. I liked it, even though it felt strange, like being intimate with a different species.

I looked down at his face; it was all screwed up. I felt a lump deep in my chest, a definite physical presence, that painfully and slowly started to move upwards until I felt this same lump in my throat. The lump rested there a while, before starting my lips off quivering and my eyes blinking and then, as the lump came into my mouth and finally out into the world, my body started shaking and a whole series of little gulps and cries came up out of me. I was panting and blubbing and holding onto Dale, stroking his head, thinking of him as a lame frog who was magically gifted to save me from my unhappiness.

It must have been very late, may be 3 am. Dale was still licking and sucking, making little, 'Ohh, ohh, ohh!' moaning sounds; then he stopped and got very serious.

"Touch my penis, Lou. You'd know: is that hard enough?"

"Don't worry about it. I'm not even on the pill."

"Just tell me though; is that hard enough?"

I did touch it and it wasn't really hard; sort of gumbi hard.

"It feels nice."

He made another strange sound and was still.

"What is it?"

"I gotta stop this."

"What's up?"

"Nothing. I just gotta stop, that's all."

He pulled his BUMM-ER t-shirt down and fitted the sheet around himself.

In the morning when I woke Dale wasn't there. I lay still and listened. In the next room I could hear Dale moving. I found him on the floor next to the sofabed with his jeans halfway up his legs. He didn't take any notice of me and continued pushing each dead leg further down the jeans.

"Do you want tea?"

He just kept on.

"Dale, do you want tea?"

"No thanks."

I went through to the kitchen to start my breakfast. I couldn't work out what he was about. Watching him from the kitchen he looked odd and deformed. A baby with hairy arms.

"Dale tell me what I can do to help you."

His face was so stiff he couldn't talk. I went over to him and knelt beside him.

"What's going on? Why are you so silent?"

Dale didn't look at me.

"Shall I get your chair?"

He nodded. I went into the bedroom to fetch it for Dale but I couldn't work out how to get it out of gear.

"Sorry Dale, how do you get this thing moving?"

"I'll do it."

I went back to the kitchen and made myself a peppermint tea. Dale turned himself over and began dragging himself along the floor to my bedroom. His legs rocked to and fro making skid marks on the carpet. I waited for him to get to my room then followed him in there.

"Can I help you into it?"

"Yeah."

I supported his weight around my neck and hoisted him up over the chair.

"What's going on with you Dale?"

He fussed about with his chair turning levers.

"Silly," I said, ruffling his hair. He moved his head away from my hand.

"I gotta call a taxi. I'm on a city tour this morning."

He dialled a number and looked down at the telephone table.

"I don't wanna miss on it; this tour goes all over: Bondi, the Zoo, Centrepoint Tower."

"I could've dropped you off Dale."

"Thanks, but I'm in a hurry and I don't wanna interfere with you."

When the taxi came, I helped the driver with Dale and the stairs. I took a kitchen chair and put it down on the landing. Then the driver carried Dale down the steps and put him on the chair. We went back up and together we carried Dale's chair to the very bottom. The driver went back up the steps to the landing and carried Dale back down to his own chair. It seemed impossible that I had, last night, hauled Dale and his chair up the two flights of stairs all alone.

"Have a good tour, and Dale, give me a call."

"Okay."

From my front door I watched him being lifted into the taxi. I couldn't hear, but I could see him leaning forward and talking and I could see the driver leaning back, nodding and talking animatedly. They were getting on very well.

I rang the shell shop and told them I couldn't come in, then I cleaned up the flat and went back to bed. I slept till the afternoon. When I woke up I telephoned the shell shop. No one had rung. I started to write Dale a letter. By 12 pm he hadn't rung and I was still trying to get the letter right. When I went to bed I could see Dale's drag marks on the carpet. When Trevor was alive, we had those marks all up and down our hall.

Before work at the shop, I took my letter to his hostel. It was early, 8 am, so I just left it at the desk. The girl there said she'd make sure he got it. I wish now I'd gone up and given it to him myself. I can't believe that if he got the letter, he wouldn't have contacted me.

The day before I left the shell shop I had a dream about the big shell. I dreamt that Dale was inside it and all I could see of him was his thin legs. I was talking to him but he didn't answer. In my dream I wasn't sure he could hear from inside the shell.

On Sunday I left the shell shop for good. The shell was definitely a giant, but nobody could possibly fit in it. Not even a child or a baby.

BLUE SKY

(2002)

A memoir of grief
Inspired by the events of September 11, 2001

On September 11, 2001, I woke early at 7.30 am in my Los Angeles hotel room, got up and fed a VHS tape into my TV. The television hummed into life and before the video began a news item played. It was New York City and what was happening looked like an atom bomb had exploded. Perhaps I was watching a news section inside a movie or even a mocumentary? I glanced at the banner running along the bottom of the broadcast, finding what I was seeing hard to believe. It read however, "CBS News, New York City." What I was in fact watching was the first of the World Trade Center towers collapsing.

I rang my friend in her room, waking her up. "You won't believe this. Turn your television on. Something serious has happened in New York City." I went to her room, 721. The empty corridors of the hotel seemed suddenly ominous. Together we sat on the end of the bed in our silk dressing gowns, mine electric blue, hers olive green, and watched.

We saw the towers fall, people looking, people being carried out dead, tiny people falling from windows like dolls, head first. They didn't, however, show the body parts of the burning people that eyewitnesses said were everywhere, too horrible to describe.

And then the black silhouetted plane went into the second World Trade Center tower, again and again, exploding all day long on more and yet more angles as people delivered their home-video material to the newscasters.

As I saw the first person falling, streaming head first down the side of the tower, I realised I didn't know and no-one knew what was going to happen now or even ever. The man alive in the air was already a body, a dead body, the aeroplane was about to become a missile and the two tallest twin buildings in America were rubble.

This is the problem. It's now a month later, over a month since the 24 hours of television spectacle "Attack on America." A month since I absorbed the image of the two aeroplanes embedded in the country's two tallest buildings. And I am still in shock.

I have been taken hostage, my psyche trapped in amazement, as if I myself swallowed the aeroplanes. I wait to explode. But it doesn't happen, nothing happens. Just the little black plane and the explosion, over and over, insistently separating me from the compassion and feeling, human feeling for all the dead, the frightened, the grieving, the motherless, the fatherless and the Afghani innocents daily facing a justice meant for someone else.

I take myself back to the scene of the crime. I imagine the roof for a while. The young man on the roof, talking to a friend on his mobile, searching for water. Next I imagine those heated concrete stairs, dark and parched, the choking, the panic, and the people, all the people, and I count. Am I counting people? Yes. It's a gesture towards meaning.

In some way I am wondering if even the time it takes to count 5,000 will help me understand. I begin: 1, 2, 3, 4, 5, 6,... At 180 I start to sob, not from compassion but from frustration. I can't keep count. I can't mentally multiply tragedy. Once again I am too overwhelmed by the sheer pornographic spectacle of the disaster to feel for it.

And then it happens quite without plan: my mind drifts to the little black plane, its stop-frame movement and the better-than-average, movie-styled explosions, but this time I remember past it to the sky that day. The brilliant blue sky, cloudless, heavenly, limitless, eternal.

I am not a novice at grief. I had a son eight years ago who died on his eleventh day. A baby son we wanted to call Jude or Shelley, but when we realised he might die, my husband and I called him Jasper after the George Burrow war poem "Lavengro." The sky during those eleven days was that blue of the sky behind the 727 on the eleventh of September, and the explosion that went off in my life as he died ended everything as it was, as it had been, forever.

The explosions made my heart beat and feel and I wept so, I didn't believe I could bear it. Wave upon wave of sadness. People asked me how my baby was; my breasts leaked milk; my stomach still stuck out so some people didn't know and asked if I was pregnant.

I looked in amazement at ordinary people who crossed a road, shopped, chatted, picked through the apples for a good one. I sobbed when I watched Aboriginal women talk of their land being taken, of their babies stolen. I cried for all who died anywhere and everywhere. I was grateful when friends invited me to sit at their table, while they laughed, joked and ate, reminding me of life, eternal life and the old days of the old blue skies.

Grieving is a business like anything else. But when I was grieving, there wasn't anything much that was helpful said about it. I read C. S. Lewis's grief journal, written after his wife died, on which the film *Shadowlands* was based. I read about Elizabeth Kübler-Ross's five stages of grief. I read medical articles about the death of babies and the prognosis of recovery for the mothers. It was not good, and it also outlined the probable breakdown of the marriage. And so it went on, distractingly, fulsomely and bitterly. I cried, I sobbed every day for six months.

My sister suggested a counsellor. I rang one in London but I didn't like the sound of her voice and I couldn't imagine that if I began to describe my grief I would ever finish. It was so big, so encompassing, so without end that to talk about it was to be re-burnt, re-wounded. My story in itself seemed dangerous, hopelessly leaking inky despair. So I stayed trapped in my ghastly, ghostly memories of when I first saw my husband's face grey-white with tears springing from his eyes like a cartoon character, 'Our baby's fitting. The doctor's say he's got brain damage.' The baby's last gurgling painful breaths and hours later, in my arms, his baby body with its golden downy hairs turning black.

These images haunted me day after day, month after month. After an exhausting and passionate six months, I tried another counsellor. I made, not very hopefully, a two-hour appointment. The day of the appointment, though I never would have believed it, marked a remarkable new beginning.

The process was very simple, almost invisible in its naturalness. My counsellor, Win Childs, took me through the story of Jasper's short life and, while I wanted to tell her about the things that haunted me, like the moment I heard he was terribly brain damaged or the horrifying blackness of his skin, she continually and gently steered me back to a day-by-day, even-handed account of events. "And then what happened?" "You invited your friends to come in?" "And how was that?" "Okay. They were wonderful, they dropped everything." "So they really were able to support you." "So what happened when you knew your baby was unable to live, what did you do then?"

I told her that when my baby was clearly going to die, I was encouraged to take him out of the humidicrib, something I couldn't believe possible. My shocked mind had me believing that he belonged to the hospital. He was not my baby. But that night, a patient nurse whose face I can remember even now, helped me make Jasper my own. I could do much more than peer at him in his little Perspex crib. Gently she asked if I would like to put the baby on my chest. "Yes I would," but I didn't know how to make it possible. I didn't know how to undress a baby, let alone one with all those tubes. "I can do it," she said. So one night, the most romantic of my entire life, my baby slept naked on my chest as a candle flickered and he and I floated in and out of consciousness. I stroked his head and held his hand. I fell in love. It was just in time; twenty-four hours later he was dead.

There were moments, hours even, I realised, of incredible spiritual intimacy, both with my baby's delicate hovering presence and, ten days after his death, a strange embodiment, an absolute, definite, spiritual ecstasy, in which for two hours I experienced a psychic inhabiting of myself by my baby as Jesus. While the imagery was Christian, the sensation was purely energetic and transformational, a tremendous excitement as if every cell was alive with a strange, perfect, full quietness, a grace.

And so I began to see past my personal horror, to appreciate the kindness, the good and the beauty that had arisen during and after my tragedy.

Tragedy brings suffering; it also brings the meaning of our lives closer to us, the reality of death and loss and eventually our own deaths. It shows us the value of people to each other, their capacity to comfort and show kindness to the suffering. These are the riches of grieving.

From the accounts I have read in newspapers and seen on television, New York City has risen in just such a way to support and comfort the suffering and grieving survivors. Many have commented that they have never witnessed so much kindness in the once proudly tough city.

It's strange for me to realise I had so long helplessly cleaved to those images of shock, both in my baby's death and in the events of September 11, disallowing anything else to emerge.

My baby died and nothing will make that good. Just as the terrorists did hijack those four planes causing the deaths of perhaps 5,000 people that can only be a disaster, a tragedy. But in my baby's case, what happened during and after his death was the common but strange miracle of my awakening, the expanding, deepening and softening of my humanity. It was a gift of profound proportions and the cost for me at the time was piteously outrageous: the death of my only child.

It's eight years since Jasper's death; a time within which I had another child, a beautiful daughter, and also in which my marriage did break up. But what has persisted after his death is not the horror but my awakening, my increased capacity for feeling and compassion.

Compassion does not come cheaply, as the people of New York City know. Fantasies of retaliation are inevitable, but they keep our humanity separate from us. This is why the terrorist attack on New York City is so challenging. Redemption is not won by way of revenge or even justice. Justice after tragedy is the tiring grind towards a proper conclusion, and if it is done well, then there is dignity in completing the exercise. But very often justice is not well performed and new problems are laid over the top of the old. No, the unique possibility after tragedy is that it be well managed, that kindness, help and gentleness be present, and through this our humanity is confirmed and enlarged.

For me, the greatest irony is not that humanity has power, it is that humanity has so much power. The world's great prophets—Abraham, Jesus Christ, Buddha and Mohammed—deliver us to our humanity, but poor scholars of the prophets, like bad interpreters of poetry, have delivered themselves to some very unexpected conclusions. The humanity of Jesus Christ and Mohammed was not meant to be used as justification for destruction; it was to be found afresh in each of our hearts. To defend a prophet of love with hatred and death is a mistake. Jesus Christ and Mohammed are not literally alive to defend but they live again when we feel their inspiration in our hearts, and that inspiration is full of compassion.

Today as I look at the sky, clouds are skidding through it. Some are big with grey underbellies threatening rain, but the blue patches are that deep bright blue like that sky behind the World Trade Center's towers, and that same blue sky of baby Jasper's eleven days. That sky is the air we breathe in and out, in and out, exactly the same for all people. The single thing we can be sure of in our lives. For when it stops, as it did for my baby, life is over.

To me, America and the world have a challenge in replying to the tragedy of September 11. Justice is required, but if it cannot be justly done, then it must be admitted and explained. Killing innocent, undefended Afghanis as a political display of justice or frustration at not being able to capture the actual perpetrators is a crime.

"Life is sweet, Jasper. There's day and night, Jasper, both sweet things. There's sun, moon and stars, brother, there is likewise a wind on the heath. Who would wish to die?"

MY JOHN KEATS

(2009)

I would not have read Keats's poems if I had not been avoiding adapting a book for the screen where the protagonist was a creative writing teacher. The thought was that before proceeding with my script I should enlarge my knowledge of English poetry and literature. It was on this account that I bought a biography of Keats by Andrew Motion and set about reading it. It was a very big book and I really could not escape learning quite a bit about John Keats and his poems. I worked studiously through the first half of the biography, amazed at Keats's insights and emerging philosophy and reading and rereading Motion's analysis of his early poems. Nothing prepared me for the last third. Here Motion outlined a love affair unparalleled for its touchingly detailed and weepingly tragic proportions. Almost all evidence of the love affair came from one primary source: Keats's own letters to the girl he loved. These were no ordinary letters but the staggeringly honest outpourings from one of the youngest and greatest of the English romantic poets. I still today remember finishing the biography in the blue attic room I then used as a study. I remember reading as the afternoon turned into evening, then night, sobbing pitifully as I came to the sorrowful end of Keats's life and his love affair.

For me it is a story more romantic and sad than *Romeo and Juliet* for being true. She eighteen years old, 'unformed, frisky and quick tongued', a diligent student of fashion, and he a twenty-three-year-old orphaned poet. Many things were in their favour: depth of feeling, joined hearts, steadfastness and a shared house, while much else conspired against them: Keats's lack of financial success and his bad health. The engaged Fanny and Keats were finally separated as Keats took his last chance for a cure in Rome. This last hope was unrealised and Keats, at twenty-five, died of consumption in his young friend Severn's arms.

Intrigued, I bought and began to read Keats's poems and his collected letters. I drifted into wondering if I could somehow tell his story on film, only to shake myself. Nobody really reads poetry anymore, but the cruellest blow to my hope was simply that while I was reading the poems I didn't completely understand them, or, in the case of the long poems *Endymion* or *Hyperion*, I didn't know the classical references. How could I make a film about Keats if I didn't understand poetry?

I didn't give up, but nor did my ambitions harden. Two years later, when I took a four-year sabbatical break from filmmaking, I found myself daydreaming in a soft and wafty way of Keats and Fanny. I would sit in a paddock by the Colo River with a rag-tag collection of horses while I made coffee on a little burner. The sun's warmth felt like a kiss. Life slowed down: a breeze coming across the paddock arrived as an event. As I sat across a log sipping my coffee, the horses gathered around. One day a pregnant mare stayed after the others had drifted off and finally, with all the tenderness a hoof could afford, she carefully widened the opening of my bag and peered inside. I sat next to the mare, and started to read Keats's poems to myself. I read "Ode to Psyche" with its vivid description of the open poetic mind, also "Ode on Indolence," where Keats championed and wrote of the dreamy, drifty state I was enjoying:

Ripe was the drowsy hour;

The blissful cloud of summer-indolence
Benumb'd my eyes; my pulse grew less and less

Sometimes I read a poem and felt I had taken in the meaning, only to realise I had not understood it and had in fact mistaken the meaning, and would then feel quite a fool. Fool or not, actual meaning or not, the seduction by words, rhythm, atmosphere and intimacy had begun. I was loving that these words, sounds and drifts of meaning could be joined like daisy chains, like streams to rivers, like whispers that could, in Keats's hands, describe me to myself and all the while have a sensuous and delicious presence that played on my sensations.

As I read Keats's letters (he spelt badly like me), I came across his theory of negative capability: an endorsement of mystery, of developing your capacity to accept mystery without 'irritable searching after fact and reason'. I began to realise that perhaps poetry is not so much in need of understanding as loving, or being enchanted, seduced, intrigued or awed. Like eating something delicious: you don't need to know how it was made; all you need to do is enjoy it.

My journey with Keats has been longer, deeper, more intimate and more sustained over the last few years than my relationships with even my best friends. I have read his life story, I have read his poems, I have read his letters, amongst which are the thirty-two surviving letters and notes he wrote to his beloved Fanny Brawne. I have read her letters. I have lain around on couches and beds, at a beach house, a river house and a mountain hut, dreaming about the two and a half years of Fanny and Keats's brief but intense time together. Then I wrote the screenplay, *Bright Star,* based on their love affair. I know as much about those two and a half years of his life as almost anyone can. I have lent myself to imagining how things might have happened, how Keats might have first met Fanny. By thinking about all the practical aspects of their relationship and their lives I realised it was possible that Fanny may have actually slept in what was to become Keats's bed while he and his best friend Brown were away in Scotland. Also, when Fanny's family moved in to share the house with Brown and Keats, Fanny and Keats may have slept only a wall apart. I have been to Keats's house, Wentworth Place in Hampstead, I've walked the Heath and the streets of Hampstead where Keats would have walked and also several times visited the room where he died in the house (now a museum for Keats, Shelley and Byron) next to the Spanish Steps in Rome. I've looked up at the ceiling above his deathbed and seen the painted daisies he joked about to Severn, already growing over him.

I got more confident with his poems, declaring "Ode to a Nightingale" my favourite poem in the world. It has the best of Keats's immediacy, written in one sitting under a plum tree. It is a sustained, brilliant meditation on an actual nightingale in a spring garden. As natural as thought, it describes thought but it is laced with links and soft rhymes of immense grace, delight and depth. It is full of his desire for happiness and his grief for its fleeting nature:

> Now more than ever seems it rich to die,
> To cease upon the midnight with no pain,
> While thou art pouring forth thy soul abroad
> In such an ecstasy!

Five years later, *Bright Star,* based on Keats's and Fanny's love affair, has now been made into a film and I have heard almost a hundred little girls auditioning for the role of Fanny's sister Margaret, reciting by heart the opening lines of *Endymion*:

> A thing of beauty is a joy for ever:

Its loveliness increases; it will never
Pass into nothingness; but still will keep
A bower quiet for us, and a sleep
Full of sweet dreams, and health, and quiet breathing.

I was afraid of how the girls would manage the poetry. I imagined that they would perhaps be intimidated by the meaning and the unfamiliar words and that they would speak too quickly or garble the quotes. But as each girl recited the poem, she became transformed: the words seemed to find gravity and force, a shape and clarity within each of them. When later they spoke of their pets, their brothers and sisters, the glow dimmed to good behaviour and cliché. It was similar when auditioning for Fanny and Keats: all the actors were mesmerising when reciting the poems—something I wasn't expecting.

A friend of mine told me that her mother, now in her nineties and diminished by dementia, quoted, "O what can ail thee, knight-at-arms, Alone and palely loitering?" and then asked repetitively, "What is it I am saying? Where is it from?" The poem is lodged inside her, happy as a bee continuing to hum, despite her confusion.

My film journey with Keats ended the day we finished filming in Italy in June 2008. We re-enacted a version of Keats's coffin being carried from his lodgings, across the Spanish Steps and into the waiting funeral carriage before clattering along the empty morning streets, along Via Giulia, on its way to the Protestant cemetery.

After we had celebrated the end of our shoot, a few of us made the journey to the cemetery and, finally after all this time—a century or two for Keats and six years for me—I was standing as near to Keats's mortal remains as I ever could be. Cats of all kinds strolled amongst the graves and along walls. An old tomcat curled his tail around Keats's gravestone, rubbing his battered head back and forth. Someone had left a tiny souvenir bear with a red t-shirt on the grave and our designer scooped it up, explaining to the bear (and to Keats) that she would take it to her daughter in Australia. Behind the headstone was a bunch of rotting, cellophane-wrapped flowers. I knelt and kissed the grave. I felt the sun on my back, the cool of the stone; I remember the bright waxy new foliage in shadow and speckled sun, and all my many complicated human feelings and thoughts were all together there with me at Keats's grave.

Keats's poems were my portals into poetry, and his life and letters staged for me a revived creative relationship with myself as well as faith in the divine; there is no other explanation for his best poetry. The beautiful human Keats opened himself, he was "a bright torch, and a casement ope at night, to let the warm love in!" Perhaps I will be ninety-three and mumbling,

> Darkling I listen; and for many a time
> I have been half in love with easeful Death,
> Call'd him soft names in many a musèd rhyme

And if so, I hope I will savour it in my mouth and ear; I hope I will continue to enjoy this pathway Keats has opened into my senses, my soul and my imagination, a portal to the human heart.

"Scattered Memories"

By Holly Hunter
(2013)

My audition for *The Piano*.

I met Jane in 1991 in Santa Monica, California, in a hotel on the beach. I came in wearing a long green-lace dress to give myself a feel of the era, and I had prepared a half-hour tape of my piano playing to leave with her. She had such gorgeous hair and was immediately intimate in the way only Jane can be. She had her video camera and wanted me to simply talk through the opening and closing voice-over monologues from the movie. I had taken some dialect lessons from Carla Meyer, a fabulous coach in LA, to get in the vicinity of the Scottish sound. So Jane and I sat on this living room couch, and she shot and directed the two speeches while we talked together. I wonder if she still has that tape? Jane captures something about wonder and excitement when you meet her. You want her to fasten her eyes on you; you want to fasten your eyes on her; then there's a lot of laughing.

I left that meeting with a contact high. Then I didn't hear from her for at least a month. (Low point.) Then a telegram (those were the days) arrived that said she kept thinking of me as "Ada." (Oh shit.) I knew she was traveling through Europe meeting with some ridiculously gifted and beautiful actresses there. And I knew the role had been conceived visually as a tall, imposing reed of a woman, but for me that was inconsequential. Her height had nothing to do with her potency. About another month after that telegram, she called. I was living in a very empty house in Santa Monica at that time. I remember taking the call on the kitchen floor where she offered me the part and where I stayed for the remainder of the night, getting drunk solo on a bottle of Dom that had been waiting in my refrigerator for a moment no less momentous than that. Laughing, crying, laughing, crying, laughing for a few hours.

Shortly after—within days—my piano began to stalk me, haunt me from the living room, "You can't play me for shit." I did a stall dive from elation to depression as the weight of all I did not know came to live in the base of my neck, where it burrowed in and lifted my shoulders to just under my ears. My shoulders remained in that position for the entire preproduction phase, until I hired a massive man to come in with a jackhammer and break up the concrete. Michael Nyman would mail me music, much too late for my liking. He had no real comprehension of the impediments in my learning process to playing his beautiful pieces. I had played windowsills as a child for a couple of years until my parents caught on and bought me an actual piano. I had a giant passion, an enormous appetite for the piano that lasted from my early childhood into adulthood, but no real chops. I slugged it out on the bench for five to seven hours a day. My living room wood floor was pockmarked with the imprints of the stiletto heels my piano teacher wore as she paced behind my bench and stood in sentry over my hands as I stumbled around the handwritten compositions by Nyman.

I was having a less morose experience with the sign language. In Europe in the 1850s, there was no official language, only "home" languages, created by any community that had one or more deaf or deaf/mute members. So my ASL teacher and I had freedom, and we had fun. We could also make up the actual sentences my character was speaking, so we authored her voice to a loose degree, but in a language secretly known only to her and myself.

I chose an Emily Brontë poem to recite to Flora at bedtime. And then I would send Jane periodic videos to show how it looked on my hands. It was a very free-spirited process.

Once I arrived in New Zealand, though, I almost had a nervous breakdown when I was introduced to the piano I was actually going to be playing in the film. Of course, it was built in the year 1850—a Broadwood—and the deterioration was complete. It had a muffled, strangled sound, like a dying animal. Many keys didn't work. Strings were broken. Any intermediate pianist knows that if you play on a superior instrument, you get exponentially better. Unfortunately, the opposite is true with a lousy piano. Jane and Jan Chapman, the brilliant producer, employed immediate solutions: they had as much of the Broadwood's insides rebuilt as was possible, and they made a pact with me that the piano would live wherever I was, from the time of preproduction all the way through to the end of the shoot. We moved around constantly during shooting, so the Broadwood would be transported from one apartment, then to the set, then back to that apartment, then to another location, where the process would be repeated, with tunings happening after each move. It was laborious and expensive, but worth it. I grew fond of the sound and the feel.

Jane likes to establish, from the first second, an intimate thing with her actors. She likes to hang out on a bed and talk about our lives, and silly things, and our first impressions of scenes—what the characters might want from one another. She likes to go get a flat white at the coffee shop and then take a walk or a swim. And just spend time joking around and sharing stuff. We talked about the sex scene between Harvey and me, and we staged the scene ourselves, feeling quite proud about the clever solutions we'd created. Then Harvey showed up and told us all about it. We said "Aye-aye, sir," and the scene is much more the way Harvey saw it, but, of course, all through the musky filter of J. C.'s lens. She loves to rehearse and make the rehearsal hall a real destination—comfortable furniture scattered around, lunch, coffees, big windows, lots of light, a few primitive props, maybe, but mainly a positive vibe and a place for people to congregate and feel comforted. No hotel conference rooms for her. It introduces the actors to a feeling of stretching out, of luxuriating, even. It's safe here, you can try stuff and fail and it's OK. Actors as comrades. She doesn't do read-throughs of the movie. You take it one scene at a time, and talk it through, improvise, stage it casually, then chuck that out and try a new idea. Play musical chairs, Simon Says, do a talent show, whatever comes up. People start singing . . . I don't know.

The thing about Harvey is that he's perhaps the most present actor I've ever worked with. When Harvey is looking at you, you are seen. When Harvey is listening, you are heard. No bullshit. He responds to what is real. Over the years, I've missed him. He is a rare jewel. And he's got a great sense of humor in his work, his characters. And humility. He's able to combine entitlement and humility—that's a rare cocktail. Harvey knows how to make it, shake it. His vulnerability kills me. And his laugh.

Anna was a one in a million. How did I get so lucky? We hooked up; it was a natural thing. Loving her was like drinking water. Her talent was extraordinary and has survived the transition into adulthood—treacherous waters that the careers of most child actors don't survive. She was utterly natural in front of the camera. Nothing was lost in her childish/motherly portrayal. Because sometimes Flora felt like the parent. And Anna could handle it all. But mainly she was made of love.

Sam Neill is gorgeous. His wisecracking asides are adorable. He is the ambassador at any dinner table. I want Sam to preside, please! He was able to play Stewart in a way that brought the boy to the fore. You saw that in him and could forgive him his trespasses. After all, he just wanted to be loved, too. He didn't play Stewart as a psychotic but as a man who was out of his element, which required a subtle touch, and that's Sam. His knowingness was all.

Jane connects with landscape as a central character. Through her eyes there is as much mystery and unknowing, foreboding, and sexuality present in them as in any human being. The lushness and dripping rainforest of Baines's cottage, coupled with the stunted, jagged landscape of Stewart's front yard, set up a visual polemic between the two men. Jane's childhood connections with New Zealand—the bush, the wind, rain, the swaying trees, the bare branches tapping a window, the bleached driftwood piled like corpses on the black beaches, the claustrophobic vines that can grow around you practically as you watch, the moss underneath your foot—she exploits these private connections from a purely female point of view. I can't describe exactly how that is, but when you watch her movies, it's female.

She achieved the same potent expression with the South Island for *Top of the Lake*. The perspective was dizzying there. I was somewhat shocked by the vertigo-like relationship between the lake and the mountains. Human perspective in the landscape is not what's going on. And in the story, the raw and cunning adult community had no synchronicity with the place and no use for it outside of exploitation. Hanging someone from a tree. Drowning someone in a lake. Pushing someone off a cliff. Only the children retreated into it for safe harbor, and the women's camp communed with it for nourishment. Her landscapes are participants in a lot of stuff. Jane uses them to express spiritual entropy when Robyn goes wandering as a lost child/woman—and her stockings are torn and her feet muddy from the walk. Robyn brings the outside in.

The audience surely took on the visceral weight of Ada's beautiful gowns as they dragged through the mud, the handmade shoes almost getting wrenched off her feet from the sucking stuff. As always with Jane, you feel a sense of our smallness in this giant world. And yet, and yet… accompanying that inconsequential creature walking or running, there's abandonment, liberation! The character is headed somewhere. Maybe someplace not good. Despair and euphoria. The beauty of Janet Frame running and carrying her shoes through the woods has stayed with me all these years. Flora skipping across the summits as she brings the

illicit piano key to her adoptive father. The tiny figure of the tiny Tui riding her bike against the surreal backdrop of the mountains before she ditches her bike and winter coat and walks into an icy lake to perhaps solve some of her problems. The involvement of Jane's landscapes is devastating.

When Jane offered me the role of G. J., she said she envisioned the character wearing camel-colored outfits with long gray hair. That hit me. At one point during preproduction, Jane thought the wig might not be possible, and I just felt the bottom drop out. It had to happen. I loved the transformation. Stillness was possible with it. I loved the way it wrapped around my body. I felt beautiful, mysterious, cloaked. I also wanted to satisfy that prescriptive utterance made by Peter Mullan when he wondered if G. J. was a he, she, or it. G. J. is a character devoid of sexual orientation. I bound my breasts; I wore man-tailored clothes and tennis shoes at least three sizes too big. I relied on the infinite trust I have in Jane to be my guide. For *The Piano*, I had to convince Jane that I was the one to play the role. For *Top of the Lake*, Jane had to do the coaxing, because I couldn't see it. In many ways, I found G. J. in front of the camera, just as I've found large pieces of a character's puzzle only once I was in front of an audience. Some people take the time they take in being born.

Because G. J. describes herself as having suffered a "calamity," and because she considers herself a "zombie," Jane and I both wanted to see her be very earthbound—loving food and smoking and coffee—checking out the progress of stocks on the Internet—the banality of the physical world. That felt good. And true. And divorced from the hippy-dippy, yoga blah-blah of it all. Because there's another part of her that's not in that realm at all, the realm of the banal. She's other.

For me, G. J. became a world of riches—the leather underneath my hand, the sheepskin I leaned my head up against, the sound of the iron doors creaking on their hinges, the glimpse of the grass, the smoke in my lungs, the feel of the dog's weight on my lap. These things led me. Where is G. J. rolling that suitcase? Hopefully into the next episode of *Top of the Lake*.

Filmography

Short films

1980
Tissues

Director and Screenplay: Jane Campion. Unfinished.

1981
Mishaps of Seduction and Conquest

B&W video. Director and Screenplay: Jane Campion. Cinematography: Sally Bongers, Nicolette Freeman, George Perykowski, Paul Cox. Production: Jane Campion. Production company: Australian Film, Television and Radio School (AFTRS). Running time: 15 min.

With Deborah Kennedy (Emma), Richard Evans (Geoffrey), Stuart Campbell (the voice of George Mallory).

1982
Peel: An Exercise in Discipline

Director and Screenplay: Jane Campion. Cinematography: Sally Bongers. Production: Ulla Ryghe. Production company: Australian Film, Television and Radio School (AFTRS). Running time: 9 min.

With Tim Pye (Brother/Father), Katie Pye (Sister/Aunt), Ben Martin (Son/Nephew).

1983
Passionless Moments

B&W. Director: Jane Campion. Screenplay: Gerard Lee. Cinematography: Jane Campion, Alex Proyas. Editing: Veronica Haussler (Veronika Jenet). Production company: Australian Film, Television and Radio School (AFTRS). Running time: 13 min.

With David Benton (Ed Tumbury), Ann Burriman (Gwen Gilbert), Sean Callinan (Jim Newbury), Paul Chubb (Jim Simpson), Sue Collie (Angela Elliott), Elias Ibrahim (Ibrahim Ibrahim), Paul Melchert (Arnold), George Nezovic (Gavin Metchalle), Jamie Pride (Lyndsay Aldridge), Yves Stening (Shaun), Rebecca Stewart (Julie Fry).

1984
A Girl's Own Story

B&W. Director and Screenplay: Jane Campion. Cinematography: Sally Bongers. Editing: Christopher Lancaster. Sound: Veronica Haussler (Veronika Jenet). Music: Alex Proyas. Production: Patricia L'Huede. Production company: Australian Film, Television and Radio School (AFTRS). Running time: 27 min.

With Gabrielle Shornegg (Pam), Paul Chubb (Father), Colleen Fitzpatrick (Mother), Joanne Gabbe (Sister), Jane Edwards (Deirdre), John Godden (Graeme), Geraldine Haywood (Stella), Marina Knight (Gloria).

1985
After Hours

Director and Screenplay: Jane Campion. Cinematography: Laurie McInnes, Michael Edols. Editing: Annabelle Sheehan. Music: Alex Proyas. Production design: Janet Bell. Production company: Women's Film Unit of Australia. Running time: 29 min.

With Danielle Pearse (Lorraine), Don Reid (John Phillips), Anna Maria Monticelli (Sandra Adams), Russell Newman.

1986
Dancing Daze

Fifth episode of a six-episode TV series. Director: Jane Campion. Screenplay: Debra Oswald. Cinematography: Chrissie Koltai. Music: Martin Armiger. Production: Jan Chapman. Production company: Australian Broadcasting Corporation (ABC). Running time: 50 min.

With Melissa Docker (Anita), Meryl Tankard (Phoebe Green), Paul Chubb (Oliver), Norman Kaye (Stephen Issacs), Lance Curtis (Harry), Patsy Stephen (Kate Green).

2005
The Water Diary

One of eight segments that make up the film *8*, eight stories for the United Nations eight Millennium Development Goals. Director and Screenplay: Jane Campion. Cinematography: Greig Fraser. Production design and costumes: Janet Patterson. Make-up: Noriko Wantanabe. Editing: Heidi Kenessey. Music: Mark Bradshaw. Production: Marc Oberon, Lissandra Haulica, Christopher Gill, Belinda Mravicic, in partnership with the United Nations Development Program. Production companies: LDM Productions, Big Shell Publishing. Running time: 18 min.

With Alice Englert (Ziggy), Tintin Marova Kelly (Sam), Isidore Tillers (Felicity), Harry Greenwood (Simon), Genevieve Lemon (Pam), Miranda Jakich (Mrs Miles), Justine Clarke (Mother), Russell Dykstra (Father), Ian Abdulla, Di Adams, Chris Haywood, Clayton Jacobson (Lunch Guests).

2007
The Lady Bug

One of thirty-three segments of *Chacun son cinéma*. Director and Screenplay: Jane Campion. Cinematography: Greig Fraser. Editing: Alexandre de Franceschi. Music: Mark Bradshaw. Production company: Elzévir Films with the Cannes Film Festival. Running time: 3 min.

With Erica Englert (The Bug), Clayton Jacobson (The Man/ The Voices #3), Genevieve Lemon (The Voices #1), Marney McQueen (The Voices #2).

Feature films

1986
Two Friends

TV film. Director: Jane Campion. Screenplay: Helen Garner. Cinematography: Julian Penney. Production design and costumes: Janet Patterson. Editing: Bill Russo. Music: Martin Armiger. Production: Jane Campion, Jan Chapman. Production company: Australian Broadcasting Corporation (ABC). Running time: 76 min.

With Kris Bidenko (Kelly), Emma Coles (Louise), Sean Travers (Matthew), Kris McQuade (Janet, Louise's mother), Peter Hehir (Malcolm), Stephen Leeder (Jim), Steve Bisley (Kevin), Kerry Dwyer (Alison), Tony Barry (Charlie), John Sheerin (Dead Girl's Father).

1989
Sweetie

Director: Jane Campion. Screenplay: Jane Campion and Gerard Lee, based on an original idea by Jane Campion. Cinematography: Sally Bongers. Costumes: Amanda Lovejoy. Editing: Veronika Haeussler (Veronika Jenet). Music: Martin Armiger. Production: John Maynard, William MacKinnon. Production companies: Arenafilm, Australian Film Commission, New South Wales Film Corp., Television Office. Running time: 100 min.

With Genevieve Lemon (Dawn 'Sweetie'), Karen Colston (Kay), Tom Lycos (Louis), Jon Darling (Gordon), Dorothy Barry (Flo), Michael Lake (Bob), Andre Pataczek (Clayton), Emma Fowler (Sweetie as a child).

1990
An Angel at My Table

Originally a TV miniseries. Director: Jane Campion. Screenplay: Laura Jones, based on Janet Frame's *An Autobiography: To the Is-Land, An Angel at My Table* and *The Envoy from Mirror City*. Cinematography: Stuart Dryburgh. Production design: Grant Major. Costumes: Glenys Jackson. Editing: Veronika Haeussler (Veronika Jenet). Music: Don McGlashan. Production: Bridget Ikin, John Maynard. Production companies: Hibiscus Films, New Zealand Film Commission, Television New Zealand, Australian Broadcasting Corporation (ABC), Channel Four Films. Running time: 158 min.

With Alexia Keogh (Janet as a child), Karen Fergusson (Janet as a teenager), Kerry Fox (Janet Frame), Iris Churn (Mother), Kevin J. Wilson (Father), William Brandt (Bernhard), Melina Bernecker (Myrtle), Timothy Bartlett (Gussy Dymock), Hamish McFarlane (Avril Luxon), Edith Campion (Miss Lindsay), Andrew Binns (Bruddie), Glynis Angell (Isabel), Sarah Smuts-Kennedy (June), David Letch (Patrick), Martyn Sanderson (Frank Sargeson), Carla Hedgeman (Poppy), Francesca Collins (Baby Jane), Monk Morrison (Bruddie as a child).

1993
The Piano

Director and Screenplay: Jane Campion. Cinematography: Stuart Dryburgh. Production design: Andrew McAlpine. Costumes: Janet Patterson. Editing: Veronika Jenet. Music: Michael Nyman. Production: Jan Chapman, Alain Depardieu, Mark Turnbull. Production companies: New South Wales Film & Television Office, Jan Chapman Productions, CiBy 2000, The Australian Film Commission. Running time: 121 min.

With Holly Hunter (Ada McGrath), Harvey Keitel (George Baines), Sam Neill (Alisdair Stewart), Anna Paquin (Flora McGrath), Kerry Walker (Aunt Morag), Genevieve Lemon (Nessie), Tungia Baker (Hira), Te Whatanui Skipwith (Chief Nihe), Pete Smith (Hone), Cliff Curtis (Mana), Ian Mune (Reverend), Peter Dennett (Head Seaman), Bruce Allpress (Blind Piano Tuner), Carla Rupuha (Heni—Mission Girl), Mahina Tunui (Mere—Mission Girl).

1996
The Portrait of a Lady

Director: Jane Campion. Screenplay: Laura Jones, based on the novel by Henry James. Cinematography: Stuart Dryburgh. Production design and costumes: Janet Patterson. Editing: Veronika Jenet. Music: Wojciech Kilar. Production: Steve Golin, Monty Montgomery, Mark Turnbull, Ann Wingate, Ute Leonhardt, Heidrun Reshoeft. Production companies: Polygram Filmed Entertainment, Propaganda Films. Running time: 144 min.

With Nicole Kidman (Isabel Archer), John Malkovich (Gilbert Osmond), Barbara Hershey (Madame Serena Merle), Mary-Louise Parker (Henrietta Stackpole), Martin Donovan (Ralph Touchett), Shelley Winters (Mrs Touchett), Richard E. Grant (Lord Warburton), Shelley Duvall (Countess Gemini), Christian Bale (Edward Rosier), Viggo Mortensen (Caspar Goodwood), Valentina Cervi (Pansy Osmond), John Gielgud (Mr Touchett), Roger Ashton-Griffiths (Bob Bantling), Catherine Zago (Mother Superior).

1999
Holy Smoke

Director: Jane Campion. Screenplay: Anna and Jane Campion. Cinematography: Dion Beebe. Editing: Veronika

Jenet. Production design: Janet Patterson. Music: Angelo Badalamenti. Production: Jan Chapman, Fiona Crawford. Executive Producer: Harvey Weinstein. Production companies: Miramax Films, Jan Chapman Productions. Running time: 115 min.

With Kate Winslet (Ruth Barron), Harvey Keitel (P. J. Waters), Julie Hamilton (Mum, Miriam Barron), Sophie Lee (Yvonne Barron), Tim Robertson (Dad, Gilbert Barron), Genevieve Lemon (Rahi), Pam Grier (Carol), Dan Wyllie (Robbie), Paul Goddard (Tim), George Mangos (Yani), Kerry Walker (Puss), Leslie Dayman (Bill-Bill), Samantha Murray (Prue), Austen Tayshus (Stan), Simon Anderson (Fabio), Dhritiman Chaterji (Chidaatma Baba), Robert Joseph (Miriam's Taxi Driver), Jane Edwards (Priya).

2003
In the Cut

Director: Jane Campion. Screenplay: Jane Campion and Susanna Moore, based on the novel by Susanna Moore. Cinematography: Dion Beebe. Production design: David Brisbin. Costumes: Beatrix Aruna Pasztor. Editing: Alexandre de Franceschi. Music: Hilmar Örn Hilmarsson. Production: Laurie Parker, Nicole Kidman. Executive Producers: Effie T. Brown, François Ivernel, Ray Angelic. Production companies: Pathé Productions, Screen Gems, Red Turtle. Running time: 119 min.

With Meg Ryan (Frannie Avery), Mark Ruffalo (Malloy), Jennifer Jason Leigh (Pauline), Nick Damici (Rodriguez), Sharrieff Pugh (Cornelius Webb), Kevin Bacon (John Graham), Heather Litteer (Angela Sands), Patrice O'Neal (Hector), Arthur Nascarella (Captain Crosley).

2009
Bright Star

Director and Screenplay: Jane Campion, based on research and Keats: A Biography by Andrew Motion. Cinematography: Greig Fraser. Production design: Janet Patterson. Editing: Alexandre de Franceschi. Music: Mark Bradshaw. Production: Jan Chapman, Caroline Hewitt. Executive Producers: François Ivernel, Cameron McCracken, Christine Langan, David M. Thompson. Production companies: Pathé, Australian Film Finance Corporation, UK Film Council, BBC Films. Running time: 119 min.

With Abbie Cornish (Fanny Brawne), Ben Whishaw (John Keats), Paul Schneider (Mr Brown), Kerry Fox (Mrs Brawne), Edie Martin (Toots Brawne), Thomas Brodie-Sangster (Samuel Brawne), Claudie Blakley (Maria Dilke), Gerard Monaco (Charles Dilke), Antonia Campbell-Hughes (Abigail), Samuel Roukin (Reynolds), Amanda Hale and Lucinda Raikes (the Reynolds Sisters), Samuel Barnett (Mr Severn), Jonathan Aris (Mr Hunt), Olly Alexander (Tom Keats).

2013
Top of the Lake

TV miniseries. Directors: Jane Campion (episodes 1, 4, 6) and Garth Davis (episodes 2, 3, 5). Screenplay: Jane Campion and Gerard Lee. Cinematography: Adam Arkapaw. Production design: Fiona Crombie. Costumes: Emily Seresin. Art direction: Ken Turner. Editing: Alexandre de Franceschi, Scott Gray. Music: Mark Bradshaw. Production: Philippa Campbell. Executive Producers: Emile Sherman, Iain Canning. Production companies: BBC, Sundance Channel, See-Saw Films, Escapade Pictures. Running time: 350 min.

With Elisabeth Moss (Robin Griffin), David Wenham (Al Parker), Peter Mullan (Matt Mitcham), Thomas M. Wright (Johnno Mitcham), Holly Hunter (G. J.), Jay Ryan (Mark Mitcham), Kip Chapman (Luke Mitcham), Jacqueline Joe (Tui Mitcham), Robyn Malcolm (Anita), Genevieve Lemon (Bunny), Georgi Kay (Melissa), Skye Wansey (Grishina), Alison Bruce (Anne-Marie), Sarah Valentine (Prue), Robyn

Nevin (Jude), Calvin Tuteao (Turangi), Lucy Lawless (Caroline Platt), Darren Gilshenan (Bob Platt), Mirrah Foulkes (Simone), Luke Buchanan (Jamie), Jacek Koman (Wolfgang Zanic), Madeleine Sami (Zena).

2017
Top of the Lake: China Girl

Directors: Jane Campion (episodes 1, 5) and Ariel Kleiman (episodes 2, 3, 4). Screenplay: Jane Campion and Gerard Lee. Cinematography: Adam Arkapaw. Production design: Fiona Crombie. Costumes: Emily Seresin. Art direction: Mandi Bialek-Wester. Editing: Alexandre de Franceschi, Scott Gray. Music: Mark Bradshaw, Georgi Kay. Production: Philippa Campbell, Jane Campion, Hakan Kousetta, Libby Sharpe. Executive Producers: Emile Sherman, Iain Canning. Production companies: See Saw Films, Escapade Pictures, Screen Australia, Screen NSW, Fulcrum Media Finance. Running time: 360 min.

With Elisabeth Moss (Robin Griffin), Gwendoline Christie (Miranda Hilmarson), Nicole Kidman (Julia Edwards), Alice Englert (Mary Edwards), David Dencik (Alexander 'Minou' Braun), Ewen Leslie (Pyke Edwards), Yianni Warnock (Neeson), Clayton Jacobson (Adrian Butler), Kirin J. Callinan (Liam), Heath Franklin (North), Merlynn Tong (Caramel), Ling Cooper Tang (Dang), Kim Gyngell (Bootie), Lincoln Vickery (Brett Iles), Victoria Abbott (Kristy), Geoff Morrell (Ray), Christiaan Van Vuuren (Stally), Julian Garner (Mike), Helen Thomson (Felicity), Adam Zwar (Carson), Marg Downey (Isadore).

2021
The Power of the Dog

Director and Screenplay: Jane Campion, based on the novel of the same name by Thomas Savage. Cinematography: Ari Wegner. Production design: Grant Major. Costumes: Kirsty Cameron. Editing: Peter Sciberras. Music: Jonny Greenwood. Production: Jane Campion, Tanya Seghatchian, Emile Sherman, Iain Canning, Roger Frappier. Executive Producers: Simon Gillis, Rose Garnett, John Woodward. Co-producers: Libby Sharpe, Chloe Smith. Running time: 125 min.

With Benedict Cumberbatch (Phil Burbank), Kirsten Dunst (Rose Gordon), Jesse Plemons (George Burbank), Kodi Smit-McPhee (Peter Gordon), Thomasin McKenzie (Lola), Genevieve Lemon (Mrs. Lewis), Peter Carroll (Old Gent), Alison Bruce (The Governor's Wife), with the participation of Keith Carradine (The Governor) and Frances Conroy (Old Lady).

Documentaries about Jane Campion

1989
Jane Campion: The Film School Years

A video conversation between Campion and critic Peter Thompson. Production: Jason Wheatley. Production company: AFTRS. Running time: 22 min.

1990
The Grass is Greener: Interview with Jane Campion

TV programme. Director: Greg Stitt. Cinematography: Bayly Watson. Music: Jan Preston. Production company: Rymer/Bayly Watson. Running time: 23 min.

Audition

Director: Anna Campion. Cinematography: Warwick Attewell. Production: David Hazlett. Running time: 24 min. With Edith and Jane Campion.

1993
Inside The Piano

Director and Production: Colin Englert. Production companies: Jan Chapman Productions, Ciby 2000. Running time: 16 min.

1995
Cinema of Unease: A Personal Journey by Sam Neill

Direction and Screenplay: Sam Neill and Judy Rymer. Cinematography: Alun Bollinger. Music: Don McGlashan. Production: Paula Jalfon, Grant Campbell. Production companies: Top Shelf Productions, British Film Institute. Running time: 52 min.

1996
Portrait: Jane Campion and The Portrait of a Lady

Director: Peter Lang, Kate Ellis. Production: Monty Montgomery. Production company: Polygram. Running time: 54 min.

2000
Conversations in World Cinema: Jane Campion

TV programme. Host Richard Peña. Cinematography: Simon Riera. Production: Scott Hopper, Keith Keity. Production company: Sundance Channel. Running time: 28 min.

2001
With the Filmmaker: Portraits by Albert Maysles

TV series. Director, Screenplay and Cinematography: Albert Maysles. Production: Antonio Ferrera. Production companies: Genco Film Company, IFC Originals. Running time: 29 min.

With Jane Campion, Wes Anderson, Robert Duvall, Martin Scorsese.

2002
The Making of An Angel at My Table

Production: Bridget Ikin, Tiora Lowndes. Running time: 11 min.

2003
Entretien avec Michel Ciment: Premiers Plans de Jane Campion

Production company: Allerton Films. Running time: 11 min.
In the Cut: Behind the Scenes

DVD special feature. Production company: Columbia Tristar Home Entertainment. Running time: 16 min.

2005
The Water Diary: Making of

Director: Pauline Goasmat. Music: Gilles Lakoste. Production company: LDM Productions. Running time: 5 min.

2006
Making Sweetie

A video conversation between stars Genevieve Lemon and Karen Colston, DVD special feature. Executive Producers: Peter Becker, Fumiko Takagi, Jonathan Turell. Production company: The Criterion Collection. Running time: 23 min.

2012
From the Bottom of the Lake

Director: Clare Young. Production company: BBC. Running time: 51 min.

2015
The Legend of the Palme d'Or

Director: Alexis Veller. Production company: AV Productions. Running time: 70 min.

2018
The Piano at 25

Production companies: Jan Chapman production, Studio Canal. Running time: 30 min.

2021
Montana, 1925

Directors: Prisca Bouchet, Nick Mayow. Production company: Netflix. Running time: 17 min.

2022
Jane Campion, Cinema Woman

Director: Julie Bertuccelli. Production companies: Les Films du Poisson, Uccelli Production, Arte. Running time: 97 min.

Bibliography

Only publications in French and English are featured in this bibliography.

Monographs

Irène Bessière, Alistair Fox and Hilary Radner (eds), *Jane Campion: Cinema, Nation, Identity*, Wayne State University Press, Detroit, 2009.

Ellen Cheshire, *The Pocket Essential Jane Campion*, Pocket Essentials, Harpenden, 2000.

Annick Demers, *Parcours du féminisme dans l'œuvre cinématographique de Jane Campion*, University of Quebec, Montreal, 2000.

Alistair Fox, *Jane Campion: Authorship and Personal Cinema*, Indiana University Press, Bloomington, 2011.

Sue Gillett, *Views from Beyond the Mirror: The Films of Jane Campion*, ATOM, St Kilda, Melbourne, 2004.

Kathleen McHugh, *Jane Campion* (Contemporary Film Directors), University of Illinois Press, Urbana and Chicago, 2007.

Dana Polan, *Jane Campion*, British Film Institute, London, 2001.

Deb Verhoeven, *Jane Campion*, Routledge Film Guidebooks, London and New York, 2009.

Virginia Wright Wexman (ed.), *Jane Campion: Interviews* (Conversations with Filmmakers), University Press of Mississippi, Jackson, 1999.

General articles

Géraldine Bloustiev, 'Jane Campion: Memory, Motif and Music', *Continuum*, 5/2, 1992.

Michel Chion, 'La femme désarticulée: la folie chez Jane Campion', *Positif*, 581–2, July–August 2009.

Kennedy Fraser, 'Portrait of the Director', *Vanity Fair*, January 1997.

Freda Freiberg, 'The Bizarre in the Banal: Notes on the Films of Jane Campion' in Annette Blonski, Barbara Creed and Freda Freiberg (eds), *Don't Shoot Darling!: Women's Independent Filmmaking in Australia*, Greenhouse, Richmond, Victoria, 1987.

Ken Gelder, 'Jane Campion and the Limits of Literary Cinema' in Deborah Cartnell and Imelda Whelehan, *Adaptation from Text to Screen, Screen to Text*, Routledge, London and New York, 1999.

Adrian Martin, 'Losing the Way: The Decline of Jane Campion', *Landfall*, 200/2, 2000.

Kathleen A. McHugh, '"Sounds that Creep Inside You": Female Narration and Voiceover in the Films of Jane Campion', *Style*, 35/2, Summer 2001.

Patricia Mellencamp, 'Jane Campion' in *A Fine Romance: Five Ages of Film Feminism*, Temple University Press, Philadelphia, 1995.

Kathleen Murphy, 'Jane Campion's Shining Portrait of a Director', *Film Comment*, 2/6, 1998.

Eithne O'Neill, 'Voile blanc dans un arbre : Jane Campion, anthropologue de l'âme', *Positif*, 466, December 1999.

Eithne O'Neill, 'Briser les graines d'Éros dans l'œuvre de Jane Campion', *Positif*, 521–2, July–August 2004.

Barbara Quart, 'The Short Films of Jane Campion', *Cineaste*, 19/1, 1992.

Judith Redding and Victoria A. Brownworth, 'Jane Campion' in *Films Fatales: Independent Women Directors*, Seal Press, Seattle, 1997.

Eva Rueschmann, 'Out of Place: Reading Post-colonial Landscapes as Gothic Spaces in Jane Campion's Films', *Post Script*, 24/2–3, 2005.

Eva Rueschmann, 'Dislocation of Home and Gender in the Films of Jane Campion' in Ian Conrich and Stuart Murray, *New Zealand Filmmakers*, Wayne State University, Detroit, 2007.

John Slavin, 'The Films of Jane Campion', *Metro Magazine* (St Kilda West, Victoria), 95, Spring 1993.

David Stratton, 'Jane Campion, Director of the Year', *International Film Guide*, 1995, Hamlyn, London.

Ella Taylor, 'Jane Campion', *L. A. Weekly*, 14–20 June 2000.

Short films

Mishaps of Seduction and Conquest
• Eithne O'Neill, *Positif*, 458, April 1999.

Peel
• Sylvia Paskin, *Monthly Film Bulletin*, 57/678, July 1990.
• Ruth Watson, 'Naughty Girls Films', *Illusions*, 15 December 1990.

Passionless Moments
• Pam Cook, *Monthly Film Bulletin*, 57/678, July 1990.
• Jean-Luc Manceau, 'Programme Jane Campion', *Cinéma*, 355–6, 23 May 1986.

A Girl's Own Story
• Virginia Glaessner, *Monthly Film Bulletin*, 57/678, July 1990.
• Gina Hausknecht, 'Self Possession, Dolls, Beatlemania, Loss: Telling the Girl's Own Story' in Ruth O. Saxton, *The Girl: Construction of the Girl in Contemporary Fictions by Women*, St. Martin's Press, New York, 1998.
• Ruth Watson, 'Naughty Girls Films', *Illusions*, 15 December 1990.

Feature films

Two Friends
• Michel Ciment, 'Programme Jane Campion', *Positif*, 305–6.
• Debi Enker, 'The Girl's Own Story', *Cinema Papers*, 60, November 1986.
• Helen Garner, *The Last Days of Chez Nous* & *Two Friends* (screenplays), Penguin Books, Melbourne, 1992.
• Philippa Hawker, 'A Tale of Friendships… a Few Little Surprises', *The Age Green Guide*, 24 April 1986.
• David Stratton, *Variety*, 14 May 1986.

Sweetie
• Françoise Audé, 'Les malheurs de S.', *Positif*, 347, January 1990.
• Raphael Bassan, 'Le récif des sentiments', *Revue du cinéma*, 456, January 1990.

• C. Bates and R. Lang, 'Emotional Experience: Girls on Film', *On Film*, September 1990.
• Jane Campion and Gerard Lee, *Sweetie: The Screenplay*, University of Queensland Press, St Lucia, 1991.
• Vincent Canby, '*Sweetie*, a Wry Comedy by New Australian Director', *The New York Times*, 6 October 1989.
• Ann Marie Crawford and Adrian Martin, *Cinema Papers*, 75, 1989.
• Philippe Ethem, 'Femmes, famille, folie', *24 Images*, 44–5, Autumn 1989.
• Myra Forsberg, '*Sweetie* is not Sugary', *The New York Times*, 14 January 1990.
• Sue Gillett, 'More than Meets the Eye: The Mediation of Effects in Jane Campion's *Sweetie*', *Senses of cinema*, 1, 1999.
• Ann Hardy, 'A Story in the Desert', *Illusions*, 15, 1990.
• Hal Hinson, '*Sweetie*', *Washington Post*, 2 March 1990.
• Desson Howe, '*Sweetie*', *Washington Post*, 2 March 1990.
• Stephen Jenkins, *Monthly Film Bulletin*, May 1990.
• Anna Johnson, 'The Root of Evil: Suburban Imagery in Jane Campion's *Sweetie* and Bill Hanson's Series Untitled 1985–1986' in Ewen McDonald and Juliana Engberg, *Binocular: Focusing, Writing, Vision*, Moët and Chandon Contemporary Edition, Sydney, 1991.
• Shelby Kay and Megan McMurchy, 'Sitcom of the Absurd (once upon a tone)', *Filmnews*, September 1989.
• Marine Landrot, 'Les désaxés', *Télérama*, 3 May 1995.
• R. Lang, 'Passionless Moments' (interview), *On Film*, February–March 1990.
• Doreen O'Cruz, 'Textual Enigmas and Disruptive Desires in Jane Campion's *Sweetie*', *Australian Feminist Studies*, 21/49, 2006.
• Vincent Ostria, 'Une plante hystérique', *Cahiers du cinéma*, 427, January 1990.
• Philippe Rouyer, 'La mort dans le jardin', *Positif*, 347, January 1990.
• Robert Seidenberg, '*Sweetie*: Jane Campion's Maverick Family', *American Film*, XV/4, January 1990.
• Anneke Smelik, 'The Gothic Image' in *And the Mirror Cracked: Feminist Cinema and Film Theory*, St. Martin's Press, New York, 1998.
• Ellen Strain, 'Reinstating the Cultural Framework in Kay Shaffer's *Women and the Bust* and Jane Campion's *Sweetie*', *Spectator*, 11/2, 1991.
• David Stratton, *Variety*, 10 May 1989.
• Bob Strauss, 'Tart Family Ties in *Sweetie*', *San Francisco Chronicle*, 25 February 1990.
• M. Walters, 'Sweetness and Bite', *The Listener*, 3 May 1990.
• Josef Woodward, 'Family Ties in *Sweetie* and *Tie me up, Tie me down*', *Independent* (Santa Barbara), 7 June 1990.

An Angel at My Table
• Helen Barlow, 'Angels on screen', *Filmnews*, July 1990.
• Raphael Bassan, 'Mystère de la création', *La Revue du cinéma*, 47, April 1991.
• C. Bates and R. Lang, 'Emotional experience. Girls on film', *On Film*, September 1990.
• M. Borgese and L. Sangini, 'Entretien avec Janet Frame' (interview), *Jeune Cinéma*, 208, May–June 1991.

- Thomas Bourguignon, 'Les racines du moi', *Positif*, 362, April 1991.
- Alison Carter, 'Kerry's Janet moves cinemagoers to tears', *New Zealand Women's Weekly*, 6 August 1990.
- M. Cloutier, *Séquences*, 158, June 1992.
- Marie Colmant, 'Janet et Janet, face à face' (interview), *Libération*, 24 April 1991.
- Pam Cook, *Monthly Film Bulletin*, November 1990.
- Jean-Luc Douin and Gilbert Salachas, 'Lignes de vie', *Télérama*, 20 April 1994.
- Elisabeth Drucker, interview, *American Film*, 16/7, July 1991.
- Patrick Evans and Josephine Clarke, 'Filming Fiction: The Disease of Writing', *Illusions*, 15 December 1990.
- Janet Frame, *An Autobiography*, (vol. 1) *To the Is-Land*, (vol. 2) *An Angel at My Table*, (vol. 3) *The Envoy from Mirror City*, Vintage, Auckland, 2004.
- Anne De Gasperi, 'Rousseur de vivre', *Le Quotidien de Paris*, 25 April 1991.
- Bernard Génies, 'La Folie à l'horizon', *Le Nouvel Observateur*, 2 May 1991.
- Sue Gillett, 'Angel from the Mirror City: Jane Campion's Janet Frame', *Senses of Cinema*, 10, November 2000.
- Suzette Henke, 'Jane Campion frames Janet Frame: a portrait of the artist as a young New Zealand poet', *Biography*, 23–4, Autumn 2004.
- Elizabeth Jacka, 'Not a Frame out of Place', *Filmnews*, September 1990.
- Laura Jones, *An Angel at My Table: The Screenplay: from the Three-Volume Autobiography of Janet Frame*, Pandora, London, 1990.
- Stanley Kaufman, 'A Woman's Life', *The New Republic*, 22, 1991.
- Brian McFarlane, *Cinema Papers*, December 1990.
- Mariam Niroumand, *Cinéaste*, 18/4, 1991.
- Eithne O'Neill, 'Jane Campion filme Janet Frame', *Positif*, 616, June 2012.
- André Roy, 'L'ange qu'on a voulu exterminer', *24 Images*, 61, Summer 1992.
- Dominique de Saint Pern, 'Le Sceau de l'ange', *L'Express*, 25 April 1991.
- David Stratton, *Variety*, 20 June 1990.
- Camille Taboulay and Vincent Ostria, 'Sage comme un ange' (review and interview), *Cahiers du cinéma*, 442, April 1991.
- Philip Wakefield, 'Best Times, Worst Times' (interview with Kerry Fox), *On Film*, October 1990.

The Piano
- Yves Alion, 'J'aime être surprise par mes personnages' (interview), *Mensuel du cinéma*, 6, May 1993.
- Berth Althofer, '*The Piano* or *Wuthering Heights* Revisited: On Separation and Civilization through the Eye of the (Girl) Child', *Psychoanalytic Review*, 8/2, Summer 1994.
- Geoff Andrew, 'Grand Entrance' (interview), *Time Out*, 20 October 1993.
- Feona Attwood, 'Weird Lullaby: Jane Campion's *The Piano*', *Feminist Review*, 58, Spring 1998.
- Françoise Audé, 'Une expérience de femme', *Positif*, 387, May 1993.
- David Baker, 'Mud-wrestling with the Angels: *The Piano* as Literature', *Southern Review* (Melbourne), 30/2, 1997.
- Philip Bell, 'All that Patriarch Allows: The Melodrama of *The Piano*', *Metro Magazine* (St Kilda West, Victoria), 102, May 1995.
- Gregg Bentley, 'Mothers, Daughters and (absent) Fathers', *Literature/Film Quarterly*, January 2002.
- Jaime Bihlmeyer, 'The (Un)Speakable Femininity in Mainstream Movies: Jane Campion's *The Piano*', *Cinema Journal*, 44–2, Winter 2005.
- Thomas Bourguignon, '*La Leçon de Piano*: Un ange au piano', *Positif*, 387, May 1993.
- Stella Bruzzi, 'Bodyscape', *Sight and Sound*, 3/10, October 1993.
- Stella Bruzzi, 'Tempestuous Petticoats: Costume and Desire in *The Piano*', *Screen*, 36/3, Autumn 1995.
- Russell Campbell, 'Dismembering the Kiwi Bloke: Representation of Masculinity in *Braindead*, *Desperate Remedies* and *The Piano*', *Illusions*, 24, Spring 1995.
- Jane Campion, *The Piano* (screenplay), Bloomsbury, London, 1993.
- Jane Campion and Kate Pullinger, *The Piano: A Novel*, Bloomsbury, London, 1994.
- Peter N. Chumo, 'Keys to the Imagination: Jane Campion's *The Piano*', *Literature/Film Quarterly*, 25/3, 1 January 1997.
- Peter Cleave, 'Old New Zealand, New New Zealand', *Illusions*, 24, Spring 1995.
- Carol Clover, 'Ecstatic Mutilation', *The Threepenny Review*, 57, 1994.
- Felicity Coombs with Suzanne Gemmell (ed.), *Piano Lessons: Approaches to 'The Piano'*, John Libbey, Sydney, 1999.
- Isabelle Danel and Vincent Rémy, 'Regard de femmes' (interview), *Télérama*, 19 May 1993.
- Jeanne R. Dapkus, 'Sloughing off the Burdens: Parallel/ Antithetical Quests for Self-Actualization', *Literature/Film Quarterly*, 25/3, 1997.
- Alain Depardieu, 'Les notes de *La Leçon de piano* (production journal)', *Studio*, December 1993.
- Ngaire Dixon, *Ragtime* (New Zealand), 3 December 1993.
- Danielle Dumas, *L'Avant-Scène*, 424, July 1993.
- Reshela DuPuis, 'Romanticizing Colonialism: Power and Pleasure in Jane Campion's *The Piano*', *The Contemporary Pacific*, 8/1, 1996.
- Linda Dyson, 'The Return of the Repressed: Whiteness, Feminism and Colonialism in *The Piano*', *Screen*, 36/3, Summer 1995.
- Christophe d'Yvoire, 'Vertige de l'amour', *Studio*, May 1993.
- Judith Eckman-Jadow, '*The Piano*: A Revisit to the 'Dark Continent', *Issues in Psychoanalytic Psychology*, 17/2, 1995.
- David Eggleton and Ann Hardy, 'Grimm Fairytale of the South Seas/The Last Patriarch', *Illusions*, 23, Winter 1995.
- Philippe Elhem, Gilles Marsolais, André Joassin and Thierry Horguelin, 'Sur la corde raide des sentiments', *24 Images*, 68–9, September–October 1993.
- Lizzie Francke, *Sight and Sound*, November 1993.
- Carolyn Gage, 'No', *Broadsheet*, 204, Spring 1994.
- Sue Gillett, 'Lips and Fingers: Jane Campion's *The Piano*', *Screen*, 36/3, 1995.
- Annie Goldson, 'Piano Recital', *Screen*, 38/3, 1997.
- Kerryn Goldsworthy, 'What Music Is', *Arena Magazine*, 7, October–November 1993.
- Suzy Gordon, '"I clipped your wing. That's all": Autoeroticism and the Female Spectator in *The Piano*', *Screen*, 37/3, Spring 1994.
- Harvey Greenberg, *Film Quarterly*, 47/3, Spring 1994.
- Valerie Hazel, 'Disjointed Articulations: The Politics of Vision and Jane Campion's *The Piano*', *Women Studies Journal*, 10/2, September 1994.
- Cyndy Hendershot, '(Re)Visioning the Gothic: Jane Campion's *The Piano*', *Literature/Film Quarterly*, 26/2, 1998.
- Diane L. Hoeveler, 'Silence, Sex and Feminism: An Examination of *The Piano*'s Unacknowledged Sources', *Literature/Film Quarterly*, 26/2, 1998.
- Carol Jacobs, 'Playing Jane Campion's *Piano*: Politically', *MLN*, 109/5, 1991.
- Caryn James, 'A Distinctive Shade of Darkness', *The New York Times*, 28 November 1993.
- Laleen Jayamanne, 'Post-colonial Gothic: The Narcissistic Wound of Jane Campion's *Piano*' in *Towards Cinema and its Double: Cross-cultural Readings (1981–1999)*, Indiana University Press, Bloomington, 2001.
- Brian D. Johnson, 'Rain Forest Rhapsody: *The Piano* is a Work of Passion and Beauty', *Maclean's*, 22 November 1993.
- Cynthia Kaufman, 'Colonialism, Purity and Resistance in *The Piano*', *Socialist Review*, 24/1–2, 1995.
- Stanley Kaufman, *The New Republic*, 13 December 1993.
- Stuart Klawans, *The Nation*, 6 December 1993.
- Barbara Klinger, 'The Art Film, Affect and the Female Viewer: *The Piano* Revisited, *Screen*, 47/1, 2006.
- Johanne Larue, '*The Piano*', *Séquences*, 168, January 1994.
- Maria Margaroni, 'Jane Campion's Selling of the Mother/ Land: Restaging the Crisis of the Postcolonial Subject', *Camera Obscura*, September 2003.
- Harriet Marjolis (ed.), *Jane Campion's 'The Piano'* (Cambridge Film Handbooks), Cambridge University Press, 2000.
- Erin McGlothlin, 'Speaking the Minds Voice: Double Discursivity in Jane Campion's *The Piano*', *Postscript*, 23/2, 2004.
- Tania Modleski, 'Axe the Piano player' in *Old Wives Tales and Other Women's Stories*, New York University Press, 1999.
- Caroline Molina, 'Muteness and Mutilation. The Aesthetics of Disability in Jane Campion's *The Piano*' in David T. Mitchell and Sharon L. Snyder, *The Body and Physical Difference: Discourses of Disability*, University of Michigan Press, Ann Arbor, 1997.
- Harry Pearson, *Films in Review*, March–April 1994.
- Reid Perkins, 'Imag(in)ing our Colonial Past: Colonial New Zealand on Film from *The Birth of New Zealand* to *The Piano*, Part II', *Illusions*, 26, 1997.
- Leonie Pihame, 'Are Films Dangerous? A Maori Woman's Perspective on *The Piano*', *Hécate*, 20/2, 1994.
- L. Ponce, 'Le mirage de Jane Campion', *Cahiers du cinéma*, 470, July–August 1993.
- Ian Pryor, 'Piano Lessons' (interview), *On Film*, October 1993.
- B. Quart, *Cinéaste*, 20/3, 1994.
- Mark Reid, 'A Few Black Keys and Maori Tattoos: Rereading Jane Campion's *The Piano* in Post-Negritude Time', *Quarterly Review of Film and Video*, 17/2, 2000.
- Vikki Riley, 'Ancestor Worship: The Earthly Paradise of Jane Campion's Universe', *Metro Magazine* (St Kilda West, Victoria), 102, May 1995.
- Ray Sawhill and Polly Frost, 'Loose Talk', *The Modern Review*, February–March 1994.

- Naomi Segal, 'The Fatal Attraction of *The Piano*' in Nicholas White and Naomi Segal (eds), *Scarlet Letters: Fictions of Adultery from Antiquity to the 1990s*, Macmillan, London, 1997.
- Lisa Sormas, 'What Rape Is', *Arena Magazine*, 8, December 1993– January 1994.
- David Stratton, *Variety*, 10 May 1993.
- Frédéric Strauss, 'Abysses', *Cahiers du cinéma*, 467–8, May 1993.
- David Thompson, 'Harvey Keitel: Staying Power', *Sight and Sound*, 1, 1993.
- Davinia Thornley, 'Duel or Duet? Gendered Nationalism in *The Piano*', *Film Criticism*, 24/3, Spring 2000.
- Yann Tobin, '*La Leçon de Piano*: Maîtresse', *Positif*, 387, May 1993.
- Jacques Valot, *Mensuel du cinéma*, 6, May 1993.
- Jane Van Buren, 'Silences from the Deep: Mapping Being and Non Being in *The Piano* and in a Schizoid Young Woman', *The American Journal of Psychoanalysis*, 60/2, June 2000.
- Theo Van Leeuwen, 'Emotional Times: The Music in *The Piano*' in Rebecca Coyle (ed.), *Screen Scores: Studies in Contemporary Australian Film Music*, AFTRS Publishing, Sydney 1998.
- Diana Witchell, 'Return of the Native', *The Listener* (Wellington), 16 October 1993.

The Portrait of a Lady
- Geoff Andrew, 'The Lady Vanishes: Call Me Madame' (interview), *Time Out*, 12 February 1997.
- Catherine Axelrad, 'La femme peintre et son modèle', *Positif*, 430, December 1996.
- Claude Baignères, 'Au cœur du romanesque', *Le Figaro*, 18 December 1996.
- Dale Bauer, 'Jane Campion's Symbolic Portrait', *The Henry James Review*, 18/2, Spring 1997.
- Nancy Bentley, 'Conscious Observation of a Lovely Woman: Jane Campion's Portrait in Film', *The Henry James Review*, 18/2, Spring 1997.
- Samuel Blumenfeld, *Le Monde*, 19 December 1996.
- Jean-Loup Bourget, 'Montrer de l'intérieur à propos de *Portrait de femme*' in Francis Vanoye (ed.), *Cinéma et littérature*, University of Paris X, 1999.
- Stella Bruzzi, *Sight and Sound*, March 1997.
- Karen Michele Chandler, 'Agency and Social Constraint in Jane Campion's *The Portrait of a Lady*', *The Henry James Review*, 18/2, Spring 1997.
- Michael E. Connauston, 'American English and the International Theme in *The Portrait of a Lady*', *Midwest Quarterly: A Journal of Contemporary Thought*, 22/2, 1981.
- Annie Coppermann, 'Mariage fatal', *Les échos*, 18 December 1996.
- Jeanne R. Daphus, 'Sloughing off the Burdens', *Literature Film Quarterly*, July 1997.
- Olivier De Bruyn, 'La leçon de Campion', *L'événement du jeudi*, 19 December 1996.
- David Denby, 'Lady Stuck', *New York Magazine*, 13 January 1997.
- Patricia Dobson, *Screen International*, 13 September 1996.
- Maurice Elia, *Séquences*, January–February 1997.
- Howard Feinstein, 'Heroine Chic', *Vanity Fair*, December 1996.

- Lizzie Francke, 'On the Brink', *Sight and Sound*, November 1996.
- Ric Gentry, 'Painterly Touches' (interview with Stuart Dryburgh), *American Cinematographer*, January 1997.
- Rebecca Gordon, 'Portraits Perversely Framed: Jane Campion and Henry James', *Film Quarterly*, 56/2, 2003.
- Henry James, *The Portrait of a Lady*, Norton, New York, 1995.
- Laura Jones, *The Portrait of a Lady: Screenplay Based on the Novel by Henry James*, Penguin Books, New York, 1996.
- Evelyne Labbe, '"The Reality of Absent Things": La portée du négatif dans *The Portrait of a Lady*', *Études anglaises*, 51/4, 1998.
- Jean-Marc Lalanne, '*Portrait de femme*', *Cahiers du cinéma*, 508, December 1996.
- Gérard Lefort, 'La leçon de pipeau', *Libération*, 18 December 1996.
- Todd McCarthy, 'Campion's Elegant, Chilly "Portrait"', *Variety*, 9 September 1996.
- Brian McFarlane, *Cinema Papers*, April 1997.
- Pierre Murat, *Télérama*, 18 December 1996.
- Alan Nadel, 'The Search for Cinematic Identity and a Good Man: Jane Campion's Appropriation of James's *Portrait*', *The Henry James Review*, 18/2, 1997.
- Cynthia Ozick, 'What Only Words Not Film Can Portray', *The New York Times*, 5 January 1997.
- Bruno Remaury, 'À propos d'une crinoline', *Positif*, 425–6, July–August 1996.
- Marie-élisabeth Rouchy, 'Entretien', *Télérama*, 18 December 1996.
- Robert Sklar, 'A novel Approach to Movie-Making: Reinventing *The Portrait of a Lady*', *The Chronicle of Higher Education*, 43/23, 1997.
- Claudine Verley (ed.), *The Portrait of a Lady: Henry James et Jane Campion*, Ellipses, Paris, 1998.
- Christian Viviani, 'L'art d'un portrait', *Positif*, 430, December 1996.
- Priscilla Walton, 'Jane and James Go to the Movies: Post-Colonial Portrait of a Lady', *The Henry James Review*, 18/2, 1997.
- Virginia Wright Wexman, 'The Portrait of a Body', *The Henry James Review*, 18/2, 1997.

Holy Smoke
- Geoff Andrew, 'Sects Appeal', *Time Out*, 22 March 2000.
- Danielle Attali, 'La Leçon érotique de Jane Campion', *Journal du dimanche*, 14 December 2003.
- Jean-Jacques Bernard, *Première*, 1 December 1999.
- Anna and Jane Campion, *Holy Smoke: A Novel*, Hyperion, New York, 1999.
- Petra Christoph-Bokanjiev, 'La frontière chez Jane Campion: altérité et quête d'identité dans *Un ange à ma table*, *Portrait de femme*, *Holy Smoke*', *Cinéma*, 137, November 2010.
- Olivier De Bruyn, 'Please Be Kind', *Positif*, 486, December 1999.
- Clodagh Deegan, *Film Ireland*, April–May 2000.
- Gérard Delorme, 'Entretien', *Première*, 1 December 1999.
- Monia Douadi, 'Portraits de femmes', *Positif*, 458, April 1999.
- Marie Duparc, 'La leçon de cinéma' (interview), *Marie-Claire*, 1 December 1999.

- Howard Feinstein, 'The Jane Mutiny', *Guardian Unlimited*, 2 April 1999.
- Sue Gillett, 'Never a Native: Deconstructing Home and Heart in *Holy Smoke*', *Senses of Cinema*, 5, April 2000.
- Marie-Anne Guérin, '*Holy Smoke*', *Cahiers du cinéma*, 541, December 1999.
- Marie Guichoux, 'Sur l'aile du désir', *Libération*, 24 November 1999.
- Annick Le Floch'moan, 'Entretien', *Elle*, 22 November 1999.
- Marie-Françoise Leclère, 'Ruth ou le sceau de l'ange', *Le Point*, 26 November 1999.
- Judith Lewis, 'Wholly Jane', *L. A. Weekly*, 27 January 2000.
- Suzie Mackenzie, 'Beloved Rivals', *Guardian Unlimited*, 5 June 1999.
- Suzie Mackenzie, 'Campions Enjoy a Rich Friendship', *Otago Daily Times*, 2 October 1999.
- Kathleen Murphy, 'Jane Campion's *Passage to India*', *Film Comment*, 36/1, 2000.
- Hillary Neroni, 'Jane Campion's Jouissance: *Holy Smoke* and Feminist Theory' in Todd McGowan and Sheila Kunkle, *Lacan and Contemporary Film*, Other Press, New York, 2004.
- Dominique Pellerin, 'Un symbolisme excessif', *Séquences*, May–August 2000.
- Joy Press, 'Campion: *Holy Smoke* was an Essay about Love, about Belief Systems', *Village Voice*, 22 October 2003.
- Ian Pryor, 'Sister-Act', *Press* (Christchurch), 19 December 1999.
- Kate Pullinger, 'Soul Survivor', *Sight and Sound*, October 1999.
- David Rooney, *Variety*, 13 September 1999.
- Alan Samson, 'Jane Campion's Cult Fiction', *Dominion*, 14 December 1999.
- Desmond Sampson, 'Carry on Campion', *Sunday Star Times*, 5 December 1999.
- George Sandy and Rachel Turk, '*Holy Smoke*: Hallucination', *F/X Urban Cinefile*, 2 October 2000.
- Michael Sennhauser and Judith Waldner, review and interview, *Film Zoom*, May 2000.
- Amy Taubin, 'Jane and Anna Campion Make a Religious Cult Classic', *Village Voice*, 24–30 November 1999.
- Marie-Noëlle Tranchant, 'La Belle et le Gourou', *Le Figaro*, 21 November 1999.
- Sue William, 'Portrait of an Artist', *Listener*, 1 February 1999.

In the Cut
- John Calhoun, 'Interview with Dion Beebe', *American Cinematographer*, November 2003.
- Florence Colombani, '*In the Cut*', *Le Monde*, 17 December 2003.
- Florence Colombani, 'Entretien', *Le Monde*, 17 December 2003.
- Olivier De Bruyn, 'Détournement de thriller', *Le Point*, 15 December 2003.
- Olivier De Bruyn, '*In the Cut*: Le secret derrière la porte', *Positif*, 514, December 2003.
- Olivier De Bruyn, *Première*, 12 January 2004.
- Stéphane Delorme, '*In the Cut*', *Cahiers du cinéma*, 585, December 2003.
- David Denby, 'Creep Shows', *The New Yorker*, 27 October 2003.
- Leslie Felperin, *Sight and Sound*, December 2003.

- François Forestier, 'La Leçon de Campion', *Le Nouvel Observateur*, 11 December 2003.
- Emmanuelle Frois, 'Jane Campion l'effrontée', *Le Figaro*, 17 December 2003.
- Graham Fuller, 'Sex and Self Danger', *Sight and Sound*, November 2003.
- Bernard Géniès, 'La Folie à l'horizon', *Le Nouvel Observateur*, 2 May 1991.
- Sue Gillett, 'Engaging Medusa: Competing Myths and Fairy Tales in *In the Cut*', *Senses of Cinema*, 31, April–June 2004.
- Richard Glanerie, 'L'Amérique est puritaine et pornographique' (interview), *France-Soir*, 17 December 2003.
- Christian Haas, 'Jane Campion explore le désir des femmes' (interview), *Paris-Match*, 18 December 2003.
- Danièle Heymann, 'Entre *Taxi Driver* et *Alice au pays des merveilles*', *Marianne*, 15 December 2003.
- Fincina Hopgood, 'Inspiring Passion and Hatred', *Metro Magazine* (St Kilda West, Victoria), 139, 2003.
- Wendy Ide, 'In the Cut', *The Times*, 24 October 2003.
- Marine Landrot, 'La ligue des Campion', *Télérama*, 24 November 1999.
- Francine Laurendeau, '*In the Cut*', *Séquences*, 229, January–February 2004.
- Todd McCarthy, *Variety*, 15 September 2003.
- Susanna Moore, *In the Cut*, Alfred A. Knopf, New York, 1995.
- Douglas Park and Dawn Dietrich, *Film Quarterly*, 58/4, 2005.
- Gilles Renault, 'Campion repart à éros', *Libération*, 17 December 2003.
- Thomas Sotinel, *Le Monde*, 17 December 2003.
- Frédéric Strauss, *Télérama*, 17 December 2003.
- Amy Taubin, 'The Wrong Man: Jane Campion Dives in the Psychosexual Abyss and Returns with a Fractured Fairy Tale', *Film Comment*, 39/6, November–December 2003.
- Linda Ruth Williams, *The Erotic Thriller in Contemporary Cinema*, Indiana University Press, Bloomington, 2005.

Bright Star
- Nicolas Azalbert, 'Les songes de la lumière', *Cahiers du cinéma*, 652, January 2010.
- Livia Bloom, 'Destinées sentimentales', *CinémaScope*, Autumn 2009.
- Rachel K. Bosley, 'A Lyrical Love' (interview with Greig Fraser), *American Cinematographer*, October 2009.
- Lucie Calet, 'Une star est née', *Le Nouvel Observateur*, 7 January 2010.
- Isabelle Danel, 'Interview', *Première*, December 2009.
- Jean-Luc Douin, *Le Monde*, 17 May 2009.
- Jean-Luc Douin, 'Héroïne complexe', *Le Monde*, 7 January 2010.
- Nicola Evans, *Film Comment*, September–October 2009.
- Aurélien Ferenczi, 'La Leçon d'amour', *Télérama*, 6 January 2010.
- François Forestier, 'Jane Campion allume le feu', *Le Nouvel Observateur*, 20 May 2009.
- Emmanuelle Frois, 'Interview', *Le Figaro*, 15 May 2009.
- Christian Haas, 'Toujours aussi romantique' (interview), *Paris-Match*, 7 January 2010.
- S. F. Hamil, 'Poésie de la vie', *Ciné-Bulles* (Montreal), Winter 2010.

- Danièle Heymann, 'Jane Campion, la championne', *Marianne*, 2 January 2010.
- Fincina Hopgood, 'Lighting the Lamp', *Metro Magazine* (St Kilda West, Victoria), 163, 2009.
- Heike Hurst, *Jeune Cinéma*, 324–5, Summer 2009.
- Bruno Icher, 'Je suis imprégné de sa poésie' (interview), *Libération*, 7 January 2010.
- Didier Jacob, 'John Keats superstar', *Le Nouvel Observateur*, 7 January 2010.
- Nick James, 'Romantic Setting' (interview), *Sight and Sound*, December 2009.
- John Keats, *Bright Star: The Complete Poems and Selected Letters of John Keats*, introduction by Jane Campion, Vintage, London, 2009.
- Jacques Kermabon, 'Passion romantique', *24 Images*, September 2009.
- éric Libiot, 'Campion du monde', *L'Express*, 24 December 2009.
- Alain Masson, 'Et vivre ainsi toujours ou défaillir dans la mort', *Positif*, 587, January 2010.
- Todd McCarthy, *Variety*, 25 May 2009.
- Pascal Mérigeau, 'Keats par Jane Campion', *Le Nouvel Observateur*, 7 January 2010.
- Sonia Mladenova, 'Jane Campion's *Bright Star*: Conditions of Minority', *Film Matters*, 1–4, Winter 2010.
- Andrew Motion, *Keats: A Biography*, Faber & Faber, London, 1997.
- Didier Péron, *Libération*, 7 January 2010.
- Marcus Rothe, 'Jane Campion: "L'industrie du cinéma reste un club de machos"' (interview), *L'Humanité*, 6 January 2010.
- Arnaud Schwartz, *La Croix*, 6 January 2010.
- Olivier Séguret, 'Portrait de flamme', *Libération*, 16 May 2009.
- Thomas Sotinel, *Le Monde*, 6 January 2010.
- Kate Stables, *Sight and Sound*, December 2009.
- Moira Sullivan, interview, *Film International*, 7/42, 2009.
- Claire Valade, 'Destinées sentimentales', *Séquences*, November–December 2009.
- Neil Vickers, 'Bright Star', *Studies in Australian Cinema*, 3, 2009.

Top of the Lake
- Marianne Behar, 'Voyage au bout du paradis', *L'Humanité*, 7 November 2013.
- Jean-Loup Bourget, 'Le don du lac', *Positif*, 632, October 2013.
- Elise Domenach and Yann Tobin, 'Laissons l'histoire se raconter elle-même' (interview), *Positif*, 632, October 2013.
- Clémentine Gallot, 'La Leçon de télé de Jane Campion', *Le Magazine du Monde*, 26 October 2013.
- Raphaël Garrigos and Isabelle Roberts, '*Top of the Lake*, cimes passionnelles', *Libération*, 6 November 2013.
- Paule Gonzales, 'Jane Campion, nouvelle star de la BBC', *Le Figaro*, 4 November 2012.
- Paule Gonzales, 'Une série est une course de fond' (interview), *Le Figaro*, 7 November 2013.
- Olivier Joyard, 'Il n'existe aucun sujet qu'une femme ne puisse mettre en scène' (interview), *Les Inrockuptibles*, 6 November 2013.
- Olivier Joyard, 'La Leçon de Jane Campion', *Les Inrockuptibles*, 10 May 2013.
- Gérard Lefort, 'Bush à mourir', *Libération*, 25 January 2014.

- Robert Lloyd, 'Review: Jane Campion's 'Top of the Lake' mysterious, beautiful', Los Angeles Times, 18 March 2013.
- Tom Meltzer, 'Top of the Lake—TV review', *The Guardian*, 15 July 2013.
- Emily Nussbaum, 'Deep Dive', *The New Yorker*, 25 March 2013.
- Isabelle Regnier, 'Jane Campion, une reine en Carrosse', *Le Monde*, 16 May 2013.
- Laurent Rigoulet, 'Névrose au bord du lac', *Télérama*, 2 November 2013.
- Alan Scherstuhl, '*Top of the Lake* Review: Peggy Olson Goes to Hell, in Jane Campion's TV Series', L. A. Weekly, 14 March 2013.
- Amy Taubin, 'Law of the Father', *Film Comment*, March-April 2013.
- Barbara Théate, 'La leçon de télé de Jane Campion', *Le Journal du Dimanche*, 4 November 2013.

The Power of the Dog
- Thomas Baurez, 'Jane Campion au pays de Lumière' (interview), *Première*, October 2021.
- Stéphanie Belpeche, 'Jane Campion au JDD : "les femmes sortent enfin de terre"', *Le Journal du dimanche*, 27 November 2021.
- Mathilde Blottière and Sébastien Mauge, 'Jane Campion' (interview), *Télérama*, 4 December 2021.
- Lucas Charier, '*The Power of the Dog*', La Septième Obsession, 37, November–December 2021.
- Michel Ciment and Pierre Eisenreich, 'L'essentiel ne vient pas du cerveau, cela vient de plus profond' (interview), *Positif*, 730, December 2021.
- Olivia Cooper-Hadjian, '*The Power of the Dog*', *Cahiers du cinéma*, 782, December 2021.
- Manohla Dargis, '*The Power of the Dog* review: Wild Hearts on a Closed Frontier', *The New York Times*, 6 December 2021.
- Olivier Delcroix, 'Jane Campion : "sur le plateau, je me sens comme un médecin aux urgences"', *Le Figaro*, 17 October 2021.
- Clarisse Fabre, 'Avec *The Power of the Dog*, Jane Campion signe un western prévisible sur l'univers viril d'un cowboy", *Le Monde*, 1 December 2021.
- Victoria Garin, 'Jane Campion à l'assaut du mâle alpha' (interview), *Le Point*, 18 November 2021.
- Adrien Gombeaud, 'Morsures et cicatrices', *Positif*, 730, December 2021.
- Sophie Monks Kaufman, 'Beast of the Western World' (interview), *Sight and Sound*, December 2021.
- Jordan Kisner, 'Where Brutality Meets Tenderness' (interview), *The New York Times*, International Edition, November 2021.
- Sandra Onana, '*The Power of the Dog* : avec Jane Campion, un western par-delà le bien et le mâle', *Libération*, 27 November 2021.
- Nicolas Rapold, '*The Power of the Dog*', *Sight and Sound*, December 2021.
- Théo Ribeton, 'Ce que l'on ne fait pas délibérément' (interview), *Les Inrockuptibles*, December 2021.

Index

Author's acknowledgements

My thanks go to Éric Lenoir, Chairman of Cahiers du cinéma, and to Julie Lethiphu, managing director, for having agreed to this updated edition of my book. Thanks, too, to Richard Schlagmann, former owner of Cahiers du cinéma, who, from the outset, agreed to publish the first (French) edition; Catherine Laulhère, formerly managing director, who made it happen; Amélie Despérier-Bougdira, who with diligence, skill, and insight managed the project editorially, after taking it over from Valérie Buffet; Carolina Lucibello for her invaluable picture research; Melanie Mues, assisted by Amélie Bonhomme, for the design and layout; Anne McDowall, translator of the text into English, and Lise Connellan, copy-editor of the translation, who both made some wise comments on the original.

Thanks, too, to Anna Campion, Meera G. Lawrence, Jan Chapman (Jan Chapman Productions), John Maynard (Arena Film), Bridget Ikin (Hibiscus Films), Simone Nicholson (See-Saw Films), Laurie Parker, and David Brisbin for helping us with picture research.

I also wish to thank *Positif*, which opened up its photographic archives and allowed me to reproduce the interviews that I had published in the journal (with the exception of one, unpublished, on *Top of the Lake*); my friends Thomas Bourguignon, who recorded with me the filmmaker's words on *The Piano*, Pierre Berthomieu ('The Dent') and Jean-Loup Bourget ("Blue Sky"), who translated these short stories by Campion, and Eithne O'Neill, for whom the nuances of spoken English hold no mysteries; my wife, Evelyne, with whom I reviewed the films, which we discussed at length; Holly Hunter, who agreed to write her "scattered memories" for this book; and, of course, Jane Campion herself, who, for more than thirty years, has given me her trust and who has contributed much to the iconography of a book for which I alone am responsible, but that she has enabled to come into being.

The publisher thanks Anna Campion, Holly Hunter and Meera G. Lawrence for their help with this project.

Photographic credits

© 12 May 1953 *The Evening Post*/Fairfax NZ//Coll. Jane Campion and Anna Campion: 12TR; © Arena Film: 42T, 43R, 45; © 1986 Australian Broadcasting Corporation: 40, 41; © 1986 Australian Broadcasting Corporation/Coll. *Positif*: 38T; © Australian Film and Television School: 32, 33; © Australian Film and Television School 1982: 24; © Australian Film and Television School 1984 archive images 'The Conquest of Everest', A group 3 Production, Distributed by British Lion Film Corporation: 34; © Australian Film and Television School/Coll. Jane Campion: 27, 31; © Australian Film and Television School/Coll. *Positif*: 4TL, 20, 22, 26; © Barry Woods/Coll. Jane Campion and Anna Campion: 12TC; Coll. Hill-Stead Museum, Farmington, Connecticut: 179BL; © Coll. Jane Campion and Anna Campion: 12TL, 12BC, 12CR, 12BR, 15TL, 15TR, 15CL, 15CR, 15 BL, 15BR; Coll. Jane Campion: 179TR, 179TL; © Coll. Jane Campion: 17TL, 17BL, 18TL, 18TR, 151, 216; Courtesy of Jan Chapman Productions and Ciby 2000: 78, 79T, 79B, 82CR, 82B, 83R, 84T, 84B, 85T, 87B, 88TR, 88TL; Courtesy of Jan Chapman Productions and Ciby 2000/Coll. Cahiers du cinéma: 4CR, 74, 76L, 76R, 76BR, 80–1, 82TL, 88B, 91, 92–3, 94B; Courtesy of Jan Chapman Productions and Ciby 2000/Coll. Christophel:

82TR; Courtesy of Jan Chapman Productions and Ciby 2000/Coll. *Positif*: 6; © David Brisbin: 147, 150; © Davide Lanzilao/Contrasto/Agence REA: 18BL; © Dick Hofma// Coll. Jane Campion and Anna Campion: 12BL; Film Stills by Ari Wegner © 2021 Cross City Films Limited/Courtesy of Netflix: 204, 205T, 205B, 207BL; Gerald Jenkins/Courtesy of Miramax/Coll. Cahiers du cinéma: 5TL, 116, 122–3, 125B, 127B, 129, 130–1, 135; Gerald Jenkins/Courtesy of Miramax/Coll. Cinémathèque française: 118, 124, 132T, 132B; Gerald Jenkins/Courtesy of Miramax/Coll. *Positif*: 120–1, 125T, 127T; Grant Adams/© See-Saw (TOTL) Holdings Pty Ltd: 184BL; © Hibiscus Films: 60, 62, 63, 64T, 64B, 65T, 65B, 73T, 73B; James Bridges/© Pathé Productions Limited/Coll. Cinémathèque française: 158T; © Jane Campion: 94T, 112, 157BR, 173, 193, 194T, 206, 210T, 215; © Jane Campion/Coll. David Brisbin: 157TL; Jane Campion/ © Hibiscus Films: 56; © John Ashton/Coll. Jane Campion: 17CR; © John Lethbridge/ Coll. Jane Campion: 17BR; John Maynard/ © Arena Films/ Coll. Cahiers du cinéma: 17TR; John Maynard/ © Hibiscus Films: 4TR, 17CL, 58C, 58B, 66–7, 69T, 69B; John Maynard/© Hibiscus Films/Coll. Cahiers du cinéma: 58T, 70; Jurgen Teller/© Polygram Film Productions/Coll. Cinémathèque française: 102T; Kirsty Griffin/Netflix © 2021 Cross City Films Limited/Courtesy of Netflix: cover, 5CR, 198, 200, 202–3, 207T, 207BR, 209T, 209B, 210B, 213, 214; © Laurie Parker: 151B; Laurie Sparham/© Pathé Productions Limited, Screen Australia, BBC, UK Film Council, New South Wales Film and Television Office and Jan Chapman Productions/ Coll. Cahiers du cinéma: 5BL, 160, 162T, 168–9, 174–5; Lotte Hansen/© Pathé Productions Limited/Coll. Jane Campion: 18CR; Lotte Hansen/ © Pathé Productions Limited/Coll. Laurie Parker: 157BL; © Luis Buñuel: 43L; © Marc Obéron: 18CL; © Paramount: 113B; Parisa Taghizadeh © See-Saw Films: 18BR; Parisa Taghizadeh/© See-Saw (TOTL) Holdings Pty Ltd: 5TR, 182, 184T, 184CL, 184CR, 184 BR, 186–7, 188–9, 190L, 190R, 191L, 191R, 194B, 197T, 197B; © Pathé Productions Limited: 142, 146, 148; © Pathé Productions Limited/Coll. Christophel: 136, 138TR, 138CL, 138CR, 138BL, 138BR, 140–1, 143L, 143R, 144–5, 151T, 153B, 153T, 154–5, 158B; © Pathé Productions Limited/Coll. Jane Campion: 5CL, 138TL; © Pathé Productions Limited, Screen Australia, BBC, UK Film Council, New South Wales Film and Television Office and Jan Chapman Productions: 18C, 164, 165C, 165B, 170T, 171, 179BR; © Pathé Productions Limited, Screen Australia, BBC, UK Film Council, New South Wales Film and Television Office and Jan Chapman Productions/Coll. Cahiers du cinéma: 166–7, 170BL, 176CL, 176CR, 176BL, 176BR; © Pathé Productions Limited, Screen Australia, BBC, UK Film Council, New South Wales Film and Television Office and Jan Chapman Productions/Coll. *Positif*: 162B, 165T, 170BR, 176TL, 176TR, 180–1; © Patrick Swirc/ Modds: 10; © Polygram Film Productions: 98T, 98B, 101, 108, 109, 110, 113T, 115TL, 115TR, 115B; © Polygram Film Productions/Coll. Christophel: 4 BR, 96, 100, 102B, 107T; © Polygram Film Productions/Coll. *Positif*: 104–5, 107B; Regis Lansac/© Arena Film: 42BR, 44, 49BL, 50TL, 50TR, 50CL, 50BL, 50BR, 50CR, 52–3, 55T, 55B; Régis Lansac/© Arena Film/Coll. Christophel: 42BL, 49BR; Régis Lansac/© Arena Film/Coll. Cahiers du cinéma: 42, 3rd line R; Régis Lansac/© Arena Film/Coll. *Positif*: 4BL, 36, 38B, 42, 3rd line L, 46–7, 49TL; United Artists/MGM: 83L; W.F.U. Australian Film Commision, 1984: 28, 29; Warner Bros/Coll. Christophel: 157TR.

For Cahiers du cinéma:
Managing Director: Julie Lethiphu
Editorial coordination by Amélie Despérier-Bougdira
First edition designed by Melanie Mues, Amélie Bonhomme, Mues Design
Graphic adaptation of this edition by Nord Compo
Translation by Anne McDowall
Copyediting by Lise Connellan
Picture research by Carolina Lucibello
Photoengraving of the first edition by Point 4
Photoengraving of this edition by Nord Compo

For Abrams:
Editor: Connor Leonard
Managing Editor: Mike Richards
Design Manager: Danny Maloney
Art Director: Diane Shaw
Production Manager: Denise LaCongo

ABRAMS The Art of Books
195 Broadway, New York, NY 10007
abramsbooks.com